DAILY LIFE OF

WOMEN DURING THE CIVIL RIGHTS ERA

Recent Titles in
The Greenwood Press
Daily Life Through History Series

Victorian England, Second Edition
Sally Mitchell

The Ancient Greeks, Second Edition
Robert Garland

Chaucer's England, Second Edition
Jeffrey L. Forgeng and Will McLean

The Holocaust, Second Edition
Eve Nussbaum Soumerai and Carol D. Schulz

Civil War in America, Second Edition
Dorothy Denneen Volo and James M. Volo

Elizabethan England, Second Edition
Jeffrey L. Forgeng

The New Americans: Immigration since 1965
Christoph Strobel

The New Inuit
Pamela R. Stern

The Indian Wars
Clarissa W. Confer

The Reformation
James M. Anderson

The Aztecs, Second Edition
Davíd Carrasco and Scott Sessions

The Progressive Era
Steven L. Piott

DAILY LIFE OF

WOMEN DURING THE CIVIL RIGHTS ERA

DANELLE MOON

The Greenwood Press Daily Life Through History Series

 GREENWOOD

AN IMPRINT OF ABC-CLIO, LLC
Santa Barbara, California • Denver, Colorado • Oxford, England

Library of Congress Cataloging-in-Publication Data

Moon, Danelle.
  Daily life of women during the civil rights era / Danelle Moon.
    p. cm. — (The Greenwood Press daily life through history series)
  Includes bibliographical references and index.
    ISBN 978-0-313-38098-3 (hardcopy : alk. paper) — ISBN 978-0-313-38099-0
(ebook) 1. Women—United States—Social conditions—20th century.
2. Women—United States—Social life and customs—20th century.
3. Women—Suffrage—United States—History—20th century.   4. Feminism—
United States.   I. Title.
  HQ1420.M66   2011
  305.40973'0904—dc23   2011018373

ISBN: 978-0-313-38098-3
EISBN: 978-0-313-38099-0

15 14 13 12 11   1 2 3 4 5

This book is also available on the World Wide Web as an eBook.
Visit www.abc-clio.com for details.

Greenwood
An Imprint of ABC-CLIO, LLC

ABC-CLIO, LLC
130 Cremona Drive, P.O. Box 1911
Santa Barbara, California 93116-1911

This book is printed on acid-free paper ∞

Manufactured in the United States of America

CONTENTS

PREFACE

This book is part of the Daily Life Through History Series, which is focused on the ordinary experiences of American life.

In 1951, Florence Kitchelt, reflecting on her lifework to promote women's equality, wrote that all politics begins and ends at the local level and is dependent on local activists to push forward state and national legislation. Kitchelt's commitment to end gender discrimination and promote basic human rights for all people serves as a reminder of the importance of grassroots activism and the role of ordinary women in pushing for change in their local communities. Kitchelt committed her adult life to women's rights and the peace movement from the early 1900s until her death in 1961. Like many women of her generation, she became active in the early settlement house movement and the suffrage movement. After the Nineteenth Amendment was passed, granting women national voting rights, she focused her energies on securing world peace through the League of Nations Association, and following World War II she shifted her focus from the peace movement to promote the Equal Rights Amendment (ERA) and the U.S. endorsement of the Universal Declaration of Human Rights, adopted by the General Assembly of the United Nations in 1948. Kitchelt came to the belief that the promotion of the ERA was a logical extension of the UN declaration, though she had not always been a supporter of the amendment. The ERA was first introduced to Congress in 1923 by Alice Paul, leader of the National Women's Party—the radical arm of the woman suffrage and postsuffrage movements.

Alice Paul is better known as a national and international leader of the suffrage and postsuffrage movements, while Kitchelt spent the majority of her life working at the grassroots level. Like Paul, she spent her adult life fighting for gender equality, but unlike Paul, she had a much more diverse social justice agenda that included fighting for world peace, human rights, racial equality, and gender justice. Social movements are dependent on strong, charismatic leaders and rank-and-file activists to succeed, as well as diverse coalitions that bring together a variety of individuals with new ideas and strategies that can effectively produce positive change. This volume looks at the variety of women's experiences over the course of the 20th century in promoting social justice and human rights. Many of the characters of this book are unknown to general readers, though familiar to scholars who have carefully documented the experiences of the leaders and the rank-and-file members of various women's organizations and civil-rights-based organizations.

A primary goal of this project is to bring to life to a more general audience the diversity of experiences of ordinary women working for civil rights and social justice causes in the United States from 1920 to the 1980s. The scope is intentionally broad so as to expand the historical record and to encourage readers to engage in the diversity of the American experience, and perhaps for the first time, have a better understanding of the role that women have played in challenging the status quo. Moreover, younger readers will discover how the past struggles for gender and racial equality influence the rights we enjoy today, and often take for granted.

These broad categories include a diversity of subjects that include the ERA, world peace, racial and ethnic equality, human rights, education, religion, family life, transitions from rural and urban, employment, sexual preference, health care and reproductive rights, and domestic violence and rape. All of these issues reflect the specific challenges that women have and continue to face in American society. By focusing on individual experiences, we can gain a deeper understanding of the complexity of gender, class, and race in America. Moreover, this topical narrative approach makes clear that civil rights and social justice are tied together conceptually and that women have played a significant role in advancing democracy.

As a result of the scope of this book, it should be made clear that the research conducted for this volume is based on the diverse scholarship of the social history movement, and specifically the research endeavors into the subfield of U.S. women's history over the course of the last 30 years. As a women's historian, this project has led to new personal discoveries of historical scholarship that introduce new characters and new histories that have previously been hidden from view. As exciting as these discoveries are for scholars, I am more excited about the learning opportunities this volume and others of its kind can bring to the classroom and in advancing lifelong learning of the lessons of history and bring to light the valuable contributions women have made to American society across time.

This volume is broken into seven chapters, organized chronologically and by broad themes. Each chapter will integrate specific subthemes that touch upon the domestic, economic, intellectual, material, political, recreational, and religious life of women in the social movements of that era. Chapters 1–3 will focus on the emergence of early social movements that spanned the early beginnings of the Progressive Era through World War II, and chapters 4–7 will continue to build upon the African American civil rights struggle that slowly emerged following the Civil War and Reconstruction through the radicalization of the modern civil rights movement of the 1960s and 1970s. As this volume moves forward, the double bind of race and gender will rise to the surface in concert with the second wave of feminism, identity politics, and the anti–Vietnam War movement. Other emergent themes include labor rights, reproductive rights, child rearing, family life, courtship and marriage, sexuality, transformations from rural to urban lifestyles, social and class distinctions, leisure activities, and burgeoning roles in the economy, communication, education, health and medicine, literature, science, and art. In this way, readers will have a better appreciation of the diverse roles that ordinary and not so ordinary women played in improving society and American democracy.

Before investigating the complexities of women's social movements in the 20th century, it is first essential to define the terminology. When referring to *civil rights*, I use this term to convey the idea of the struggle for basic social and legal rights that is typically assigned to the African American struggle for racial justice, but I use it more broadly to convey basic civil rights that grant full equality to women, regardless of race, class, religion, and sexual orientation. I also describe at length the meaning of feminist waves and social movements

ACKNOWLEDGMENTS

Writing this volume has been a great pleasure. When first approached by my editor Mariah Gumpert, my first thought was how could I possibly represent the diverse experience of ordinary women, given the volume and scope of this project? Despite my initial reservations, I am happy that I was given the opportunity to write a book that I think expands on our understanding of the 20th-century civil rights movement and the important role that women have played in shaping national and local legislation and policies related to gender and racial justice in American society.

This project emerged from several years of research focused on the life of Florence Ledyard Kitchelt, a grassroots peace activist and lifelong feminist and promoter of human rights. Kitchelt's activism within the settlement house movement, as a suffragist and leader of the Connecticut Women's League of Voters, as a peace activist, and at the end of her life, as a promoter of the passage of the ERA, is representative of the role of ordinary women in addressing local, national, and international issues across time. My interest in documenting grassroots activism focused on feminism and peace in the early 20th century helped shape the direction of this book.

Over the course of the last eight years, I have benefited from the generous support of my colleagues, from San Jose State University (SJSU), Yale University, and Central Connecticut State University.

Various grants supported the research that undergirds this work, and I am especially grateful for the assistance of archivists and reference librarians working at the Schlesinger Library, Radcliffe Institute at Harvard University, Smith College, Cornell University Library, the Bancroft Library at University of California, Berkeley, Manuscripts and Archives at Yale University, and the Huntington Library. Moreover, I have benefited from the unwavering support and insightful editorial comments from Victor Geraci, Gordon Morris Bakken, and Glenna Matthews. I am very grateful to several colleagues from the history department at SJSU for their helpful and sometimes challenging questions that have improved my analysis and writing, including Patricia Evridge Hill, Glenn Gendzel, Jonathan Roth, and Ruma Chopra. I am also thankful for the friendship and encouragement I have received from Mary Nino, Kathy Hoyer, and Meredith Hawkins.

I write this book in honor of all the women who have come before me and struggled for women's equality, but mostly, I write in this area for the long-term benefit of young women and men who are the direct beneficiaries of the past feminist struggles and as a result of these struggles enjoy a more democratic society. Young people need to be reminded of the past struggles and honor the courage, strength, and perseverance of the women who pushed for the elimination of gender and racial discrimination in law and practice.

Finally, I dedicate this book to the women in my family, who have been good role models and have provided security, love, friendship, and support over the years. A special thanks to my grandmother, Margaret V. Craig, my mother, Peggy Cunningham, and sister's Diana Oja and Daphne Sloggett for always being there. Mostly, I dedicate this book to my daughter, Nichole Santangelo, who has lived through my personal and professional struggles, has granted me unwavering love and support, and is the joy of my life. The journey in documenting the past is the key to our future, and it is my hope that the ordinary lives of the women represented in this book will serve as a reminder of the importance of social movements and the role that women play in promoting social justice and human rights.

CHRONOLOGY OF EVENTS

1865   Civil War ends.

Thirteenth Amendment ratified ending slavery.

1868   Fourteenth Amendment ratified defining citizenship.

1869–70   Wyoming and Utah territories grant women suffrage.

1870   Fifteenth Amendment ratified forbidding disenfranchisement based on race, color, or previous condition of servitude.

1874   Women's Christian Temperance Union (WCTU) forms.

1884   WCTU under leadership of Francis Willard endorses woman suffrage.

1889   Hull House established in Chicago by Jane Addams.

1890   General Federation of Women's Clubs forms.

Jacob Riis publishes *How the Other Half Lives.*

Two suffrage organizations merge into National American Woman Suffrage Association (NAWSA).

1892   Ida B. Wells (later, Wells-Barnett) champions her anti-lynching campaign.

1893   Illinois establishes Factory and Workshop Inspection Act.

Colorado women gain equal suffrage with men.

1895   National Association of Colored Women forms.

1896   Supreme Court rules in *Plessy v. Ferguson,* establishing the "separate but equal" doctrine.

Idaho women gain equal suffrage with men.

1903   National Women's Trade Union League founded in Boston.

1908   *Mueller v. Oregon* upholds regulation of working hours for women.

1909   National Association for the Advancement of Colored People forms.

Uprising of 20,000 shirtwaist workers declare general strike.

1910   Washington State passes equal suffrage for women.

1911   Triangle Shirtwaist Factory fire kills 146 workers.

California passes equal suffrage for women.

1912   Federal Children's Bureau is established, headed by Julia Lathrop.

Woodrow Wilson elected president.

Kansas, Oregon, and Arizona enact woman suffrage.

1913   Alice Paul and Lucy Burns form the Congressional Union.

Ida B. Wells-Barnett forms first all-black suffrage organization.

1914   World War I begins in Europe.

1915   Woman's Peace Party forms.

Jane Addams chairs International Council of Women peacemaking meeting at The Hague.

Women's International League for Peace and Freedom forms.

1916   Congressional Union becomes the National Woman's Party (NWP), led by Alice Paul.

Margaret Sanger opens birth control clinic in Brooklyn.

1917   United States enters World War I.

Jeannette Rankin, first woman elected to House of Representatives, casts her vote against the war.

Women's Council for National Defense established.

NWP suffragists picket White House.

1918   World War I ends.

1919   Eighteenth Amendment ratified prohibiting sale of alcohol.

1920   Federal Woman's Bureau established.

Nineteenth Amendment ratified granting women national suffrage rights.

League of Women Voters formed under leadership of Carrie Chapman Catt.

Women's Joint Congressional Committee forms.

1921   Sheppard-Towner Act provides funding for mother and infant health.

1922   Equal Rights Amendment (ERA) first introduced to Congress.

1924   National Origins Act limits immigration.

1928   Herbert Hoover elected president.

1929   Stock market crash.

1930   Midwest draught begins, leads to "Oakie" migration west.

1933   Unemployment rises to highest recorded level.

Franklin D. Roosevelt elected president.

Francis Perkins appointed secretary of labor.

National Recovery Act passed.

Prohibition (Eighteenth Amendment) repealed.

1935   National Labor Relations Act passed (Wagner Act).

Social Security Act passed.

1938   Fair Labor Standards Act passed.

1939   World II breaks out in Europe.

1941   Fair Employment Practices Commission established.

1942   Women recruited into war industries.

Japanese Americans interned.

1945   Harry S. Truman becomes president, following FDR's death.

Japanese surrender ending World War II.

Women war workers laid off en masse.

1946   Cold War begins.

1947   United Nations Charter for Human Rights.

House Un-American Activities Committee established to investigate communistic activities.

1952 Betty Friedan writes "UE Fights for Women Workers."

1953 Alfred Kinsey publishes *Sexual Behavior in the Human Female.*

1954 *Brown v. Board of Education* overturns "separate but equal doctrine" established under *Plessy v. Ferguson.*

1955 Rosa Park's arrest sparks Montgomery Bus Boycott.

1957 President Eisenhower sends federal troops to Little Rock to enforce school integration.

Southern Christian Leadership Conference founded.

1960 John F. Kennedy becomes president.

Birth control introduced.

Sit-ins in Greensboro, North Carolina.

Ella Baker helps found Student Non-Violent Coordinating Committee.

1961 Freedom rides to force integration on interstate bus travel.

Women's Strike for Peace founded.

President's Commission on the Status of Women established.

1962 Delores Huerta and Cesar Chavez found United Farm Workers.

1963 Betty Friedan's *Feminine Mystique* published.

Equal Pay Act prohibits wage disparities based on gender.

March on Washington brings 250,000 civil rights activists to Washington, D.C.

President Kennedy assassinated.

1964 Freedom Summer.

1965 Voting Rights Act.

1966 National Organization of Women formed.

Black Panther Party forms in Oakland.

1968 Tet Offensive spurs U.S. involvement in Vietnam.

Jeannette Rankin Brigade—women march for peace in Washington, D.C.

Martin Luther King, Robert Kennedy, and Malcom X murdered.

Women's liberationists protest Miss America pageant.

1971	National Right to Life Committee founded.
	Women's Equality Day.
1972	Congress passes ERA; Phylliss Schlafly founds Stop-ERA.
	Title IX of Education Amendments Act bans sex discrimination in federally funded education.
1973	Supreme Court rules in *Roe v. Wade,* granting women constitutional rights to abortion.
1975	United Nations sponsors first International Women's Conference in Mexico City.
1977	National Women's Conference—Spirit of Houston takes place.
1980	Ronald Reagan becomes president.
1981	Sandra Day O'Connor becomes first female Supreme Court justice.
1982	ERA fails ratification.
1990s	Third-wave feminist movement begins.
1994	Anti–Domestic Violence Act.
2004	Gay marriage movement begins in California and Massachusetts.

1

WOMEN AND EARLY SOCIAL MOVEMENTS

This chapter will provide an overview of women's social movements that emerged in the 19th and early 20th centuries, with a specific focus on the early suffrage movement and the subsequent rise of women's organizations that provided the base for 20th-century social justice movements. This historical framework will provide the backdrop for understanding women's civil rights in the 20th century and will include highlights from the Women's Christian Temperance Union (WCTU), the Young Women's Christian Association (YWCA), the settlement house movement and women's clubs, the National American Woman Suffrage Association (NAWSA) and the National Woman's Party (NWP), and the League of Women Voters (LWV). While not intended to be comprehensive of every movement or group, this overview will highlight some of the activities that created a unique female space in public life that had previously been consigned to the private sphere of home and family.

The history of women's social movements is largely the history of white elite women's experience, though there were some clubs and societies that were organized and run by women of color. Elite women used social movements and higher education as a vehicle to expand their roles in society and to carve a specific professional niche where they could find employment. Yet, the class bias and privilege that allowed elite women to work for the public good opened new doors for minority and working-class women to pursue different pockets of social reform. In the following chapters, we will consider how ordinary women related to social feminist reform, what roles they played in advancing social change, and the impact of postindustrial developments like industrialization, urbanization, and immigration on reform agendas, as well as how these changes impacted urban reform and why.

REPUBLICAN MOTHERHOOD

The history of women and social movements dates back to times following the American Revolution as the landscape of democratic government began to take shape. At the onset, while the revolutionary zeal of democracy inspired Americans from all segments of society, the realization of a true democratic government for women would take three centuries to build. The new republic rested on the foundation that "all men are created equal," and a shared belief that a virtuous citizenry would shape good government. This view, while philosophically radical for the time, did not create a free society, and it would take several decades before all citizens were granted equal rights.

Despite initial inequalities, American women of the postrevolutionary period eked out a new domestic political role as mothers, referred to as *Republican Motherhood.* This new ideology endowed elite white women with a moral superiority in educating their children to become virtuous citizens. While women were not granted political rights, they contributed to the growth of the nation through education, religion, and domesticity. Women would use these methods to needle their way into public life, though it would take another century before women could claim a true political victory.

SEPARATE SPHERES

The 19th century provided new opportunities for women to press the boundaries between public and private life by forming new organizations that included literary, social, religious, and moral groups dedicated to establishing a national Christian ethos. This early period of the 1820s to the 1840s has been described as the age of association for middle-class men and women, where men and women were engaged in redefining their roles in society. Changes in commerce, industry, marriage patterns, and gender expectations reinforced the ideology of separate spheres. As America morphed from a republic of virtue to that of capitalist individualism, changes in family relationships, marriage, and child rearing challenged earlier social and legal traditions of economic arrangements. For example, prior to the 1820s, most marriages were arranged, but after this period, couples began to embrace individual choice and married for companionship and love. Men and women's roles were distinguished by the private and public spheres. The public sphere represented business, commerce, and civic and political life—the sphere of men. The private sphere represented the home and family life—the domain of women.

The concept of separate spheres created an artificial understanding of gender roles in society, though the boundaries were more philosophical than real. As the market economy developed and consumerism became a controlling influence over family prosperity, the ideal of different spheres gave order to social structure. However, while women's lives were initially confined to the home, they gradually extended their role by educating their children to become the moral arbitrators of society. In the 19th century, female moral authority began to extend beyond the borders of the home to city streets. A good example is the formation of the New York Moral Reform Society, which originated in the 1830s with the goal of eradicating prostitution in the city. Other reform societies would follow, including temperance and antislavery societies. Women would use these societies as a base to improve the morality of society. Through these public efforts, women slowly challenged the sexual double standard that existed in law and society and promoted the idea that women were entitled to the same rights and opportunities as men.

EARLY WOMEN'S MOVEMENT

The movement for women's rights began in the early 1830s with the first married women's property act that gave women control of their personal property. Influenced by the lack of control women held over their lives, including the right to own property, the right to children, and basic contract rights, Elizabeth Cady Stanton would emerge as the leader of the early women's rights movement. The year 1848 highlights the changing views of womanhood and the rise of the first women's movement. That same year, Stanton and several other women organized the first women's rights convention in Seneca Falls, New York, bringing together a small group of women and men to support the radical view that men and women were created equal and entitled to the same basic civil rights as men. Stanton wrote the "Declaration of Sentiments," which provided the foundation for the suffrage movement of the late 19th and early 20th centuries. Seneca Falls thus signaled a new beginning for women's rights—though it would take nearly 70 years before women were granted full voting rights, it provided a base for women's activism in the 19th and 20th centuries.

Early suffrage campaigns struggled to find their voice as a result of the social, economic, and religious conditions that defined women as second-class citizens. Their activism represented small numbers of elite women who committed themselves to abolition and women's suffrage. The trauma of the Civil War and the Reconstruction amendments intensified the efforts of women activists to push harder for national voting rights, and in 1866, Stanton, Susan B. Anthony, and Lucy Stone formed the Equal Rights Association. Conflicts on procedural issues to accomplish reform goals quickly erupted during the push to ratify the Fifteenth Amendment, granting black male voting rights. The resulting disagreement led proponents to split into two separate factions. The more radical Stanton and Anthony formed the National Woman Suffrage Association (NWSA), while Lucy Stone and her husband Henry Blackwell formed the American Woman Suffrage Association (AWSA). The latter organization focused on promoting the Fifteenth Amendment and adopted a state-by-state approach to women's rights. Meanwhile, Stanton and Anthony promoted a much more radical position that included granting married women property rights, liberal divorce laws, education, and national voting rights.

The early suffrage movement provided the foundation for female political activism across a broad spectrum of women and issues, and this growth of grassroots activism occurred incrementally across time. The historical experiences of women and men in the 19th century differ profoundly from our experiences today. Social and political society was sharply divided by gender roles and expectations, and women lacked basic civil and political rights as individuals. Thus, this early women's movement provided the philosophical and grassroots foundation to push for the Nineteenth Amendment, which eventually granted women national voting rights, basic equal rights in marriage, legal status, and guarantees as citizens of the United States.

ANTISLAVERY SOCIETIES

The history of the early women's movement had roots in the antislavery movement and Christianity. In the 1830s, a handful of women bravely challenged the social view that women were to remain silent in public and were not entitled to the same political rights as men. Quaker women like Lucreita Mott from Philadelphia, sustained by a long-term belief in egalitarianism, entered the public sphere to promote abolition and women's rights. Mott and others, drawing from the support of female voluntary societies, raised money to support the American Anti-Slavery Society, while women like Sarah and Angelina Grimke, from South Carolina, began rattling the equal rights sword in the 1830s by speaking to mixed-sex audiences by means of their radical publication "Letters on the Condition and the Equality of the Sexes." Drawing on Christian scripture and the Bill of Rights, they declared that men and women were created equal, and had moral obligations as human beings, and therefore women had a moral obligation to be politically active. Many of these early pioneers made connections between slavery and the condition of women in society, for which they were ridiculed. In the case of the Grimke sisters, they became exiles from their family home in South Carolina.

The antislavery activism of the 1830s and 1840s would provide an important base for the emerging women's rights movement, which included both white and black women. For example, former slave and popular abolitionist speaker Sojourner Truth challenged the social prescriptions of the day that placed white women on a pedestal while subjugating black women to a life of slavery and sexual abuse. The voices of Lucreita Mott, Sarah and Angelina Grimke, and Sojourner Truth illustrate the convergence of the antislavery movement and the women's movement to question the political, legal, economic, and social culture of the early republic. Their work laid the foundation for 20th-century struggles.

WOMEN'S LEGAL STATUS IN THE 19TH CENTURY

The legal status of women at this time was based on the system known as *coverture*, which defined women as legal possessions of their husbands, rather than defining them as legal beings. Coverture prohibited women from owning property, limited their rights to their own earnings, eliminated their ability to make contracts and to construct a will, and most painfully denied them rights of guardianship over their children in marriage and divorce.

As the abolition movement gained momentum, women like Lucreita Mott and Elizabeth Cady Stanton began to question their own lack of status. Together they organized a small group of New York activists to discuss the social, legal, and political rights of women. This group of some 300 women and men assembled at the Seneca

Falls Convention, where they laid bare their grievances in the now famous "Declaration of Sentiments." Modeled after the Declaration of Independence, this document laid out the list of violations and demanded equal citizenship rights, including the right to vote (suffrage); a most radical idea for the time. The "Declaration of Sentiments" verbally codified a new movement for women's rights, though it would take several decades to form a cohesive women's rights movement. Progress was indeed very slow, but the eventual victory of the Nineteenth Amendment granting women the right to vote was shaped by the growth of female voluntary societies, female benevolence, and moral reform.

FEMALE INSTITUTION BUILDING, 1870–1920

Women's social movements consisted of pockets of social activism that included participation in the abolition movement and maternal and religious organizations, from the WCTU to the General Federation of Women's Clubs, the NAWSA, and the NWP, among others. The following section will explore the emergence of female institution building and will focus on these organizations to illustrate the groundswell of social movements that resulted from past organizing and that would propel the movements into the 20th century.

Nineteenth-century gender prescriptions were culturally constructed and rested on the belief in separate spheres of influence, whereby men dominated the public sphere and women the private. Women's sphere of influence was based on the belief that women were morally superior to men, less corruptible, and more pure, pious, and virtuous than men. Men and women played very specific roles in society, but under the law, women were subordinate to men at all levels despite their role as moral guardians. Despite the inequality of 19th-century society, most men and women believed that men and women were biologically different and that women were morally superior. Even the more radical women like Stanton and Anthony maintained a belief in a separate autonomy predicated on female virtue, piety, and domesticity. Cultural practice determined societal behavior, and in the 19th century, the formation of separate voluntary organizations gave women an opportunity to contribute to politics and policy making from the backdoor—that is to say, they could not make legal changes because they lacked the right to vote and ability to participate in politics, but they influenced legal change as wives, mothers, and sisters and created and joined organizations that pressured men to address social issues.

Historian Paula Baker illustrates how the home served as the basis for political action. Women succeeded in using motherhood and moral authority as a rationale to demand political change. Throughout the 19th century, women championed social reform by addressing poverty, public health, prostitution, child welfare, drunkenness, and domestic violence. As a result, by the end of the century the number of associations increased rapidly, though the majority of women could still be found in religious organizations. As the new modern era of industrialization, urbanization, and immigration grew in intensity, the moral chasm expanded and required additional direct political action from elite white women, while advances in women's educational opportunities permanently fused domesticity with politics. As Anne Scott has articulated, only a few women ventured outside the cultural milieu, while the majority of women joined organizations and tested some of the boundaries without breeching social custom.[1]

WOMEN'S CHRISTIAN TEMPERANCE UNION (WCTU)

The WCTU is a primary example of an organization focused on correcting the societal abuses that tolerated male drunkenness (intemperance) and the sexual double standard. Saving souls and temperance reform dominated the agenda of the organization, but by the 1880s, the WCTU added numerous other social problems to its list of reform issues, including campaigns for the protection of young women, age of consent laws, prison reform, settlement house movement, child abuse, kindergarten movement, and suffrage.

The success of the WCTU has been largely attributed to the charisma and force of the organization's founder, Francis Willard, and her "Do Everything" policy. As part of the social purity movement, the WCTU women negotiated the public space demanding reform of family, work, and community. They identified drunkenness as the primary cause of family violence and the economic problems of the working class. Temperance reform provided a gateway to address the sexual double standard that limited women's ability to earn a living and subjected them to a life of poverty as dependents of drunken men. Reforming male behavior required new laws that protected women. While these protective measures were not intended as equal rights legislation at the time, the attack on the sexual double standard reinforced the need for the right to vote. The WCTU became an important base for the suffrage movement in the 20th century and for women's legal rights. The slogan "Do Everything" highlights the diversified platform that the organization took to transform social behavior in an expanding industrial and urban environment. Cleaning up society required women's moral insight to address the ills of society. Every state in the Union had state and local branches with specific reform agendas connected by evangelical gospel reform. The social gospel movement, an intellectual movement, focused on addressing the variety of social problems, from crime, poverty, child labor, alcohol abuse, education, and other social justice issues. The movement represented a spectrum of male and female activists and organizations. The WCTU focused on social problems connected to alcohol abuse and the family. By the 20th century, the WCTU would move from an evangelistic movement to a political movement, with a membership base of more than 150,000 women.

Moreover, the organizational structure of the national union allowed for grassroots autonomy in determining the local reform goals and did not require that each local chapter adapt every platform item, thus providing women the flexibility to work on a variety of reform efforts, including suffrage. From New York to California, and in between, the branches slowly came to the realization that prayer and good deeds alone could not reform society. This philosophical transformation led to successful political campaigns for women's legal rights, prohibition, and women's suffrage. In one such example, the Minnesota WCTU leadership likened women's status to slavery and clearly connected equality, purity, and prohibition together. However, it became increasingly clear that the only way to beat the saloons and liquor producers was through politics and the ballot. In response, the Minnesota union president, Susanna Fry, encouraged local branches of the WCTU to join the political party system so as to pressure politicians to act on prohibition, purity legislation, and women's equality. A key area of interest focused on addressing the problem of the fallen woman and the white slave trade. Education programs that focused on sexuality, science, and moral values educated young women on their moral responsibilities and the consequences of male temptation. Concerned by the growth of prostitution and vice in Minneapolis and the apparent endorsement of prostitution by the mayor, who required weekly medical exams of all prostitutes and protected the business interests that supported vice, the women organized group prayer meetings in front of the

brothels, and they flooded government officials with letters and petitions protesting the mayor's policies. In this example, the women's
protests prevailed, and the mayor was forced to resign. The social
purity campaigns to eliminate vice, eradicate prostitution, and reform sexual double standards in law led to major revisions in legal
statutes that related to sexual age of consent across the United
States. The Minnesota WCTU is a good example of how regional
social movements have influenced policy making.

The genuine efforts of the WCTU women provided an activist
force that improved family life, but like many other organizations,
the ideology was grounded on nativism and a firm belief in white
superiority. They shared a common belief that immigrants and the
working class lacked the correct moral values and needed cultural
uplifting, while connecting the problem of low wages to cultural
inferiority and immorality. Social purity reform represented a response to the dramatic changes brought on by industrialization,
immigration, and the growth of urban cities across the United
States. Age of consent legal reform illustrates the rose-colored view
of the reformers and the clash of class relations over sexual purity.
The role of the WCTU in advancing legal reform originally focused
on the exploitation and victimization of young women, but by the
1900s, the WCTU shifted the victim notion to female sexual delinquency. The rise of the immigrant workforce, the increase in job
opportunities for single young women, and new pursuits of leisure
time at amusement parks and other theater pastimes raised the interest of the WCTU to reform and regulate sexual behavior. The
WCTU worked to change the rape laws across the United States
and they succeeded in reforming state laws governing rape of underage females. Legislation reform focused on challenging the age
of consent laws, which varied by state and in some jurisdictions
permitted girls as young as age 10 to legally consent to sex; most
states repealed these laws and set the age of consent at age 18.

On the other side of the reform lived the young women and men
for whom these reform measures were intended. The implementation of new laws regulating sexuality created conflict not only
for the young people involved but also within their family structures. As Mary Odem has shown in her study, many of these young
women who engaged in premarital sex, even if they had intentions
to marry, were placed in girls' detention homes while awaiting
statutory rape trials. While the reformers were responsible for the
laws, parents played a key role in the enforcement of age of consent laws. In short, reformers and parents used legal measures to

regulate the new sexual autonomy of young women and men. In one such case, a young couple moved in together in 1915 prior to marriage, only to be charged later under the new statutory rape law. This case, like many others, originated from parental complaints; between the years 1910 to 1920, the majority of statutory rape prosecutions in Alameda County, California, were initiated by parents. Other reform measures similarly added new layers of protection for women, but at the same time, the social values and belief in middle-class superiority placed severe limits on those for whom the reforms were intended. Statutory rape laws were also designed to keep men in-line, even if the sex was consensual, but also controlled young women's ability to make choices about their own sexuality and potential partners. These laws were intended to protect the virtues of women, while regulating the sexual behavior of less virtuous women, and checking the sexual behavior of men.[2]

YWCA

Similarly, the YWCA founded in England in 1855, as a missionary-based society, erupted in the United States, first in Boston. Local associations soon appeared and provided housing, moral guidance, and religious support to young working women. The YWCA provided important services to young women in the expanding urban cities of the United States, and as such they prided themselves on crossing class lines early on, but of course, access to Y services, including the well-known training schools, focused on middle-class values and Christian service. The organization flourished throughout the 20th century and continues to the present day to have national and international programming. A good example is the YWCA of San Jose, California (now named the YWCA of the Silicon Valley), which formed in 1903 and continues to provide services to poor and working women in Santa Clara County. Some of the early programs included the Girl Reserves, a club that provided organized activities and leadership development for young women. The Business Girls League, founded in 1930, offered vocational counseling, classes, and clubs for working women.

By the 1950s, the local San Jose Girl Reserves program had become the Y-Teens, which reflected local youths' interest in more social and coeducational activities. The Hi-Spot (1944–1959, reopened briefly in 1961) was a popular teen center governed by a council of high school students with an adult advisory board that became a model for youth-leadership programs. The YWCA also served the needs of older women in this period through programs such as Ladies

San Jose Normal School, YWCA students, 1910. The YWCA of Silicon Valley Records, MSS-2006-01-01, San Jose State University Library Special Collections and Archives. (Courtesy of San Jose State University, Special Collections and Archives)

Day Out and clubs such as the Y-Wives. More recently, during the 1960s and 1970s, the YWCA offered a number of innovative programs, including the Young Mother's Education Program (1967), which partnered with the San Jose Unified School District to keep young mothers in school; the 24-hour Rape Crisis Hotline (1973); and the Hispanic Outreach Program (1978), which offered childcare, youth programs, clubs, and citizenship and English courses. In the 1980s and 1990s, YWCA programming expanded to include Child Assault Prevention (C.A.P.), Parent Education, and Career Development. More recently, organizational activities and programs include Walk a Mile in Her Shoes (2003); the Social and Racial Justice Program (2006), an anti-bias education program; and TechGYRLS (2007), an after-school program that teaches girls technological and engineering skills. The YWCA's organizational philosophy of diversity shaped the 20th-century platform, and it became one of the first national organizations to publicly support racial integration and civil rights.

Cities across the United States benefited from the services provided by the local Ys. The benefits even extended to women of color who lived under the yoke of Jim Crow laws that mandated segregated organizations. The experience of the Baltimore YWCA illustrates the constraints of this racial divide by their formation of the first colored Ys in the United States. Formed in 1906, the Baltimore Colored club did not receive recognition as an official branch until 1920. Of particular interest is the fact that like white branches, the majority of the black women who worked for the YWCA came from a middle-class background and held similar concerns for female purity and educational programs. But more importantly, the YWCA became a venue to promote racial uplift and civil rights, an area that the National YWCA and other locals would embrace later. The experience of women of color in the YWCA and other organizations, from the suffrage movement to settlement work, provides a different lens from which to view social movement reform. Black women, in particular, had a much larger agenda that included an anti-lynching campaign, eliminating racial violence and Jim Crow, while pursuing an interracial movement. The YWCA provided one venue, while other organizations like the National Association of Colored Women, focused on the moral education and cultural uplift of the African American community. The anti-lynching campaigns and the struggle to eliminate racial violence in the South raised awareness of gender and race discrimination, but more importantly, they highlighted the lack of economic equality and opportunity that women of color faced. All women shared in the everyday struggle for economic equality.[3]

SETTLEMENT HOUSE MOVEMENT AND WOMEN'S CLUBS

From 1880 to the 1920s, the settlement house movement emerged as a significant branch of the social gospel movement. The social gospel movement was a Protestant intellectual religious movement that looked to improve society through a variety of social reform agendas, it was frequently connected to the progressive movement—a liberal political and social movement that used the law and government policymaking to improve society. The progressive impulse of this period was a response to the grim realities of urban and industrial society. Rapid growth and the expansion of immigration to the United States during this time period pushed the demands on cities to address housing, transportation, public health, garbage removal, and access to public schools and parks. The rise of tenement housing projects and severe overcrowding, coupled by the lack of city services to address the filth, disease, and poverty, led progressive reformers to push for changes to improve the lives of immigrants and the poor.

Women played a key role as municipal housekeepers in their neighborhoods, towns, and cities. This term was used regularly during the Progressive Era to characterize the role of women as public housekeepers of civic morals through their social reform efforts to fight corruption in government, to promote city bonds to establish parks, schools, and libraries, as well as promoting social programs for working women, immigrants, and child welfare. Through civic action, women extended the boundaries of the home to include the entire community—thus paving the way for large-scale female reform. The heart of the settlement house impulse began in Chicago and New York, but it would spread across the United States. In 1891 there were only 4 settlement houses in the United States, and by 1910, there were 400. The main leaders of the movement included Jane Addams, Florence Kelly, Lillian Wald, and Alice Hamilton. All of these women shared similar backgrounds as members of the white middle class, and all were college educated, though they pursued different professional careers. Unified by the belief in the excess of American industrial capitalism and urban growth, and armed with new social science methods, these reformers promoted collective civic responsibility to improve the lives of immigrants and workers through a variety of means. Whereas in previous reform generations, the focus on personal failure dominated, the progressive reformers believed that through social and economic uplift, people could improve their lives. Progressive reformers had a more optimistic view of the human spirit, and they believed in social cohesion and direct civic participation.

Settlement houses provided single college-age women with new career options, beyond the standard professions in teaching, nursing, and librarianship. College-educated women accounted for 36 percent of the undergraduates in the United States in 1900, yet professional opportunities in medicine, law, and higher education were very limited. Thus, college-educated women had to create independent career paths that utilized their training. The formation of Hull House in 1889 and Henry House Settlement in New York in 1891 provided many of these women with new fulfilling careers and unprecedented autonomy as leaders in social work, while offering poor immigrant communities important cultural and social resources. Located in the slums of the cities, settlement houses provided a rich array of services, from day nurseries and medical care to art and music; they lobbied for day lunch programs in the public schools and promoted child labor legislation. More importantly, the leaders in the movement agitated for public reform and new legislation on a variety of levels. For example, Lillian Wald formed Henry House for visiting nurses, operating one of the first public nursing services in the country, while Florence Kelly led the state and federal movement to impose an eight-hour work day for women, to ban hiring children under the age of 14 to work in the factories, and to abolish tenement labor. John Peter Altgeld, the governor of Illinois, appointed Kelly to serve as the chief factory inspector of the state in 1893, and within a few years, she and Lillian Wald worked tirelessly to build support for the formation of the U.S. Children's Bureau. President Theodore Roosevelt sponsored several professional conferences on child welfare in 1909 and the National Child Labor Committee (NCLC) helped to draft the legislation that came to pass in 1912.

Not all of the women involved in the settlement house movement achieved national acclaim like Jane Addams, Lillian Wald, and Florence Kelly. Florence Cross Kitchelt, for example, worked closely with the Italian communities in Rochester, New York, and in New Haven, Connecticut. She never became a leader of the national movement, but she was well known in the local area of Rochester and particularly for her work helping to settle a large labor dispute in 1910. Kitchelt's participation in progressive reform mirrored the experience of many women of her generation. She held memberships in multiple organizations, participated in the suffrage movement, helped form the Connecticut League of Women Voters, held a long-term position with the Connecticut League of Nation's Association, and late in life, joined the struggle for an equal rights amendment.

WOMEN'S CLUBS

The settlement house movement success was dependent upon the generosity of wealthy benefactors and the work of women's clubs, across the United States. A good example of this model was the Chicago clubs' activism and municipal housekeeping funded by philanthropic donors. The Chicago Women's Club formed several agencies including the Women's & Children Protective Agency, School Children's Aid Society, and the Political Equality League to name a few. Cities of women worked on projects to address poverty, spreading slums, overcrowded schools, political corruption, and the spread of disease. As Americans moved to the western frontier, women applied similar public housekeeping measures to improve the quality of life of their youthful communities. In El Paso, Texas, the Women's Club led the charge to clean up the city and provide a healthier environment for their children. This same progressive impulse flourished in California, and between the years 1909 and 1918, progressive reform dominated state politics. The club women from San Francisco to San Diego exacted their civic influence in a number of ways, including building settlement houses, providing kindergartens and playgrounds, and promoting new legislation that included suffrage, child welfare, age of consent laws, and education reform. Similar to the Midwest and eastern regions, California's immigrant population expanded from 1.5 million in 1900 to 3.4 million in 1920. As a result of this expansion, state educational reformers developed adult assimilation education programs to teach newcomers English, politics, and culture. This program was referred to as the Americanization Program, which included a Home Teachers program directed at the large Mexican population, with a specific focus on women. The California program was modeled after adult education programs in Chicago and New York.

From Texas to California to the far reaches of the Northwest, women transformed their neighborhoods, towns, and cities by building schools and libraries, establishing after-school programs, and creating playgrounds and parks. All this while simultaneously reforming education and upgrading public health programs and basic services provided by municipal government. Commonly referred to as the gentle tamers, western women's voluntary associations from the General Federation of Women's Clubs (GFWC) to the WCTU and YWCA duplicated municipal housekeeping reform efforts that originated in the East and Midwest. As importantly, they provided the membership base to move women's suffrage to the national forefront.

WOMEN'S SUFFRAGE

The early campaigns for women's rights provided a firm intellectual foundation for the 20th-century movement. From the early 1860s forward, women focused on a host of injustices that included child custody, married women's property rights, divorce, and other sexual double standards to argue for the right to vote. Suffrage symbolized American democracy, and it became the beacon for women's reform. These early women believed that the vote would address other legal status issues that prevented women from participating in the democratic process.

The early movement represented a very small subset of activists, but by the early 20th century, the success of women's organizations and the growing number of western states granting women voting rights created the right environment to push for a national amendment. A combination of factors led to the final victory. Firstly, the success of the western suffrage campaigns granting women voting rights in Wyoming (1869), Colorado (1893), Utah (1896), Idaho (1896), Washington (1910), California (1911), Oregon (1912), Arizona (1912), Nevada (1914), and Montana (1914) strengthened the demand for federal voting rights. These western victories can be partially tied to settlement patterns in the western regions, the push for statehood, and growth of urbanization in these states and territories. Women played a key role as pioneers and settlers, and as suffrage leaders, western women utilized different strategies to win support from farmer-labor reformers, while lessening the emphasis on prohibition in large cities. As a result, the success of the western movement laid the groundwork for a national amendment.[4]

Leaders from the NWP traveled across the West to support various campaigns and, in 1915 following the Panama-Pacific Exposition, convinced local suffrage leader Sara Bard Field to deliver a suffrage petition to President Wilson via an automobile. The ride was intended to dramatize the demand for suffrage, with a petition of half a million signatures. Field with two Swedish feminists, traveled 5,000 miles, meeting organized crowds in Reno; Salt Lake City; rural areas of Wyoming; Colorado Springs; Kansas City; Lincoln, Nebraska; Cedar Rapids, Iowa; Chicago; New York; and finally, Washington, D.C. Along the way, local women staged parades and rallies to help dramatize the potential power of the women's voting bloc.

At the turn of the century, the NAWSA was in a state of reorganization. The old guard leadership style of Elizabeth Stanton and Susan B. Anthony, the matriarchs of the movement, shifted to younger more progressive suffragists to move the organization forward. In the late 1890s, NAWSA shifted its focus from a national amendment to winning state voting rights. While these efforts were successful in the west, state efforts east of the Mississippi river failed; a seed change in leadership was needed to fight for a federal amendment. In her final years as president of

Women march in a rally supporting the right to vote, 1912. (AP Photo)

NAWSA, Anthony recognized the talents of the Carrie Chapman Catt, a longtime suffragist and elite member of the NAWSA. After succeeding in leading the Colorado suffrage struggle in 1893, she quickly worked her way up the organizational hierarchy. In 1895 at the national convention, she outlined the organizational failures and argued for new modern strategies to advance fundraising and lobbying activities of the members. Catt's direct approach created some controversy among the elder leaders, but her organizational and public-speaking skills earned her the favor and support of Anthony. She became known as "the General" of the organization. She served as president from 1900 to 1904 and in 1916 agreed to return as the president, demanding complete autonomy over all programs, lobbying efforts, and fundraising. Catt offered her "Winning Plan," which focused on state level campaigns to build momentum for a federal amendment. Through nonpartisan lobbying, the women would convince Congress but more importantly convince American women that they needed the vote. While she supported the state approach, she was frustrated by the lack of progress at the national level and believed that NAWSA needed to move toward a more aggressive national program. In her words, she said, "We care not a gingersnap about anything but that federal amendment." Catt promoted woman suffrage in a nonpartisan fashion, but she provided unrelenting organizational skills and demanded that the membership fall in-line according to her visions. She ran the organization in a military fashion and created an efficient publicity machine designed to sway public opinion and one based on optimism that women could improve society through the ballot. A determined pragmatist and charismatic speaker, she galvanized women to act. By 1920 she was one of the most popular speakers for suffrage, banking more than 7,000 speeches and traveling more than 100,000 miles for the cause. Catt tempered her speeches according to the audience. In the South, she reinforced racism against male black voters, describing them as illiterate to gain support of Southern society, while in separate black meetings, she described suffrage democracy as having no bias based on race or sex. Like many of the suffrage leaders of the earlier generation, Catt maintained a pragmatic approach to building support, which meant sometimes playing the race card, but she also understood that she needed male politicians to endorse the amendment and she used her political savvy to influence them.

Catt recognized that winning the vote from Congress was critical, but she needed suffrage soldiers at the local level to pressure ordinary citizens and politicians to support the amendment. She formed Suffrage Schools to educate ordinary women on the history of the suffrage movement, the issues, and the skills needed to participate. Students learned how to work with municipalities, politicians, and the press, while learning public-speaking techniques. This professional network eventually penetrated every level of society and directly contributed to the growth of the membership to 2 million by 1920. The schools provided a base to unify every kind of women's group and local association across the country. She would take a similar approach following the suffrage victory to form the nonpartisan League of Women Voters.

WORLD WAR I

The 20th century opened up new opportunities for women to pursue social reform and social justice. Female moral authority allowed women to push from their domestic space to influence politics as municipal housekeepers. Housekeeping took many forms and women's activism converged with the emergence of the Progressive Era reform movements. The argument for women's political equality became increasingly difficult to deny, as reformers identified the abuses of industrial society and connected women's

political participation to the betterment of society. Indeed, the suffrage movement became more diverse and socially progressive in
a period of time when great ideological, economic, and political
shifts transformed the global landscape. World War I thus set the
stage for the final suffrage victory and for a modern civil rights
movement for women.

World War I provided a unique opportunity to build a stronger
national directive. By utilizing the groundswell of American patriotism, Catt doubled the membership base of NAWSA, while pursing lobbying policy to swing congressional support. Meanwhile,
the more radical branch of suffrage organized by Alice Paul and
the NWP protested President Wilson for his failure to grant women
voting rights during a period of intense patriotism. This group of
younger women used more radical tactics to gain attention, including picketing the White House, burning copies of the president's
speeches, and chaining themselves to the White House fence, resulting in mob violence and police brutality. In one incident, the police
arrested the female protesters for obstructing the sidewalk, and the
legal system sent them to prison. While in prison, the women went
on hunger strikes and were brutally force fed with iron devices designed to hold their mouths open, leading the papers to call them
"the Iron-Jawed Angels." The NWP was one of the first groups in
the United States to use nonviolent protest for a political cause, and
these methods, while militant for the time, forced the hand of justice.
Between the years 1918 and 1919, police arrested 168 suffragists for
peacefully protesting. In a show of support, new groups of suffragists appeared with new banners that read "Kaiser Wilson" and took
the place of their incarcerated colleagues. More arrests, court trials,
and 60-day prison terms followed. The prisoners demanded to be
treated as political prisoners with access to legal counsel, books,
and better food. The hunger strikes brought sympathy and support
from the Left, and the blame for police suppression and abuse of
these women rested at the feet of the president. Catt was outraged
by the partisan tactics of the NWP, but she later admitted that they
gave credibility to NAWSA and helped push the cause forward.
The NWP clearly influenced Wilson to compel Congress to support
suffrage, but Catt's restraint and constant reminder of the sacrifices of American women in the war effort turned the tide. In 1918,
Catt's "Winning Plan" reaped results when the House of Representatives passed the amendment, and in 1919, the Senate followed
suit, with final ratification taking place in 1920.[5]

By the end of the 19th century, women's social activism expanded
across the United States. Social organizations from the WCTU to

the General Federation of Women's Clubs, and reform organizations emanating from the social gospel movement, the social settlement houses movement, and the unification of suffrage movement, paved the way for women's full participation in American society. These early organizations laid the groundwork for women's rights in the 20th century and helped shape public policies that specifically addressed gender discrimination.

The ratification of the Nineteenth Amendment was a milestone victory for American women because it gave women new legitimacy and opportunity as voters, office holders, and social activists. Typical of the suffrage years, these women belonged to a variety of organizations and held overlapping memberships but were loosely tied together by a commitment to women's rights. The immediate aftermath of the suffrage victory had mixed results in terms of women's voting behaviors, but as political scientist Kristi Anderson reminds us, women had to learn the mechanics of government and exercise their rights as "newly enfranchised voters." Suffrage was the stepping stone that secured women's rights as political members of society, and it would take several decades before the political infrastructure allowed full female participation through voter registration, voter education, and political party participation. Women also had to learn the habit of voting. Through the newly formed League of Women Voters, women provided new learning opportunities to understand the mechanism of government and policy making.[6]

NOTES

1. Paula Baker, "The Domestication of Politics: Women and American Political Society, 1780–1920," *The American Historical Review* 89 (June 1984): 620–47; Anne Firor Scott, *Natural Allies: Women's Associations in American History* (University of Illinois Press, 1991), p. 81.

2. Fran Smith, *Breaking Ground: The Daring Women of the YWCA in the Santa Clara Valley, 1905–2005* (YWCA of Silicon Valley, 2005); Mary Odem, *Delinquent Daughters: Protecting and Policing Adolescent Female Sexuality in the United States, 1885–1920* (University of North Carolina Press, 1995).

3. Smith, *Breaking Ground;* Lizabeth Cohen, *A Consumers' Republic: The Politics of Mass Consumption in Postwar America* (Vintage Books, 2003), pp. 41–54.

4. Rebecca J. Mead, *How the Vote was Won: Woman Suffrage in the Western United States, 1868–1914* (New York University Press, 2004), pp. 1–52.

5. Jean H. Baker, *Votes for Women: The Struggle for Suffrage Revisited* (Oxford University Press, 2002).

6. Kristi Anderson, *Women in Partisan and Electoral Politics Before the New Deal* (University of Chicago Press, 1996).

2

WOMEN AND REFORM IN THE PROGRESSIVE ERA, 1880s TO 1930

This chapter will focus on women's reform during the period known as the Progressive Era, from the late 1880s through 1930. As we shall see, women played a significant role in this era of reform, which spanned the years from 1880 to 1930. The variety of reform that took place can be framed around the continued struggle for women's rights and specifically the 20th-century suffrage movement. From 1901 to 1920, more than 2 million women demanded national voting rights. These women fought side-by-side with progressive reformers to improve American society. Some women worked to create protective labor laws for women and children, influenced public policy in labor employment, birth control rights, while others fought to end racial discrimination and address the lynching crisis of African Americans in the South. Historians writing about women's history have used the wave metaphor to represent the eruptions of activism across time.

WAVES OF FEMINISM

Historians have used the metaphor of waves to describe the complex history of women's rights and feminist activism. The first wave refers to the activism that began with the Seneca Falls Convention in 1848 through 1920, when women finally were granted federal voting rights under the Nineteenth Amendment. The second-wave generation includes women who were active in the postwar years and younger women who came of age during the 1950s and 1960s.

French historian and feminist Karen Offen in her exploration of international feminism across time writes that "...many 'waves' and 'eruptions' many 'feminisms'—can be identified."[1] She traces back the emergence of the use of the wave metaphor to 1884 when Irish activist Frances Power Cobbe, writing about social movements, applied the metaphor of oceans, waves, and tides to express the movement of women. By 1968, feminists used the term *first wave* to recognize the contributions of these foremothers, yet in doing so, they lumped together multiple decades dating back to the 1840s.

The ideological framework for this chapter is based on this idea of the first wave, though the historical chronology begins with the rise of women's reform through settlement house work in the 1880s through the formation of National American Woman Suffrage Association (NAWSA), and the building momentum of the suffrage movement under the leadership of Carrie Chapman Catt and, to a lesser extent, Alice Paul and Lucy Burns as members of the Congressional Union (CU) and the National Woman's Party (NWP).

This chapter will thus incorporate multiple themes that encompass suffrage, Progressive Era politics, union activism, public health, working conditions, childbirth and pregnancy, reproductive rights and health, sexuality, religious beliefs, education, housing, clothing, food, government, as well as leisure time activities. As we have seen in chapter 1, women's social reform took many forms of which one promoted women's civil rights and its extension to children and family life. This chapter will investigate Progressive Era reforms such as measures to improve municipal government, public health, labor legislation, educational reform, sexual legal reforms, maternal and infant health, birth control, and postsuffrage politics that affected both women and families. First, let's have a better understanding of the Progressive Era politics.

HISTORICAL OVERVIEW
OF THE PROGRESSIVE ERA

Between the 1880s and the 1920s, the vast industrialization that transformed all layers of society forced many Americans to embrace a diverse series of reform efforts. Many progressives, angry about the excess of industrial capitalism and urbanization, pointed to the dangers of factory life and the squalor of tenement housing. They believed that social and economic conditions could be improved and were optimistic that American democratic government had the potential to address these social ills. They also firmly believed that the best way to change society was through voting, litigating bad practices in the courts, and congressional legislation. In contrast to the individualistic ideology of the 19th century, progressive reformers believed that collective action was necessary to produce a viable society whereby big government provided the resources to take care of the collective whole. Some reformers focused on the expansion of legislation regulating government, business, and labor, while others focused on expanding civil rights, expanding education, building kindergartens, creating local playgrounds and national parks, improving public health including infant, child, and maternal health, and eradicating poverty in urban areas.

What did it mean to be a progressive? The early histories of the progressive movement focused on the role of the great white male leaders and their battle with the Republican Party and the railroads. New histories have illustrated a far more complex view of what it meant to be a progressive reformer in this era. The initial historical body of literature by writers like George E. Mowry, in his seminal work *The California Progressives* (1951), focused entirely on a handful of male leaders in the state and regretfully overlooked the role that women progressives played in state and national politics. Newer historical literature illuminates, at the micro and macro levels, reform histories of socialists, journalists, environmentalists, welfare reformers, public health and labor reformers, and educators of the era, many of whom were women.

INTELLECTUAL ROOTS

While new developments in journalism highlighted the flaws of unbridled capitalism, a new set of intellectual solutions provided the base for the ongoing movement. The emergence of new theories in education, economics, law, and politics transformed the social landscape. New academic fields in the social sciences, sociology, anthropology, psychology, and economics focused on social behaviors and action. Reformers and intellectuals used new scientific thought to understand the relationship of the individual to the community. Many of the thinkers of the period began to critique the concept of *social Darwinism*, which equated social status and inequality to Charles Darwin's theories of natural selection and survival of the fittest. In addition was the work of sociologist Lester Frank Ward who significantly influenced modern views of social structure and biology by arguing that biological evolution was different from social evolution, and that the theorists of social Darwinism, such as William Sumner, wrongly applied theories of evolution to the human experience. In short, humans had the ability to overcome the forces of nature through rational thought and human interaction. John Dewey similarly criticized the rigidity of education and advocated for creative intelligence as a method to improve society. Dewey believed that teaching children to think creatively and to encourage imagination through formal education would produce social progress and reform.

The subsequent rise of political science and sociology also had a significant impact on all reform movements in the United States and around the world. The rich cross-fertilization of intellectual thought in Europe and the United States influenced reform work. Jane Addams, for example, modeled the Hull House settlement after the Toynbee Hall settlement house in England, which served as a living center for university men in a working-class neighborhood. The purpose of this arrangement was designed to improve understanding between classes and to provide education and culture to the local population. Addams replicated this approach, and she became the leader of the settlement house movement in the United States. The settlement house movement and the rise of new academic disciplines gave women new access to higher education and provided needed professional jobs that women could dominate in a period of time where most women worked in factories as unskilled laborers.

NEW JOURNALISM

New journalism played an important role in raising national awareness of the exploitation of industrial capitalism. One of the most significant contributions of the era came from Jacob Riis through his famous book *How the Other Half Lives.* Riis produced a photographic exposé of New York's poor and helped shape the emergence of an urban reform movement. Thereafter, newspapers and magazines began to barrage American readers with news stories highlighting the problem of urban poverty, labor abuses and impact on the industrial workforce, the immorality of business practices, and the need to reform corruption in government. Several new magazines like *McClure's, Colliers,* and the *Saturday Evening Post* emerged. Each took advantage of the growing readership by hiring talented reporters to write stories about social problems and running stories using photographs and illustrations. Some of the most well-known *McClure's* stories included Lincoln Steffen's "The Shame of City" (1903) and Ida Tarbell's "History of the Standard Oil Company" (1904). Similarly, novelists used literature as a vehicle to expose the abuses of capitalism. For example, Upton Sinclair's novel *The Jungle* (1906) exposed the gritty side of the meatpacking industry, from poor working conditions for the meatpackers to the filthy unsanitary conditions in meat processing. These stories enraged many to action and eventually led to new government regulations. On the other hand, many issues, like those mentioned by Ida B. Wells-Barnett in her study on lynching and racial bias against black men in Memphis, seemed to fall by the wayside by a white press that failed to address the Jim Crow violence of the time.

FEMALE EDUCATION

Education played a key role in the development of the settlement house movement in the United States and for the first time offered middle-class women new opportunities to work in professional environments that they actually controlled. As historian Robyn Muncy and others have shown, middle-class women used moral authority to improve their social and economic position. In the post–Civil War years, women established clear connections between raising children to be good citizens and betterment of their own lives through education. Between 1865 and the 1890s, several women's colleges opened, and many colleges instituted coeducational programs. This growth of college and universities programs provided new opportunities for both men and women. By 1870, almost one-third of American colleges admitted men and women, and by 1890, more than two-thirds of the colleges operated as coeducational institutions. Despite this impressive increase in opportunities by the turn of the 20th century, women only represented 36 percent of the undergraduate college population and 13 percent of graduate programs. Even more worrying was the fact that college-educated women continued to have limited employment opportunities. Pink-collar professions as teachers, nurses, and librarians continued to be their assigned professions, while only a few exceptional women pursued advanced degrees in medicine and law and found employment in these male-dominated professions. A couple of examples include Dr. Alice Hamilton, who was the first woman appointed to the Harvard Medical School; Clara Foltz, the first woman to practice law in California; Florence Kelley, who received her law degree in 1894; and Alice Paul, who received her PhD in 1912.

LABOR AND WORK—SETTLEMENT HOUSE MOVEMENT

College-educated women during this time period faced tremendous discrimination in professional fields, and for many, the rise of the settlement house movement offered new, exciting opportunities for different careers. As early as the 1880s, the establishment of the Settlement House Association (SHA) at Smith College opened the gate for the establishment of local chapters on Rivington Street in New York City, and in 1889, Jane Addams and Ellen Starr founded the Hull House Settlement in Chicago. These were soon followed by the Henry Settlement House for visiting nurses in New York City, founded by nurse and social reformer Lillian Wald in 1900. The settlement house movement quickly spread through New York and New England, and most followed the leadership of Addam's Hull House. The Hull House model became a philanthropic path and a vital part of the engine of social reform.

The subsequent work of Addams and other progressive women helped establish a female dominion in charity and reform work. Located in a rundown neighborhood in Chicago, Hull House offered the poor urban community a variety of needed services including medical aid and advice, a boarding house, and educational and cultural programs; in addition, they built kindergartens and parks for the community. Equally important, the settlement house movement offered an acceptable environment where women could serve the community and engage in a rich professional life. The cloistered nature of settlement house life replicated the friendship and networking experience that most of these women had experienced in women's colleges. From these close female friendships, women forged lifelong intimate relationships with settlement house colleagues as they shared common bonds as new professionals.

Addams often referred to the "subjective necessity" of the settlement house movement, by which she meant that these houses provided young educated women with the opportunity to satisfy professional ambitions and at the same time provide important resources and support to poor communities. In effect, settlement houses provided one solution to the social and economic problems created by industrialization. The idealism and sacrifice of the settlement house movement, funded by the patronage of wealthy donors, successfully empowered a new era of professional women. One successful example was the women's clubs in Chicago that provided Hull House with the resources needed resources to expand their services and employ professional women. Indeed, Hull House and its core leaders emerged as the model for social reform work in the United States.

PROTECTIVE LABOR REFORM: INFANT, CHILD, MATERNITY HEALTH

For many middle-class women, the settlement house concept represented an extension of Christian philanthropy adapted to a model for social reform work. Florence Kelley, a Hull House resident, played a significant role in Chicago and beyond by focusing on solving social problems through social scientific investigation and publicity. Kelley's entrance into social science research began with a fellowship with the Illinois Labor Bureau, and within a short period of time, she convinced the bureau to hire her to study the labor conditions in the garment industry sweatshop system. Her work exposed the terrible conditions in which women and children worked and led to a female attack on the legislature to force regulation of the sweatshops. Through the combined effort of Hull House and the Illinois Women's Alliance, Illinois enacted legislation that ended child labor and regulated working hours for women and working conditions. Kelley went on to become the chief factory inspector in the state and became the leader for protective labor legislation reform. She not only succeeded in changing public policy, she carved out a professional position for herself and other women dependent upon paid employment.

Through Kelley's careful mentorship, she opened the eyes of the residents to the horrors of unregulated industrial labor and the subsequent impact on women and children. She taught residents many investigative social science research methods and in turn gave them opportunities to make a difference in their lives. In the midst of the poverty and destitution of the 1893 depression, she sent Julia Lathrop out to investigate numerous relief agencies. Lathrop's work in turn led to her appointment to the State Board of Charities. Of note, she visited every county in the state and became an expert in mental health and eventually wrote numerous reports and papers on the problem of the asylums for the insane and disabled.

Moreover, Kelley provided a training ground for the emerging field of social science research. Her role as the state chief factory inspector allowed her to mentor new students in the field of social work and together they gathered substantial data to support new labor legislation. A good example is her 1895 research study

"Hull House Maps and Papers," where the residents conducted a survey to determine the ethnic makeup of the community and collected data on the occupations and income of residents. This study literally placed Hull House on the map as a social laboratory on working-class life and social behaviors. As such, university students engaged in the new field of social science flocked to Hull House to put theory into practice and duplicated their new programs in settlement houses across the country.

NATIONAL CONSUMERS LEAGUE (NCL)

During this time period, women's organizations worked collaboratively to support different municipal reforms, pushed for legislative change, and implemented a variety of programs. The diversity of women's social networks and their overlapping membership patterns provided another important base for social reform. For example, in 1899 Kelley accepted an offer to serve as the executive secretary of the newly formed NCL that was committed to improving industrial labor conditions by educating consumers on working conditions and encouraging them to purchase products that were produced by humane conditions. Under her leadership, the NCL focused on promoting legislation to force fair labor practices that improved working conditions, particularly for women and children. Kelley moved from Chicago to the Henry Street Settlement House in New York to pursue this work, and she made Henry Street her home base for more than 28 years. Together, the NCL, the Hull House, and the Henry Street Settlement House provided the support to promote many social programs. Moreover, other alliances between the national Women's Trade Union League (WTUL), the GFWC and Parent Teacher's Association (PTA, which was previously known as the Mother's Congress), pressed the social boundaries of women's public role. These organizations represented more than 1 million women.

The history of the settlement house movement has largely focused on Chicago and New York City, yet by 1911, there were approximately 215 settlement houses across the United States. While the residents of these houses did not reach the acclaim of Addams, Wald, Kelley, and Lathrop, they provided the backbone to the movement through research and investigation, and by providing real services to their communities; frequently, they found themselves embedded in the labor movement as they worked closely with working-class women. For example, Florence Ledyard Kitchelt worked in the Rivington

Street college settlement house and later moved to Rochester, New York as resident of the Little Italy House, where she played a key role in the final arbitration of the Rochester Strike of 1910. As part of her training to better understand the Italian immigrant population, she traveled to Italy to learn more about the culture and language and later worked closely with the Italian community in Rochester and in New Haven, Connecticut, to build social services around the needs of the community. The Denison House in Boston, Massachusetts, located in the heart of Boston's south end, served the working-class community and likewise formed bonds with union women and men as they investigated factory conditions. While in the West the movement focused on different immigrant communities, from Chinese immigrants living in San Francisco to Mexican women living in the barrios in Los Angeles.

CHILD LABOR; INFANT AND MATERNAL HEALTH—CHILDREN'S BUREAU

The crowning achievement for the progressive female reform movement took place when Congress created the Children's Bureau (CB) in 1912. Under the Department of Commerce and Labor, it became the first female-dominated agency in the federal government. The creation of the CB represented the apex of female public power in the Progressive Era and directly praised the Hull House as a social research institution. The story of the CB highlights the success of the settlement house movement in building cross coalitions to work toward social reform and the rise of female dominion in policy making.

In *Some Ethical Gains Through Legislation* (1905), Kelley wrote, "...the noblest duty of the Republic is that of self-preservation by so cherishing all its children that they in turn, may become enlightened self-governing citizens....The care and nurturing of childhood is a vital concern of the nation."[2] Indeed social welfare studies documented the need to regulate child labor and highlighted the impact that poverty had on family life. The most glaring issue was the increase in death rates of children in the summer of 1903 due to the croup. Kelley and Lillian Wald concluded that more studies were needed to address the death rate and to provide health services. The idea to create an official bureau originated from Wald and Kelley, both longtime advocates for child welfare. Wald pushed for the creation of the CB as a means to gather data on childhood disease. Drawing on Republican ideology, she too argued that the state had an obligation to ensure the health and well-being of the nations' children. Her promotion of the CB came at an ideal political moment, as Theodore Roosevelt, a committed progressive, took over the office of the presidency. Roosevelt shared the view that the federal government needed to take a more active role in social and economic reform. He convinced Congress to create new executive agencies, new investigative commissions, and conferences on specific issues. Wald's promotion of a new federal agency to address child labor and health fit perfectly into the Roosevelt platform.

In reality, the idea also required a collaborative effort with Congress in order to write the legislation and to get the bill through the legislative process. Wald and Kelley worked closely with the male-dominated National Child Labor Committee (NCLC), and the women succeeded in convincing the committee to support the legislation. This was a testament to the power of female leadership and recognition that women should take a public leadership role in developing public policy for child welfare. As lobbying work began to take shape, the NCLC demonstrated its role in policy making at regional and state levels, by bringing to the attention of local municipalities the problems of juvenile delinquency, education, and child labor and emphasizing their expertise in the area of child welfare reform. It would take some time before child welfare would become a national issue, but with the support of President Roosevelt and the convening of the White House Conference on the Care of Dependent Children, the door had been opened for a national debate on child welfare. Designed to increase awareness of the problem, a group of more than 200 professionals identified some of the problems and outlined possible solutions. One of the core questions related to dependent care of children and what should happen to children when their parents were unable to care for them. The standard view of the day supported keeping children with their biological parents rather than placing them in foster care. Thus, the group promoted government-sponsored maintenance programs that were signed into law in 1912 by President Taft.

PARENTING AND CHILDCARE

The broadly conceived mandate of the CB emphasized the need to "...investigate and report on all matters pertaining the welfare of children and child life among all classes of people."[3] Julia Lathrop became the first bureau chief and thus the first woman to be appointed to a federal agency. It was through the establishment of the bureau that the term *female dominion* first entered into the lexicon of American reform terminology. The CB replicated the gendered identity of the settlement house movement, with a female-dominated workforce committed to work on maternal policy issues. These women branded a new form of policy making, while not overstepping their male counterparts. In this way, women dominated in all areas of child welfare reform. Through Lathrop's careful management and diplomacy, she used her new position to boost new employment opportunities for women, and the agency quickly hired mainly women from the settlement house movement. All of the division heads, except one, were women, and all of the field-workers were women. Lathrop skillfully danced around the civil service merit-based hiring process by emphasizing that the programs and fieldwork required an ability to ask very personal questions about motherhood and infant care. Lathrop successfully demonstrated the need to hire female field agents, as men were not suitable to ask questions about breast-feeding, maternal health, and childcare.

Once firmly established as a government agency, women across America wrote letters to the bureau asking for support. Women confided some of the most intimate details of their lives, from breast-feeding, domestic violence, pregnancy outside of marriage, questions about birth control, and so on. Many of these letters were directed to Lathrop, demonstrating her importance as the leader of the bureau, but more importantly illustrating the needs of everyday women in rearing their children. Moreover, she made sure that the program continued to study the problem of infant mortality, and she used government publications to provide information on birth registration and other issues.

In 1910, these publications, authored by Mary Mills West, a mother of five children and a widow, became the best-selling publications from the Government Printing Office. The titles included *Prenatal Care, Infant Care, Child Care and Milk*, and *Indispensable Food for Children*, among others. The demand for these publications made it difficult to keep them in stock. Between the years 1914 and 1921, the CB distributed more than a million copies of *Infant Care*. The demand for educational information on childhood and parenting meshed perfectly with the rise of new higher education programs in home economics and childcare. The CB publicity arm worked the press at all angles to produce articles on the work of the bureau. All of the major newspapers and women's magazines carried stories on the CB programs and publications. The public relations program worked, and the volume of personal letters increased to more than 125,000 letters per year that represented every region and social class in the United States. By 1917, the CB was known as the national expert on child welfare issues and held a monopoly over policy making.

The birth registration drive program dominated in the early years of the bureau, supported by a diverse group of women's organizations from the League of Women Voters (LWV), GFWC, and the NCL. These groups provided the local campaign work needed to survey the population and to lobby in local areas through the support of voluntary groups. Club women from Ohio, Texas, Iowa, and Vermont enthusiastically surveyed their communities and sent back more than 13,000 reports, while the Association of Collegiate Alumnae conducted similar tests from New England to the West Coast.

SHEPPARD-TOWNER MATERNITY AND INFANCY ACT

As we have seen, the power and prestige of the CB grew incrementally under the care and leadership of Julia Lathrop. The bureau managed several reform efforts, but it was the Sheppard-Towner Maternity and Infancy Act that was her crowning policy achievement before her 1921 retirement from the agency. This act was no small fete given the patriotic frenzy of World War I and the fact that many of the settlement house women were pacifists who objected to U.S. involvement in World War I. Despite being a recipient of the Nobel Peace Prize, many shunned Jane Addams for her antiwar position. Lathrop similarly objected to the war but kept her views to herself in order to protect her job and the bureau. She walked a tightrope between politicians and antiwar activists. She quite literally milked the war to gain support for the campaign known as the "Children's Year." Pointing to the military physical data that denied one-third of the male population from serving in the military because of physical problems, Lathrop expertly connected child welfare to military service by demonstrating a link between infant care and physical development.

Working through the Women's Committee for National Defense and in her capacity as the executive director of the Child Welfare Department (CWD), she expanded the national program for child welfare reform. Ingeniously conceived, the "Children's Year" provided a platform to promote a national agenda to protect children as a patriotic duty. The program focused on building an American welfare state capable of eradicating poverty, providing mothers' pensions, giving workers living wages, supporting prenatal and maternity health care, enforcing pure milk laws, providing for baby clinics and childhood education, and mandating birth registrations in every state. Through an expanded educational programming and the organization of child health conferences, CWD provided infant examinations and literature on childcare, and some 6.5 million children received free medical exams. While the recipients were mostly middle class, Lathrop intended to extend the program to rural areas and to help establish a presence in every state through a public health nursing program and Child Hygiene Division. By 1920, her vision encompassed 35 states with Child Hygiene Divisions, and at the conclusion of the war, Lathrop laid the foundation for the Sheppard-Towner Act.[4]

The suffrage victory and the activism of women's clubs and other social movements helped expedite the legislation through both houses of Congress. The bill won by a landslide and was signed into law by President Harding on November 23, 1921. Under the bill, each state retained the ability to accept or reject the act, and with the added incentive of federal funds, within one year 42 of the 48 states accepted the program and its funding. By 1927, only Illinois, Connecticut, and Massachusetts refused funding.

The funding brought important public health services to 45 states that included the hiring of public health nurses and doctors. Overwhelmingly, women dominated these jobs, and some 812 public health nurses were hired throughout the United States. Between 1922 and 1929, more than 300,000 children had received care, and more than 30,000 women received prenatal care and thousands more attended prenatal conferences. Also important was the extension of visiting-nurse programs to poor and rural areas. However, visiting nurses also distributed literature on the proper care of children, based on mechanized routines and standardized care; they were frequently critical of housekeeping skills of their charges, large families and overcrowded homes, which they believed promoted promiscuity. In turn, these nurses demonstrated proper white progressive ideals on housekeeping and cooking, in order to speed the process toward the goal of assimilating immigrant families to adopt middle-class American values.

LABOR AND WAGES: THE 8-HOUR DAY

The CB's promotion of the Sheppard-Towner Maternity and Infancy Act, child welfare policy reform focused on a variety of issues, but the condition of factory work and the exploitation of children dominated the reform issues during the Progressive Era. In part, the movement represented a cross-section of new journalists, politicians, and female reformers. New journalism graphically illustrated the horror of industrial labor. In the publication *How the Other Half Lives* by Jacob Riis, the plight of the working poor became an important exposé for the movement.

Lewis Hine similarly earned a reputation as one of the pioneers of social documentary photography. Hired by the NCLC to document the abuses of child labor, he visited the New South, and his work became an important representation of the brutality of child labor conditions. While visiting nearly every Southern city from Virginia to the Gulf Coast, he documented the labor abuses in the textile mills, coal mines, cotton fields, canneries, tobacco, and glassworks. Together, journalists and the CB raised public awareness of child labor abuses and the need for national legislation. In one photograph taken in Dunbar, Louisiana, March 1911, children were depicted shucking oysters with their mothers. In another view, a mother is depicted holding her sick infant while working for $1.50 per day. These photographs highlight the poor working conditions that poor women and children labored in, the constant stream of health problems created by limited factory regulation, and the lack of childcare. Many of these women and children worked 60-hour weeks, earning below subsistence wages.

The settlement house movement provided the base to promote legislation that would outlaw child labor, introduce minimum wage laws, and champion the 8-hour workday for women in industry. The problem of child labor transcended all industries. In 1900, approximately 2 million children worked for wages. In 1893, the Illinois legislature passed factory limits on the working hours of women, prohibited child labor, and controlled the sweatshops inside the tenements. The initial success of this legislation can be attributed to Florence Kelley's role as the chief inspector of factories in the state. Kelley and her small staff of 12 investigated violations of these laws, and she wrote annual reports that detailed the violations and described the hazards of factory work. Despite the endorsement by the governor and initially the legislature, the garment industry vigorously opposed the 8-hour workday for women, and in 1895, the Illinois Supreme Court ruled against the legislation based on the argument that it violated individual freedom and the individual's right to contract for their personal labor. Immigrant families likewise resisted government control over their children's lives. It would take more than 30 years before child welfare

Oyster shuckers in Biloxi, Mississippi, 1911. Lewis Hine Photograph. (Library of Congress)

reformers would succeed in pressing labor protections for children. Finally, in 1938, Congress passed the Fair Labor Standards Act that moved to eliminate child labor in manufacturing.

Frustrated by the state lawmakers and the Illinois Supreme Court, Kelley pursued her law degree at the Northwestern University Law School and was conferred with her juris doctorate and admitted to the Illinois state bar in 1894. She used her skills as a lawyer to press for legal change. In *Some Ethical Gains Through Legislation* (1905), Kelley described the abuses against children in industry. She prefaced this work with a dedication to the "Right of Childhood." In her book, Kelley described the various degree of abuses, including the denial of providing children with compulsory education. As a result of her demands for a living wage in tenement sweatshop work, she was able to tie the exploitation of children to tenement work, and she fought to end this form of labor. Because most of this work was paid by the piece, it was impossible to regulate child labor abuses. Other areas of abuse included street occupations that included selling a variety of goods, including paper flowers, pencils, chewing gum, and newspapers. She and Wald established the New York Child Labor Committee in 1902 to address some of these issues, and with the success of the creation of the CB, she continued to support CB findings and backed legislation for child welfare. A prime example of the fruits of this successful work was the Keating-Owen Child Labor Act of 1916, though, regretfully, two years later the Supreme Court declared the act unconstitutional. Other defeats in child labor and minimum wage law reform experienced similar legal defeats. Kelley despaired that Congress cared more about protecting animals than the nation's children and mothers. She spent the next phase of her life petitioning for a child labor constitutional law.

In 1916, the first phase of legislation related to child labor restrictions was drafted, but opposition from the Southern congressmen derailed the legislation. It was not until 1938, when President Franklin D. Roosevelt signed into the law the Fair Standards Act, that child labor was finally regulated. To fully appreciate the obstacles of social welfare legislation, it is important to have a sense of the female workforce. Between 1900 to 1920, the female workforce was less than 22 percent, and more than half of the workforce was foreign born or nonwhite. Typically, most women earned half of what men earned, and the workforce was largely segregated by gender, with women, immigrants, and blacks working in mostly unskilled jobs and low-paying jobs. At this time, most of the women working in factories in the North were single women, while married women and mothers typically worked in tenement sweatshops. Factory life was hard; women worked 10–12 hours per day, lacked union representation, had to pay for their sewing machine needles and other supplies in the needle trades, were not aloud to talk, and had limited bathroom breaks. In contrast to women and foreign-born factory workers, middle-class white women gained new employment opportunities as clerical workers and in professional careers as nurses, teachers, librarians, and social workers. While their wages were still low, they did not face the same hazards and hardships that working-class and immigrant women faced in the workforce.

WOMEN'S TRADE UNION LEAGUE (WTUL)

By the year 1903, foreign-born industrial workers represented 25 percent of the female labor force, many of whom worked in the needle trades. In contrast to the male workforce, women lacked representation in the male dominated American Federation of Labor (AFL). In response, they formed a separate union known as the Women's Trade Union League (WCTU). The WTUL provided a needed structure in the fight for improved wages and working conditions for white and immigrant women. The organization followed the racist practices of the AFL by not admitting African Americans as members. Thus, the WTUL ended up operating as a coalition between trade women, social reformers, and upper-middle-class women of leisure. Many of the leaders came from the settlement house movement, and the organization depended on the generous donations from the male progressive elite. Most of the rank-and-file leaders like Leonora O'Reilly had strong roots as garment workers and labor activists. A true coalition of white and immigrant women, the WTUL worked closely with the National Women's Bureau (NWB) (formed in 1920) to promote new state regulations limiting the workday and minimum wages.

The labor union movement in the United States has a long history, but the political and economic environment in the early 20th century produced a period of extreme labor unrest, and a series of strikes took place in different industries. The growth of immigrant-based labor and the continued abuses by factory management and their owners created a powder keg for protest and violence. The WTUL took part in one the most famous garment industry labor strikes in New York City. What became known as the "Uprising of the 20,000," the International Ladies Garment Workers Union (ILGWU) walked off their jobs, picketing against declining piece rates, hiring and pay inequities, charges for materials, and fines for lateness.

The strikers were mostly Jewish and Italian workers who faced constant harassment from their bosses for their union activism, and the strikers faced arrest, jail, and expensive fines for their protest. The ILGWU turned to the WTUL for help, bringing a fresh group of protesters consisting of working-class and elite women. Elite women protesters faced the same treatment from law enforcement and from the legal system, but their social prominence and wealth helped support the movement and brought needed media attention to the strike issues. As manufacturers subcontracted the work to smaller shops, the ILGWU and the WTUL called a general meeting to encourage a general strike of shirtwaist workers. Clara Lemlich, a 17-year-old shirtwaist maker, gave an impassioned speech in Yiddish to a crowd of 15,000 workers. By the next day, nearly 30,000 workers walked off their jobs and remained on strike throughout the winter of 1910–1911. Supported by WTUL and a list of wealthy female donors, the strikers prevailed. Most of the companies agreed to a 52-hour workweek, eliminated charges for materials, and gave some agency to the workers in establishing wages. This strike demonstrated to the AFL that women were committed and worthy opponents. Moreover, the ILGWU emerged as an important labor organization, and key working-class women like Clara Lemlich and Rose Schneiderman became significant labor leaders.

Despite the success of the uprising of 20,000 women, it would take a more tragic event to force national industrial reform of the abusive labor practices within the needle trade. On March 25, 1911, the Triangle Shirtwaist Company fire killed 146 workers. In order to eliminate union interference in the factory, the company started locking the women in after arriving to work. A fire broke out on the 10th floor, but the women could not escape; 25 percent of the workforce jumped to their deaths from the rooftop. This tragic event led to the creation of the first New York State Factory Investigation Committee, led by Florence Kelley and Frances Perkins, and it was supported by political leaders such as Al Smith and Robert Wagner. A series of public hearings and on-site inspections led to a dramatic change in factory safety and working conditions and limited the working hours of women and children. This committee secured the first national industrial legislation to reform business practices.

PROTECTIVE LABOR LEGISLATION

Reformers invested a great deal of their time and energy promoting welfare legislation that protected women and children in the labor force. Illinois reformers pioneered this type of legislation in 1893, but the legal climate did not fully support specific legislation that protected women until the 1908 *Mueller v. Oregon* Supreme Court decision. Prior to this time, the court ruled that any attempt to regulate male or female labor violated individual constitutional rights to make their own contracts. In 1908, the court reversed this position and affirmed the legality of limiting the maximum hours women could work based on the view that women were fundamentally weaker than men and needed special labor protection. At the time women's working hours were limited in all but nine states. Regretfully, these new protective laws did not generally apply to agricultural workers or to domestic servants, which comprised the largest percentages of workers who were immigrants or African American. For women like Florence Kelley and members of the WTUL, the *Mueller v. Oregon* decision represented a watershed victory, yet for laboring women who needed to work overtime or in the evenings, these laws prohibited their contractual rights and defined women as unequal in the workforce to men, thus limiting their ability to unionize effectively.

Different groups supported or opposed these new labor restrictions. Female printers, for example, protested night restrictions, and management claimed that minimum wage laws resulted in higher labor costs. By 1923, the Supreme Court, in the case of *Adkins v. Children's Hospital*, ruled that women had the same right to contract as men, based on the success of the Nineteenth Amendment that granted women equal voting rights with men. Between World Wars I and II, it became increasingly clear that protective labor legislation limited women's agency as workers more than it protected them from long hours and poor working conditions. Moreover, protective labor issues proved counterproductive to a united women's movement and resulted in a protracted struggle over the Equal Rights Amendment (ERA).

BIRTH CONTROL

Labor legal reform and infant and maternity legislation clearly improved the lives of women workers, but birth control reform would have a long-lasting impact on reproduction rights for women in the 20th century. The birth control options and rights that we enjoy today as modern Americans is a result of the early reform work of birth control advocates in the early 20th century. While settlement house reformers focused on the problems of female and child labor, they had sympathy for immigrant and poor women, who lacked education about birth control devices to limit the size of their families. Religion also played an important role in how different immigrant groups dealt with pregnancy, abortion, miscarriages, and the high rate of death among birthing mothers. Another group of activists emerged to advance birth control and reproductive health. The pioneering work of Margaret Sanger and Mary Ware Dennett, among other more radical women, laid the foundation for modern-day freedoms over reproductive rights.

The modern birth control movement emerged during the hey-day of Progressive Era reform. Rapid urbanization and overcrowding in the tenements highlighted the need to educate and provide birth control devices to control family size. Sanger, educated in the field of nursing, closely observed the problems of family life in the New York tenements as a visiting nurse. A labor activist and Socialist, she became a member of the radical Left, writing articles on women's sexual liberation in the socialist weekly paper *The Call*. In 1913, she published an article on the problem of syphilis, but because of the Comstock Act of 1873, this publication was banned as unmailable.

At this time, contraception literature and the distribution of birth control devices was an illegal act by New York statute and federally illegal under the Comstock Act, which prohibited sexually explicit information from being distributed through the U.S. mail. In addition to state and federal laws, the American medical profession did not support contraceptives and believed that the distributors of birth control were quacks.

As a result of state and federal laws, birth control activists faced persecution under these laws for distribution of obscenity, and they lacked support of the male medical community to promote and distribute contraceptive devices. Sanger played a key role in redefining birth control as a medical condition by battling the social purity laws that defined contraceptive use as a vice used by prostitutes. Moreover, the religious and social-cultural beliefs from different immigrant communities, particularly Catholicism, perpetuated this view. Sanger's work as a midwife and nurse on the Lower East Side radicalized her to action. She made birth control her lifelong cause, and she challenged the Comstock Act by mailing out contraceptive information through the mail. Part of Sanger's goal was to eliminate the stigma attached to birth control and to separate the act of sex from procreation—a counterpoint to the religious viewpoint that the purpose of sex was for procreation and not sexual pleasure. As a woman before her time, she believed that women lacked a voice in their ability to define their sexuality and that distribution of educational material on contraceptives and family planning would liberate women.

In 1914, Sanger mobilized her campaign first with the publication *The Woman Rebel*, which the post office declared obscene. While the publication gave no specific contraceptive advice, she was indicted for violating the postal code. She left for Europe to escape prosecution, while her husband William Sanger continued to distribute a pamphlet titled *Family Limitation*, a how-to guide that educated readers on birth control devices and practices. Sanger returned to United States and with her sister Ethel Byrne opened the Brownsville Clinic and continued providing women with contraceptive literature. Just nine days after opening the clinic, Sanger was arrested and served a 30-day jail term. She unsuccessfully appealed the Comstock Law, until a significant ruling by the New York appeals court ruled that doctors had the ability to provide women with contraceptive information. Sanger used this justification to build doctor-staffed birth control clinics.

In 1921, Sanger organized the American Birth Control League (ABCL)—the precursor to Planned Parenthood (1942)—but it would take years before birth control clinics and the distribution of contraceptive information and devices would take root. Nevertheless, the ABCL provided the first process to expand acceptance of birth control as a civil right, though women would not fully enjoy access to birth control until the Supreme Court case of *Griswold v. Connecticut* (1965). The work of the CB in the 1920s further illustrates the concerns that average women had in limiting their family size. Some of these women wrote the agency asking for advice on how to prevent pregnancy, and they cited health problems and concerns of economic support. Many of these women requested copies of Sanger's birth control pamphlets, but in the 1920s, the CB shied away from providing any birth control information as a result of the laws and attitudes of the government against birth control.

SUFFRAGE AND THE LEAGUE
OF WOMEN VOTERS (LWV)

As we have learned from chapter 1, the mid-19th-century suffrage movement got off to a slow start as result of the Civil War and the Reconstruction amendments. Elizabeth Cady Stanton, Susan B. Anthony, and Lucy Stone organized the Equal Rights Association (1866). However, conflict over the Fifteenth Amendment, granting black male voting rights, resulted in the first feminist schism and the creation of two separate woman suffrage organizations. The more radical Stanton and Anthony formed the National Woman Suffrage Association, while Lucy Stone and her husband Henry Blackwell formed the American Woman Suffrage Association. By 1890, the factions came back together to form the National American Woman Suffrage Association (NAWSA) to push for a national suffrage amendment.

As the first two decades of the 20th century wore on, women worked to secure a permanent public space as progressive leaders, as policymakers, and as citizens. The combination of labor militancy and the work of female reformers in all areas of society provided the engine needed to drive the final push for voting rights. NAWSA, the NWP, the WTUL, and other women's organizations created a 2-million-women groundswell.

Under the able leadership of Carrie Chapman Catt, NAWSA became the primary suffrage organization in the United States. Catt promoted woman suffrage in a nonpartisan fashion, and she created an efficient publicity machine designed to sway public opinion by arguing that women could improve society through the ballot. A determined pragmatist and charismatic speaker, she galvanized women's organizations to promote national suffrage. While Catt

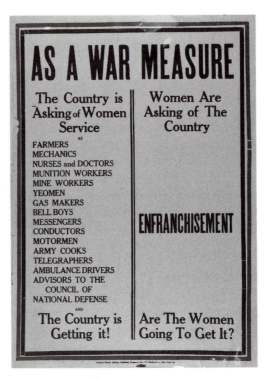

Women suffragists used the momentum of World War I to demand voting rights, circa 1917. Women's Heritage Museum/ International Museum of Women Records, MSS-2010-02-18, San Jose State University Library Special Collections and Archives. (Courtesy of San Jose State University, Special Collections and Archives)

succeeded in building a strong national organization, supported by state and local suffrage branches, not all women supported suffrage. Many women, particularly in the South, maintained an anti-suffrage platform. Meanwhile, more radical, younger women, led by Alice Paul, had their own ideas on how to win the vote, and they separated from the NAWSA to form the NWP. It would take the combined effort of mainstream women's organizations and the NWP to push suffrage forward during the strain of World War I.

Building the momentum for a final suffrage victory required building bridges with working-class women, social reformers, and middle-class and elite women, though overall, the movement remained racially segregated. Both the NAWSA and the NWP refused to make any political waves in the South, yet African American women continued to support universal voting rights. Moreover, World War I provided the right political environment to force the hand of President Wilson and Congress to support suffrage.

The groundswell of suffrage activism was also aided by the success of western state suffrage referendums. By 1918, 10 states granted women state voting rights, which meant that they could influence the outcome of national races in Congress, and in these states, women could run for political office. The California victory in 1911 highlights the impact that different groups of women had on state politics. Clubwomen, socialists, trade union activists, and college-educated women contributed to the state victory. Similarly, women in Washington, Oregon, Nevada, and Montana pressed for equal suffrage. Women such as Sarah Bard Field, suffragist and poet, became an important suffrage campaigner in Oregon and later stumped in the Nevada campaign, where she worked closely with Ann Martin, who helped form the NWP, and she ran unsuccessfully for the U.S. Senate in 1916 and 1918. Jeannette Rankin worked in the Washington State campaign and in her home state of Montana, and her success as the first elected female to the U.S. House of Representatives presented her the opportunity to vote in favor of the Nineteenth Amendment. The national movement thus received an important boost from suffrage activists in the West. By 1919, the majority of states had passed full suffrage.

In 1920, the Nineteenth Amendment granting women equal suffrage was finally ratified. This watershed victory ended 72 years of lobbying activities for the right to vote. As one long chapter closed, new chapters opened granting women full participation in politics, as voters, office holders, and lobbyists. While suffrage brought together some 2 million women and represented an important milestone, women had made considerable progress as social activists, lobbyists, and policymakers prior to the suffrage victory. As we have seen, organizations like the YWCA, WCTU, GFWC, Hull House, CB, NWP, and NAWSA played a key role in American politics and changed state and federal laws on a variety of issues including moral reform, public health and safety, labor and welfare reform, and finally suffrage.

The ratification of the Nineteenth Amendment recognized women as voters, but more importantly, it gave women activists' new legitimacy as potential office holders and increased their visibility and credibility as lobbyists at all levels of local, state, and federal government. There was much work yet to be done in the aftermath of the suffrage victory—women had to learn how to become voters; the political infrastructure had to be reformed, from

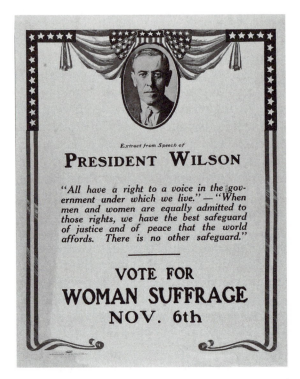

Suffrage poster encouraging male support of
the suffrage amendment, circa 1920. Women's
Heritage Museum/International Museum of
Women Records, MSS-2010-02-18, San Jose
State University Library Special Collections
and Archives. (Courtesy of San Jose State University, Special Collections and Archives)

basic voter registration to voter education; and the political party
system had to reform as well. In a nutshell, women had to learn to
navigate the male sphere of politics and develop new expectations
and roles as enfranchised citizens. In contrast to the majority of female voters, female activists were well versed in government civics and had been working for years as lobbyists for suffrage, social
reform, education, and many other issues.

LEAGUE OF WOMEN VOTERS (LWV)

Prior to the final vote for ratification, it became clear that a suffrage victory was inevitable, and many of the leaders of the suffrage movement began to think about the next steps for women's

rights. Carrie Chapman Catt took the lead to transform NAWSA into the LWV. This organization was created as a nonpartisan political action group to initially educate women in the art of voting and civic responsibilities but today is focused on educating all citizens on political issues at the local level. The state suffrage association morphed into state leagues.

The Connecticut State league became one of the best organized in the nation and provided specific leadership in educating women to become voters. Florence Kitchelt served as the first citizenship director (1920–1924), establishing citizenship schools for women throughout the state. Kitchelt developed techniques to encourage women to vote, and in her 1920 pamphlet, *The Mechanism of Law-Making in Connecticut* (reprinted in 1927), graphically depicted the various paths by which bills traveled through the Connecticut legislature to become laws. She successfully forged a third nonpartisan path for women independent of the Republican and Democratic parties. A 1921 article in *Good Housekeeping* praised her success with citizenship schools, saying that her "ability, tact, and fearlessness, accompanied by an unsuspected spark of wickedness, have made her handling of the delicate nonpartisan campaign meetings a real art." Described as "a small person with a wealth of dark hair and demure eyes that give her face a Madonna-like look," Kitchelt was an appealing speaker who effectively dispelled the mysteries of male-dominated politics. The article said that one seasoned politician was speechless when scheduled to speak after her: "He cast a sort of pleading glance back at the men on the platform behind him, and said, 'Boys she's laid us bare!'"[5] Kitchelt's activism is representative of the ordinary experiences of grassroots leaders, and while she is not well known as a national activist, her contributions to progressive reform, to suffrage, to the peace movement, and to the ERA campaign in the 1940s–1950s illustrates interconnections among different social movements and the overlapping reform interests.

EQUAL RIGHTS AMENDMENT (ERA)

Another important development following the suffrage victory of 1920 was the emergence of a new lobby movement for an equal rights amendment, led by Alice Paul and the NWP. The ERA proved to be a divisive issue among social and more radical feminists. Social feminists opposed the ERA based on the fear that it would nullify protective labor legislation. Social feminists asked Paul to consider adding language to the draft amendment that would include an exemption for protective labor legislation, but she refused. The ERA was first introduced to Congress in 1923, and every year thereafter until it passed Congress in 1972.

While the NWP focused almost exclusively on passing the ERA, an immediate anti-ERA opposition group formed. The membership base of the NWP prior to the ERA debate included a number of women who had worked for suffrage and protective legislation, and many feared that the ERA would undermine their work to improve working women's rights. A small group of the leaders, including Florence Kelley of the NCL and Maud Wood Park, president of the national LWV approached Paul to include an exemption for protective legislation. Paul's absolute refusal to include an exemption alienated social feminists. Park accurately predicted that the ERA would divide the first-wave movement. Other predominant figures including Carrie Chapman Catt, Mary Anderson of the CB, and Dr. Alice Hamilton, champion of industrial medicine and labor advocate, opposed the ERA. It would take several decades before a cohesive movement would form in support of a constitutional amendment. Despite the lack of support from major women's groups and from laboring women, Paul committed the next 49 years of her life to the ERA movement.

Protective labor legislation became the central area of disagreement. However, it became increasingly clear that protection was a double-edged sword due to the impact of the Great Depression, and the labor needs created by World Wars I and II, which highlighted the inequities that women faced in the labor market. The reliance on the unique role of women as mothers limited their ability to contract independently and to live by the same labor laws as mentioned, thus creating a separate and unequal workforce, with women at the bottom of the employment ladder, legally incapable of making decisions over their work lives, including working swing shifts or overtime.

AFRICAN AMERICANS (RACE—JIM CROW)

Where middle-class white reformers focused their attention on urban poverty, African American women activists, concentrated in Southern rural communities, provided a range of services including schools, homes for the aged, medical services, and other community programs. Because of the racism within white organizations, from the suffrage movement to social reform, black women formed separate organizations that supported the needs of their communities, while maintaining some connection to national organizations. For example, the YWCA maintained separate white and black local organizations. This is not to suggest that some interracial coopera- tion did not take place, but for the most part, black women's orga- nization had to go it alone. Even in organizations where black and white women worked together, black women rarely held positions of power. Moreover, white women's clubs frequently avoided or trivialized the real-life issues of Jim Crow racism, which further alienated black women who were actively working toward anti- lynching legislation and racial uplift of their communities.

In the African American community, education dominated as the primary reform effort, from the building of kindergartens to the establishment of trainings schools and colleges. For example, Nan- nie Burrough's National Training School for Women and Girls pro- vided black women opportunities to develop skills as teachers in Washington, D.C. According to one study, by 1907, there were some 151 church-connected schools and 161 private "Negro" schools. Their initiatives included providing homes for the elderly, black hospitals, and visiting-nurse programs.[6]

The aftermath of the Civil War and Reconstruction Era (1865– 1877) created a situation whereby Southern whites looked for new racial and economic measures to control the black population. The creation of Jim Crow laws enforced segregation and institutional- ized discrimination of African Americans. These laws were used by mainstream white society to intimidate and dominate the black population. Segregation laws negated all of the gains made in the earlier Reconstruction amendments and made it nearly impossible for African Americans to exercise their civil rights, isolating them through segregation legislation that created separate facilities in education, transportation, theaters, restaurants, banks, and hospi- tals. Throughout the South, states imposed new literacy tests and property requirements to vote. Blacks were also barred from public office and could not serve on a jury. The suspension of basic civil liberties was reinforced by extreme racial violence and race riots, and lynchings of men, women, and children became commonplace.

It was under the yoke of Jim Crow that black women reformers worked to improve the social and sexual morals of their community, which was a more pressing concern, because of the racial violence they faced on a daily basis. In part, the need to improve moral values stemmed from the breakdown of the family under slavery, and the continued sexual exploitation of their race by white sexual assaults and false accusations of rape by white women. Thus, racial uplift and racial equality were intertwined. Despite the racial violence in the South, a number of exceptional women emerged as leaders, including Ida B. Wells-Barnett, Mary Talbert, and Mary Church Terrell. Black women were the first to protest lynching in the United States, and several different organizations worked to eradicate the practice through federal legislation.

The National Association for the Advancement of Colored People (NAACP), National Colored Women's Association (NCWA), and the short-lived Anti-Lynching Crusaders (ALC), an auxiliary of the NAACP, worked together to address the problem through publicity campaigns and by supporting federal legislation to address these extreme civil rights violations. The degree of the problem was made public through the activism and writings of Wells-Barnett, who published *Southern Horrors: Lynch Law in All Its Phases, A Red Record*, and *Mob Rule in New Orleans*. Wells began her early career as a journalist and investigator into the crime of lynching in Memphis, Tennessee, where she co-owned the *Free Press*. Her activism with the anti-lynching movement began after three of her good friends were shot to death by a white mob. Like many other Americans at the time, Wells at first believed that lynching resulted from rape and similar crimes. However, after the death of her innocent friends, she realized that lynching was act of terror intended to subdue the black population and prevent them from seeking social, economic, and political progress. Her writings forced her to leave Memphis for Chicago where her campaign gained momentum. Wells became the voice of the national and international movement. In the *Red Record*, she made clear what was needed to help the cause, when she wrote, "When the Christian world knows the alarming growth and extent of outlawry in our land, some means will be found to stop it."[7] She compiled law statistics to drive home the epidemic. Between the years 1880–1930, approximately 5,000 blacks were lynched compared to 700 whites.

Wells' writings and publicity tours provided the foundation for more direct action by the ACL and other groups. Mary B. Talbert, the president of the NCWA, organized the formation of the ACL with the express purpose to campaign for the Dyer Anti-Lynching Bill. Authored by Congressman Leonidas Dyer (Missouri), the bill was designed to penalize state, county, and local law enforcement agencies who failed to provide equal protection to all citizens, to deter the practice of mob rule, and to prosecute the participants. The bill passed the House in 1922 but failed to pass the Senate. In response, Talbert organized the campaign "A Million Women United to Stop

Lynching." The objective was to get 1 million women to donate one dollar toward the NAACP's campaign to support passage of the Dyer Bill. While they never reached their original goal, they did succeed in publicizing the terror of mob violence and the problem of lynching. They also helped dispel the myth that lynching was a result of the crime of rape and showed that women and children were lynched along side men; the entire community suffered under the yoke of so-called Southern justice.

The ALC quickly expanded from 16 members to 900 within the first three months of the campaign and they worked to educate white women on the reality and scope of the problem resulting in some 2,000 white women joining the cause. Racial uplift and reform in the black community centered on religion, and the ALC and other groups utilized the church as the center for their fundraising efforts, through bake sales and prayer meetings. The NAACP programs depended on grassroots efforts to raise awareness of the legislation. One woman from Cleveland sold fruit cake to raise money for the NAACP; bake sales, while small in scale, provided important funds to sustain many of the legal initiatives of the NAACP. While the ALC campaign did not succeed in meeting its original goals, the contributions of many local women highlights how black women tried to shape civil rights policy and more importantly how they worked to better their community. The anti-lynching crusade continued for several decades, resulting in numerous legal cases that provided an important foundation to eliminate Jim Crow laws and to promote civil rights. The history of lynching in 20th-century America is a very sad chapter in our history. Jazz singer Billy Holiday memorialized the impact of lynching in the South with the famous song "Strange Fruit." The song originated from a Lewis Allen's poem protesting the racial violence against African Americans. The poem and song describes the blood on the leaves and trees that resulted from the strange fruit on the trees—the lifeless bodies of countless African Americans who were brutally lynched.

CONCLUSION

Progressive Era reform provided the early foundation for civil rights activism in the 20th century. Social movements, like the ALC, NAACP, WTUL, and many other organizations, pushed the boundaries of female appropriate behavior to extend from the home to local, state, and national government. These early pioneers succeeded in creating a female dominion in policy making and community building. The variety of issues addressed illustrate the diverse needs of Americans in the early 20th century, while highlighting the important and needed role of women as municipal housekeepers, as leaders in politics, government, and society.

These movements provided ordinary women with new benefits from the 8-hour workday, access to nursery schools and kindergartens, and legal protection in the workforce to new access to information about birth control, infant and maternal health, childbirth, and child rearing. This first wave of feminist activism centered on basic equal rights for women, initially through the ballot and later through legislation that provided important social services, and the struggle for equal rights in employment opened a pathway for a modern civil rights movement. As we move forward in this study, we will see the interconnection between social movements, women's activism, and the role of the Fourteenth Amendment's guarantee of due process and equal protection. It would take several generations before African Americans and women achieved basic civil rights, but this period of progressive reform provided a firm foundation to push the boundaries of law and society forward.

NOTES

1. Nancy A. Hewitt, ed., *No Permanent Waves: Recasting Histories of U.S. Feminism* (Rutgers University Press, 2010), pp. 1–7; Karen Offen, ed., *Globalizing Feminisms, 1789–1945* (Routledge, 2010), p. xxix.

2. Florence Kelley, *Some Ethical Gains Through Legislation* (The Macmillan Company, 1905), p. 3.

3. Robyn Muncy, *Creating a Female Dominion in American Reform, 1890–1935* (Oxford University Press, 1991), pp. 46–47.

4. Muncy, *Female Dominion*, pp. 94–101.

5. Ruth E. Finley, "Laying Politics Bare," *Good Housekeeping* (October 1921): 69, 101–102, 106, found in Florence Ledyard Cross Kitchelt Papers, MS-A-1, Schlesinger Library, Radcliffe Institute for Advanced Studies, Harvard University, Cambridge, Massachusetts.

6. Linda Gordon, "Black and White Visions of Welfare: Women's Welfare Activism, 1890–1945," in *Unequal Sisters: A Multicultural Reader in U.S. Women's History*, 2nd ed., eds., Vicki L. Ruiz and Ellen Carol DuBois (Routledge, 1994), p. 161.

7. Jacqueline Jones Royster, ed., *Southern Horrors and Other Writings: The Anti-Lynching Campaign of Ida B. Wells, 1892–1900* (Bedford/St. Martin's, 1997), p. 157.

3

FROM WORLD WAR I
TO A NEW DEAL

The focus of this chapter is centered around the historical themes of World War I, the Great Depression, and New Deal policies, which span three decades from 1914 to 1940. During this time period, Americans faced the horror of war and had a slight reprieve during the 1920s, which offered the promise of prosperity but ended in 1929 with the Great Depression—the worst economic crisis in American history. The election of President Franklin Delano Roosevelt (FDR) gave rise to his New Deal policies that were designed to restore the confidence of the nation, to enact legislation that addressed the banking crisis and unemployment rate, and to provide relief for general recovery in the states, while increasing federal authority over banking, labor, agricultural production, environmental protection, and production through various public works projects.

This chapter will explore the various experiences of women through the different lenses of social protest, women's labor, consumer culture, gender identity, suffrage, gender politics, and marriage and family. Each of these components helped shape the rich diversity of women's experiences in the first half of the 20th century. In turn, the challenges brought on by the events of this period set the stage for the intensification for the struggle for women's civil rights that led to the eventual rise of modern feminism in what scholars have labeled the second wave. Progressive Era reform would continue to grow during this time period as well, and after suffrage was finally won in 1920, new pockets of social activism emerged. We will learn how pacifists and feminists worked to change legislation locally and nationally, while also influencing international politics. From a women's rights perspective, the single most important outcome of this era was the final passage of the Nineteenth Amendment, granting women federal voting rights. More importantly, this milestone victory marked the beginning for social, political, and economic change for American women. Armed with new voting rights, various groups of women leveraged the suffrage victory to push for deeper equality reform for women in employment, marriage, politics, and society at large. It took 72 years of women's activism to secure the national voting rights, but a new era of feminist activism emerged to address equality legislation in all areas of politics, employment opportunities, and social and family life.

The postsuffrage years (1920–1945) highlight the different paths that women took to secure full equal rights in society. Not all groups or individuals sought the same path to equality. Some women focused on singles issues, while others maintained membership in multiple organizations. The variation in participation, ideology, and solutions to equality legislation created some tension between groups, but the output of new legislation that addressed employment discrimination, equal rights, citizenship entitlements, jury service, segregation, and racism provided the base for coalition formation in the second-wave movement.

The debate over the Equal Rights Amendment (ERA) dominated as the primary conflict between radical feminists and moderate social feminists in the postsuffrage years. Following the suffrage victory, the National Woman's Party (NWP) focused exclusively on the ERA, while moderate feminists worked to maintain protective labor legislation. The conflicts that emerged between women over the ERA further fragmented the earlier suffrage coalition. The history of the ERA helps us better understand the diversity of women's views during this time period and will show how different coalitions formed to promote specific legislation that would over time improve women's civil rights.

The early scholars who wrote about the postsuffrage years by and large believed that the suffrage movement failed because it did not lead to a united women's movement or create a women's voting bloc. The conflict over the ERA helped to stigmatize feminism, which limited the effectiveness of women's groups, but the energy of equal rights feminists and those who opposed it, confirms that different pockets of feminism continued to promote specific issues. The suffrage victory may have ended two decades of energy and collective spirit, but feminist activism continued to flourish, and old and new pockets of social activism took place that provided the foundation for groups to pursue different social policies that would benefit the collective whole of American women. Not every woman engaged actively in these movements, but all women were beneficiaries of new legislation that improved both their lives, as citizens and as individuals, and the lives of their families. The hodge-podge of social movements during this period helped to advance human rights for women and men alike. In so doing, they helped build a stronger and more diverse feminists consciousness for the future.

BACKGROUND TO WORLD WAR I

Women's lives would face a whole new set of challenges between the world wars. Much of the Progressive Era reform efforts, from the creation of the Children's Bureau (CB) to the final success of the suffrage movement, helped set the stage for women's advancement in society at large. The suffrage momentum and subsequent constitutional victory occurred midstream during World War I, also known at the time as the Great War (1914–1919). The United States under the leadership of Woodrow Wilson maintained a policy of neutrality, but Germany and England made it next to impossible for the United States to remain passive. Germany used U-boats to target British passenger ships, declared the waters around the British Isle part of the war zone, and declared unlimited submarine warfare. Mounting tensions in Europe combined with continued infringements on U.S. shipping rights forced Wilson and the American Congress to act, and on April 6, 1917, the United States declared war on Germany. A polished public speaker and academic, Wilson effectively convinced Congress that U.S. commercial interests and diplomatic interests were tied at the hip, and that the United States needed to become a world power in order to spread American democracy and capitalism. The U.S. support of the Allied Powers (Britain, France, and Russia) offered a new opportunity for the United States to become a world power and a key broker for peace.

The United States played a supportive role in the actual war effort, but a central role in the peace settlement process. Wilson articulated a new vision of world peace via his famous Fourteen Points speech, which he delivered to Congress on January 8, 1918. In this speech, he summed up the U.S. war aims, based largely on his belief in self-determination and free trade. He also promoted a League of Nations to maintain collective security, enforce free navigation, lower trade barriers, facilitate reduction of armaments, and provide a stage for peaceful negotiations between squabbling nations. Wilson believed that international alliances and the balance of powers would improve international relations. Self-determination and open covenants (agreements between nations) were a central part of Wilson's plan, but the Paris negotiations took place in secret between the Big Four (United States, England, France, and Italy), and the victors of the war ignored Wilson's call for the independence and self-determination of the defeated nations. Moreover, Wilson failed to convince Congress to endorse the League of Nations and to ratify the peace treaty. The League of Nations eventually failed, but it would later become the blueprint for the creation of the United Nations after World War II.[1]

American women played an important role in the war effort, and as we shall see, social activists and pacifists pushed for legislative change that addressed women's second-class status. In addition, some women provided important relief to war-torn Europe, and a few exceptional women traveled to Paris to try to influence the peace process.

SUFFRAGE

As we have learned in chapter 2, the suffrage movement had a slow start in the mid-19th century and was organized primarily by anti-slavery advocates. Following the Civil War and the period known as Reconstruction, suffrage advocates splintered into two separate organizations: the National Woman Suffrage Association founded by Elizabeth Stanton and Susan B. Anthony, and the American Woman Suffrage Association founded by Lucy Stone and Henry Blackwell. In 1890, these two rival groups came back together to form the National American Woman Suffrage Association (NAWSA). In 1900, Anthony resigned as the president, and Carrie Chapman Catt of Iowa took over the leadership. Prior to this time period, only four states had granted women voting rights: Wyoming (1869), Colorado (1893), Idaho and Utah (1896). While almost every western state and territory had granted women voting rights by 1914, the Midwest, East, and South lagged far behind in recognizing women's rights. The early NAWSA campaign focused on winning the vote state by state, but progress was slow. Many of the eastern and southern suffragists promoted prohibition (outlawing alcohol consumption) and suffrage together, which limited male endorsements of the ballot for women, and particularly among immigrant and working-class communities where alcohol consumption was cultural. Thus, state suffrage initiatives failed in large part. In contrast, western suffragists used a variety of techniques to increase support from wary urban voters, from the immigrant and working class population. They also deemphasized prohibition, and as a result, key state victories in the West inspired eastern women to promote a national amendment rather than the state-by-state approach.

The formation of NAWSA and change in leadership at the turn of the century converged with Progressive Era politics and activism within urban centers. The new generation of suffrage leaders rallied under the banner "Votes for Women." Catt served as the president from 1900 to 1904 and again from 1916 to 1920. Catt joined the Women's Christian Temperance Union (WCTU) and from there launched her career as social reformer and suffragist. Between 1899 and 1890, she served the Iowa Woman Suffrage Association, where she quickly made a name for herself, and from 1890 to 1895, she worked on a number of state suffrage referenda with Anthony. In 1900, Anthony handpicked Catt to take over the presidency.

Catt's direct approach created some controversy among the elder leaders, but her organizational and public-speaking skills earned her the favor and support of Anthony. She became known as "the General" of the organization. Demanding complete autonomy over all programs, lobbying efforts, fundraising, and programs, Catt offered her "Winning Plan," which focused on state-level campaigns to build momentum for a federal amendment. Through nonpartisan lobbying, the women would convince Congress but more importantly convince American women that they needed the vote. While she supported the state approach, she was frustrated by the lack of progress at the national level and believed that NAWSA needed to move toward a more aggressive national program. Catt promoted woman's suffrage in a nonpartisan fashion, but she provided unrelenting organizational skills and demanded that the membership fall in line according to her visions. She ran the organization in a military fashion and created an efficient publicity machine designed to sway public opinion and one based on optimism that women could improve society through the ballot.

A determined pragmatist and charismatic speaker, Catt galvanized women to act, but she also understood that women needed to understand why they needed the vote. Moreover, she needed suffrage soldiers at the local level to pressure ordinary citizens and politicians to support the amendment. She formed suffrage schools to educate ordinary women on the history of the suffrage movement, the issues, and the skills needed to participate. Students learned how to work with municipalities, politicians, and the press, while learning public-speaking techniques. This professional network eventually penetrated every level of society and directly contributed to the growth of the membership to 2 million by 1920. The schools provided a base to unify every kind of women's group and local association across the country. The suffrage schools provide an important step toward building a national amendment platform.

Prior to Catt returning to the helm of NAWSA, Anna Howard Shaw, who served in the presidency from 1906 to 1916, maintained a conservative approach that focused on state chapters, and she was not of the mind to financially support a national campaign. Many of the younger members of NAWSA believed that it would be more expedient to pursue a national amendment. Lucy Burns and Alice Paul led this movement and convinced the leadership to allow them to take over the national campaign. Both women were influenced by radical British suffragists, and they organized one of the largest suffrage parades in the history of the movement. Paul and Burns strategically planned the parade to take place in Washington, D.C., during the day before President Wilson was inaugurated. The parade was a spectacular success and included suffrage chapters from across the United States. Florence Kitchelt, a well-known regional suffragist in New York and Connecticut, traveled to Washington to participate. She later reflected on the excitement and success of the parade and what it meant to her to be involved in the suffrage movement and to work toward a national amendment.

Within weeks of the parade, the suffrage amendment was introduced to the House of Representatives for the first time. Thus, the national movement to secure an amendment was born. In 1916, Burns and Paul formed the Congressional Union (CU) as a branch of NAWSA to pressure Congress to pass the amendment. Paul and Burns began to build a coalition of working-class and elite women to pursue the amendment. They also became expert fund-raisers, which created a conflict among the leaders of NAWSA. In part, the leadership of NAWSA disliked the more aggressive tactics of the younger women, and they wanted to use funds raised by CU to promote the state chapters. As a result of this conflict, the CU split from the organization and in 1917 was renamed the NWP. The parting of ways created a permanent schism between suffragists, but both groups would play a significant role in the final suffrage victory.

The NWP represented a small, yet focused group of younger women who supported the national amendment. Paul and Burns built a coalition of activists composed of elite and working-class women. The organization was sustained by generous donations from elite women like Alma Belmont. The NWP focused entirely on the national amendment, but it also supported western suffrage campaigns in California, Nevada, Montana, and other western states. The 1915 Panama-Pacific Exposition in San Francisco provided an interesting opportunity for Alice Paul and the members of the NWP to promote suffrage. Many California suffragists became active in the state campaign but also participated in parades and picketed the White House in 1917. Sarah Bard Field became a central figure in the western campaigns.

Field first became involved in several western state/territory suffrage campaigns while living in Oregon. In need of an income after divorcing her husband, she became a paid suffrage organizer in Oregon, where she worked closely with pioneer feminists Emma Wold and Abigail Scott Duniway. Field spent hours working in rural locations giving speeches, for which she received good press. Typical of western suffrage work, the women traveled from town to town. They focused on all groups in the state, including the mining camps, farmers, and labor groups. She tried to arrange to speak from her car or on the street, which she found most effective in getting people to listen. She recruited men and women and handed out pamphlets and literature that she begged them to read. Following the Oregon victory, she traveled to Nevada to support Anne Martin's senate campaign in 1912 and 1914, while working with Martin to secure women's suffrage in the state. Their efforts paid off, and Nevada granted women voting rights in 1914.

Early on in the Nevada campaign, Field met Mabel Vernon of the CU. Vernon sold Field on the goals of the NWP to push for a federal amendment, and she offered to help with the upcoming 1915 Panama-Pacific Exposition. As Vernon described, "...we are going to have a booth with great signs, and there will be hundreds of women from all over the western states, as well as everywhere, and we're going to have a great petition to President Wilson."[2]

It was at this meeting that Field came to the realization that a federal amendment would save women money and energy. Field agreed to do what she could to help with the exposition, and she joined the ranks of the NWP and became a primary speech writer and speaker. She worked with Vernon, Doris Stevens, and Inez Milholland; 1915 proved a busy time for her, as she worked the suffrage booth at the Panama-Pacific Exposition. The exposition attracted visitors around the globe, and Alma Belmont, a significant financer of the booth, spoke daily. The energy and enthusiasm generated by the fair and the convening of the first Women's Voters Convention revitalized the determination of the women present to fight for a federal amendment. Field wrote the culminating speech delivered by Belmont.

The suffrage attendees believed that the success of western suffrage and the power of 4 million women voters would force the president and Congress to support the suffrage amendment. The NWP organized a cross-country automobile ride from California to Washington, D.C., to hand deliver a suffrage petition to President Wilson and to Congress. The ride was intended to dramatize the demand for suffrage, with a petition of half a million signatures gathered during the trip. Paul selected Field to ride with two Swedish feminists who had recently purchased a new car that they planned to drive back to Rhode Island. Field described herself as a reluctant angel. When Field suggested to Paul that they lacked sufficient knowledge of auto mechanics, Paul responded in her typical way, "Oh, well if that happens I'm sure some good man will come along that'll help you."[3] Field further objected that she was writing a book. In the end, she could not say no to the violet-eyed Paul, even though it meant being separated from her two children and facing unknown dangers on the road.

The women left on September 16 and finally arrived on December 6, 1915, after facing bitter weather, poor road conditions, and mechanical problems. They traveled more than 5,000 miles, meeting organized crowds in Reno; Salt Lake City; rural areas of Wyoming; Colorado Springs; Kansas City; Lincoln, Nebraska; Cedar Rapids, Iowa; Chicago; and New York. Vernon organized each city tour and with the help of local women staged parades and rallies and built new support for suffrage. The cross-county ride and the publicity it generated helped dramatize the potential power of women's organizational abilities and the power of a women's voting bloc. Field arrived in Washington exhausted but gave her crescendo speech before Congress and with much fanfare. Field attended parades and speeches in Newark, Philadelphia, and Baltimore. The envoy ended at the steps of the capitol, where Field gave a speech and was escorted with 300 guests to the White House to meet with President Wilson. She presented the 18,333-foot-long petition roll with half a

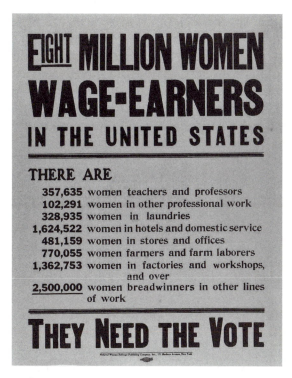

Suffrage poster highlighting the role of working women and their support of suffrage, circa 1917. Women's Heritage Museum/International Museum of Women Records, MSS-2010-02-18, San Jose State University Library Special Collections and Archives. (Courtesy of San Jose State University, Special Collections and Archives)

million signatures. Despite the fanfare, the president still opposed the suffrage amendment.

Field continued to work with the NWP until the suffrage amendment was finally ratified by the states in 1920, which included more speech writing and making, lobbying senators, and working on gaining support of the Democratic Party.

Meanwhile, Jeannette Rankin, a native of Montana, began working on the Washington State suffrage campaign and moved back to Montana in 1912 after suffrage passed. In 1910, Washington granted women voting rights. Inspired by this success, Rankin returned to Montana and joined the Montana Equal Franchise Society. It was at this juncture that she began to exercise her public-speaking skills and became the first woman to speak before the all-male legislature. In her first speech to the Montana legislature, she asked the men to consider the 6 million working women who scraped and scrimped to support their families. Referencing the ideology of the American Revolution, "taxation with no representation," she declared that women everywhere needed the vote to be productive homemakers and citizens. While she received great applause after this speech, the legislature was not quite convinced. The women faced several challenges in promoting the state campaign. First, the size of the state and small population made it difficult to reach the voters. Second, the women had to combat anti-suffrage sentiments from the powerful Anaconda Copper Mining Company and anti-prohibition constituents.

Montana's early suffrage campaign originated in Helena in the 1890s, and by 1895, the Montana Woman Suffrage Organization formed but did little to expand the state movement. In 1902, Catt, a regional representative of NAWSA, traveled to the state to revive the suffrage movement, but her attitude toward western ways offended the state organizers, and they withdrew their membership from the NAWSA. Western suffragists and especially Montanans were extremely independent, and the local women resented the interloping of the NAWSA. Despite the combined support of local and national women, the legislature resoundingly defeated the suffrage resolutions in 1903 and 1905.

Sensitive to the feelings of the local women, Rankin established a loose suffrage organization unconnected to the NAWSA. She traveled across the state to help form local organizations and spent time canvassing political candidates, speaking at political meetings, and mentoring local women in lobbying techniques. In 1913, the suffrage bill passed overwhelmingly, with 26–2 in the senate and 74–2 in the house.

Rankin's work on the state campaign led to an appointment as a field secretary for NAWSA, but she returned to Montana in 1914 to campaign for the popular referendum, and in November of that year, suffrage rights were granted, as in Nevada. Montana now shared victory with other western states including Washington (1910), California (1911), Arizona (1912), Kansas (1912), and Oregon (1912). Rankin ended her relationship with the NAWSA when Catt became president and after the CU, run by Alice Paul, separated over tactics and goals. Within in a few short years, the CU became the NWP, representing the radical branch of the movement. Western women embraced the NWP strategy for a federal amendment, and they worked collaboratively with Paul and the

NWP. Rankin developed close ties with the NWP, but she maintained her independence and never adopted the single-issue approach of the NWP.

In 1916, she began to mark her next steps by organizing local support for her congressional campaign, while her brother Wellington Rankin managed her campaign. She began by soliciting advice from key NAWSA leaders including Anna Howard Shaw and Catt. Both women discouraged her, but Catt made clear her view that an eastern lawyer or more commanding woman should become the first congresswoman, but only after suffrage was won. Catt's condescension only served to alienate Rankin and reinforce her negative opinion of NAWSA. Despite the lack of support from NAWSA leaders, she won the Republican ticket for the House, and in 1917, she became the first woman elected to Congress. Shaw had advised her to aim for the state legislature as a first step, and when Rankin won Congress, Shaw sent a belated apologetic letter and finally congratulated her several months after her victory election. Rankin and Catt never became friends, but Rankin used her political position to fight for suffrage.

Rankin focused her campaign on social issues. She told her constituents that she would continue to fight for federal suffrage and for child welfare legislation. Running as a nonpartisan, she appealed to the farmers, miners, small businessmen, and labor. Rankin's victory can be attributed to the change in election of two congressmen at large and to state suffrage rights. In contrast to Anne Martin's congressional campaign, Rankin did not focus solely on women's issues, and while she supported feminist goals, her philosophies were less direct and oriented toward political freedom and social responsibility.

At age 30, Rankin was young and attractive, and like Alice Paul, she represented a younger generation; the press frequently commented on her smart looks and pleasing personality. Her landmark victory made her an immediate political celebrity. Her first months in Congress were crowded with social events, speeches, newspaper stories, and numerous celebrations. On the opening day of Congress, the suffragists honored Rankin with a congratulatory breakfast, attended by NAWSA and NWP women. This breakfast highlighted the conflicts between the two organizations. Catt and NAWSA pledged full suffrage support for the war, while the peace activists objected to Catt's promise. Rankin sympathized with the pacifists and supported Paul but quickly accessed the importance of nonpartisanship in her role as congresswoman.

Rankin became a controversial figure on several fronts—foremost as the first woman in Congress, but secondly, her votes against World War I and World War II marked her political future. A committed pacifist and founding member of the Woman's Peace Party (WPP), led by Jane Addams, Rankin voted according to her conscience. Before her election victory, she believed President Wilson when he said he would keep American out of the war. To her disappointment and shock, she entered Congress just as the Germans resumed submarine warfare on U.S. merchant ships. Her brother encouraged her to vote as man, and Catt privately wrote that Rankin's vote would "lose a million votes."[4] Several suffragists feared that to vote no would jeopardize the campaign. Rankin's vote reverberated across the country, despite the fact that 50 men also voted against the war. She faced harsh and immediate criticism for her vote. Many of the papers falsely reported that she cried giving her vote. Fellow congressman Fiorella LaGuardia of New York told the press that he did not notice any tears, but for the fact that he had tears in his own eyes. Rankin recalled that she did not cry at that point but cried for an entire week until no tears would come. In retrospect, the criticism she faced reflected the expectation that women were not suited for politics and that they lacked the constitution to make important decisions, and especially on issues of foreign policy and war. She received harsh criticism from men and women, though she also received hundreds of sympathetic letters from men and women across the country who opposed the war.

While in Congress, Rankin demonstrated her commitment to social policy, and she introduced a variety of bills focused on women, children, and fair labor practices for men and women working for the government. She also introduced a bill supporting women's citizenship separate from their husbands, and she authored a bill creating a hydroelectric plant run by a federal board—a precursor to the Tennessee Valley Authority Act. Most significantly and closest to her heart, she introduced the first bill mandating maternity and child hygiene. This bill, known as the Rankin-Robinson bill, focused on rural health education and became the forerunner to the Sheppard-Towner Act, which provided federal funding for maternal and infant health. In 1918, Rankin focused on her reelection campaign but lost the Republican primary, and later as a third party candidate, she also lost. Rankin's unpopular vote against the war did not help her, but her support of the Anaconda miners' strike in

1917 placed her placed her at odds with the financially and politically powerful Anaconda Copper Company.

World War I provided a unique opportunity to build a stronger national directive for the suffrage movement. By utilizing the groundswell of American patriotism, Catt doubled the organization's membership, while pursing a moderate lobbying policy to swing congressional support. Meanwhile, Alice Paul and the NWP protested President Wilson for his failure to grant women voting rights. This group of younger women used more radical tactics to gain attention, from picketing the White House to burning copies of the president's speeches to chaining themselves to the White House fence, resulting in mob violence and police brutality. In one incident, the police arrested the female protesters for obstructing the sidewalk, and the legal system sent them to prison. While in prison, the women went on hunger strikes and were brutally force fed with iron devices designed to hold their mouths open, leading the papers to call them "the Iron-Jawed Angels." The NWP was one of the first groups in the United States to use nonviolent protest for a political cause, and these methods, while militant for the time, forced the hand of justice. Between the years 1918 and 1919, the police arrested 168 suffragists for peacefully protesting. In a show of support, new groups of suffragists appeared with a banner that referred to President Wilson as "Kaiser Wilson," implying that his treatment of women was no better than the Germans. More arrests followed, and the protestors received 60-day prison terms. The prisoners demanded to be treated as political prisoners with access to legal counsel, books, and better food. The hunger strikes brought sympathy and support from the Left, and the blame for police suppression and abuse of these women rested at the feet of the president. Catt was outraged by the partisan tactics of the NWP, but she later admitted that they gave credibility to NAWSA and helped push the cause forward. The NWP clearly influenced Wilson to compel Congress to support suffrage, but Catt's restraint and constant reminder of the sacrifices of American women in the war effort turned the tide. In 1918, Catt's "Winning Plan" reaped results when the House of Representatives passed the amendment, and in 1919, the Senate followed suit, with final ratification taking place in 1920.

The contributions of the radical NWP, the firm leadership of Carrie Chapman Catt, and the individual contributions of Sarah Bard Field, Jeannette Rankin, and Anne Martin helped build the momentum for the Nineteenth Amendment. The conflicts over U.S. participation in World War I provided the right political timing to shame the president and Congress to support national voting rights for women.

PACIFIST ORGANIZATIONS

Peace societies in the United States have a long history, dating back to the early 19th century. Following the Spanish-American War, a number of peace societies emerged, though most were male-dominated societies. Female peace activists found it difficult to develop leadership roles within these organizations, and as educated women and social activists, they were unwilling to defer to male leadership. Thus, the formation of the WPP offered women new opportunities to pursue new solutions to international and national problems; Jane Addams and Carrie Chapman Catt were founding members. Emily Greene Balch, a leader in the WPP and in Women's International League for Peace and Freedom (WILPF), connected the concept of peace to femininity—the opposite to war and masculinity. The formation of female-based societies illustrates the biological and maternal nature of social and political reform. WILPF shared separate organizational space with the Women's Peace Union, the National Conference on the Cause and Cure of War (organized by Catt), the League of Women Voters, the Young Women's Christian Association (YWCA), and the American Association of University Women.

In 1915, Addams articulated the importance of women's role in peacemaking while attending The Hague—International Conference of Women, when she wrote: "WE DO NOT THINK we can settle the war. We do not think that by raising our hands we can make armies cease slaughter. We do think it is valuable to state a new point of view. We do think it is fitting that women should meet and take counsel to see what may be done."[5] The conference was composed of women from the United States and Europe. Most of these women were well educated, feminists, and pacifists. Prior to the meeting in 1915, Catt presented a petition to President Wilson calling for the establishment of world court to remediate international disputes without military sanctions. Out of this initial work, the WPP was born.

Many Americans objected to U.S. participation in World War I, and peace activists and those who maintained a position as isolationists, in particular, criticized Wilson's policies. To counter this criticism and help sell the war to the American public, Wilson created the Committee on Public Information (CPI) to create poster art and magazine advertising to bolster the nation's democratic values and convince Americans that our democratic ideals needed to be exported to and used throughout the world.

Under the leadership of journalist and social reformer George Creel, the CPI hired 150,000 people to run the agency, and collectively they produced more than one million pieces of the literature that included pamphlets, articles, and books that explained the U.S. war aims. They also produced visual images that included movies, slides, advertisements, and war posters. The war posters depicted patriotic visual representations through a variety of programs, from food conservation, military service, and war industries work. As part of the campaign, Wilson called upon American women to protect the American way of life through patriotic war service, which included working in the munitions factories, sewing clothes, knitting, cannery and meatpacking work, creating victory gardens, and conserving natural resources. The CPI succeeded in framing Wilson war aims, and by defining the war as moral crusade for democracy and American interest, much of the opposition to the war faded.

Protest against U.S. involvement in the war was very controversial, and very few groups considered attacking Wilson's policies. Those who did faced a serious backlash from pro-military groups and individuals. The peaceful protests organized by the NWP illustrate this point. Their White House campaign was designed to shame President Wilson to endorse suffrage, and their use of provocative banners fostered hostility and violence from American servicemen. This radical approach brought controversial publicity to the suffrage cause, while patriotic citizens attacked them as traitors. Other women found themselves similarly maligned for their pacifist position, including Jeannette Rankin, the only member of the House to vote against the war. Other prominent women lost theirs jobs for protesting, others were attacked as American Socialists, and a handful of protesters faced the threat of prison. Radical feminist and Socialist Emma Goldman faced prison for exercising her right to free speech and protesting the draft. World War I thus gave birth to a renewal of pacifist and antiwar demonstrations, and the Iron-Jawed Angels, as they became known, helped push the suffrage ballot forward.

The devastation of World War I and the peace process that followed encouraged the formation of new groups such as such as the

Back our girls over there: YWCA United War
Work Campaign. Underwood, Clarence F.
(artist), 1918. World War I Charles B. Burdick
War Poster Collection, MSS-2010-02-02, San
Jose State University Library Special Col-
lections and Archives. (Courtesy of San Jose
State University, Special Collections and Ar-
chives)

WPP. The WPP membership included Jeannette Rankin, Jane Addams, Alice Hamilton, and Lillian Wald. Representing the United
States, they traveled to Europe to participate in an international
peace conference of women in 1915, and together with women from
other nations, they formed the WILPF.

As the war wound down and preparation began for the making of the peace treaty, international pacifists organized the Zurich
Conference through the International Committee of Women for
Permanent Peace (ICWPP). In April of 1918, American delegates
Jane Addams, Emily Greene Balch, Alice Hamilton, Lillian Wald,
and Jeannette Rankin sailed for Europe to participate. Rankin had
finished out her term in the House of Representatives and in 1918

focused her energies on peace activism. She and the other delegates strategically scheduled the Zurich Conference to coincide with the Paris Peace Conference in Versailles. As part of their trip, the women toured the French battlefields, where they witnessed firsthand the horrors of war-torn France, and they were struck by the devastation on the population and staggering number of starving children. One of their primary goals was to influence a positive outcome in the peace settlement. The conference dealings were done behind closed doors and were dominated by the Allied nations, who objected to colonial independence and demanded distribution of German colonial territories in Turkey, Africa, and western Asia. The American peace delegates at the ICWPP articulated their disappointment over the terms of the treaty. In their resolution, they cited the denial of the principles of self-determination and the need to stay true to President Wilson's original Fourteen Points, which they believed would have encouraged peace and harmony. While these activists did not support the war; they did support Wilson's vision of a League of Nations. Instead, the treaty condemned Europe to a life of poverty, disease, despair, and anarchy. The women rightly predicted that the settlement agreements would increase hostilities between nations and would lead to future wars. The secrecy of the Paris Peace Conference reinforced their distrust of the peace process. It should also be noted that Wilson was very disappointed by the peace process and the harshness of the economic reparations against the Central Power, and especially the reparations against Germany.

ANTIWAR SUPPRESSION AND THE RED SCARE

World War I created a tense atmosphere in the United States. The government played a heavy hand in trying to quell antiwar sentiments. In June of 1917, the government enacted the Espionage Act to suppress dissent, which had a prison sentence up to 20 years for anyone convicted of aiding the enemy or for anti-draft protests. Emma Goldman was prosecuted under this act, where she was forced to serve a 2-year prison term. Eugene E. Debs of the AFL-CIO Labor Union was sentenced to a 10-year prison sentence for defending antiwar protesters but served only 32 months after President Harding issued a presidential pardon in 1921.

During and after the war, both male and female pacifists were criticized and treated as traitors. Addams, who won the Nobel Prize in 1931, is a good example. She maintained an antiwar position all of her life, and she regularly spoke out against World War I,

and the Red scare that followed the war resulted in a media backlash against her. The *Red scare* is a term used by historians to de-
note the hysteria that evolved after the Russian Revolution and the
fear of the spread of Bolshevism to the United States. Socialists and
Communists in the United States were targeted as traitors and they
were blamed for many of the social problems in the United States
after the war. Individuals and groups who protested, unionized, or
were defined as radicals were made scapegoats during this period.
Later, the same anti-Communist hysteria would take hold in the
post–World War II era.

During the war, feminist organizations were also targeted as
subversive. The Military Intelligence Division of the War Department had been collecting files on various feminist groups, including the NAWSA, NWP, WPP, WILPF, Women's Joint Congressional
Committee, Parent Teacher Association (PTA), YWCA, WCTU, and
other religious organizations. In May of 1923, an ambitious librarian from the Chemical Warfare Service complied and published a
chart of subversive women's organizations. Nearly every prominent female social activist and organization was listed, including
Jane Addams, Alice Paul, Jeannette Rankin, Carrie Chapman Catt,
and many others. The publication was called the *Spider-Web Chart*
and was circulated widely. The librarian Lucia R. Maxwell anno-
tated the chart with inflammatory statements indicting all branches
of feminists for supporting the spread of Bolshevism, and she wrote
an equally scathing poem. The first verse reads:

> Miss Bolsheviki has come to town,
> With a Russian cap and a German gown,
> In women's clubs she's sure to be found,
> For she's come to disarm AMERICA.[6]

HYPERPATRIOTISM

The work of librarian Maxwell is an example of the hyperpatriotism that some Americans expressed during and after the war. The
majority of Americans supported the war, and some of the most extreme patriotic groups included the American Foreign Legion and
Daughters of the American Revolution (DAR). Both organizations
believed that pacifists were infiltrators of Communism. In their
minds, failure to support the war was treason and un-American.
Ironically, women who offered clear support to Wilson and the
war effort found themselves attacked by the extreme Right. Carrie Chapman Catt offered Wilson the full support from NAWSA,
and clubwomen, the YWCA, and the WCTU also supported the

war effort. The Women's Council for National Defense (WCND) organized local branches to educate women on food conservation, raised relief funds, and created land armies that supported the war effort. Ironically, Catt's support did little to stop the wave of Red-baiting that came out of the hyperpatriotism movement.

The lobby work of WILPF to promote arms limitations, to eliminate a standing military, and specifically the formation of the Women's Committee for World Disarmament led the government to use blacklisting as a mechanism to intimidate peace activists. Members of President Harding's military cabinet struck back through vicious Red-baiting techniques. Secretary of War John Weeks started the campaign to blacklist all pacifist groups. The most famous example is the response by Brigadier-General A. Amos Fries, who objected to any arms limitation, reduction in a standing army, and naval reductions. Fries counterattacked by accusing WILPF of being subversive and accused the National Council for the Prevention of War (NCPW) of being a Communist front organization. His sentiments were reinforced by conservative politicians who dismissed the talk of disarmament as "silly pacifists" and suffragists interfering in government. As noted, through the Chemical Warfare Service Division, Fries authorized the creation of the *Spider-Web Chart* implicating nearly every pacifist organization and women's groups as Communist traitors. The chart was first published in the *Dearborn Independent* in 1924, a paper owned by Henry Ford. Fries had close connections to military intelligence and went as far as to implicate the PTA; the chart named nearly every major and some minor women's organizations. Fries pointed to the work of the Children's Bureau and the promotion of social welfare legislation as an example of the insidious nature of the Communist infiltration, and he accused WILPF of spreading Communism.

Hyperpatriotic groups jumped on the bandwagon to attack women's organizations, feeding into the hysteria of the era. The DAR, a conservative women's patriotic organization, identified Bolsheviks as a major enemy of the United States, and they established the National Defense Community to respond to the spread of pacifism. They directly attacked WILPF as "Red radicals," and began publicly attacking notable women's organization leaders, including Carrie Chapman Catt, Jane Addams, Dorothy Detzer, Mary Anderson, Emily Balch, Jeannette Rankin, Sara Bard Field, Julia Lathrop, and more. Catt responded to the *Spider-Web Chart* and to the accusations, slander, and lies produced by DAR. In *Poison Propaganda,* Catt made clear that the accusation that women's organizations were being financed by Moscow was outrageous, and through her own investigation, she discovered that the chart was actually produced by the government. WILPF was at the center of the attacks, and the Military Intelligence Division of the Department of War colluded with DAR to secretly investigate WILPF. Moreover, the organization and its leaders were followed by military intelligence investigators, and their headquarters were frequently broken into. This surveillance continued throughout the 1920s. Ironically, DAR was listed on the original *Spider-Web Chart,* but once they offered to act as private investigators, their name was removed from the chart.

Despite the Red-scare environment, pacifists groups continued to work toward world peace. Moreover, the results of the Treaty of Versailles highlighted the need to continue as a pacifist organization to support a just and humane peace. The U.S. branch of WILPF created a national lobbying arm to promote peace and to demand that Congress act against continued military sanctions. From the 1920s and 1930s, WILPF focused their lobbying efforts to promote universal peace and complete disarmament worldwide. They also supported neutrality legislation that treated all nations equally. In the United States, WILPF focused its attention on the violation of the munitions industry, which was fueled by economic instability and aggressive action by Japan as it invaded Manchuria. WILPF's belief in universal disarmament, and Japan's violation of China, presented them with a new world crisis.

Through the lobbying activities of Dorothy Detzer and other peace advocates, WILPF took direct action and sent telegrams to President Hoover and Secretary of State Henry Stimson and urged them to support the enforcement of the Nine Powers Act, which safe-guarded the rights and interests of China, to which Japan and the United States were signatories. When these efforts failed, they petitioned Hoover to send a "strong public message" to Japan, which eventually led to an arms embargo against Japan and China.[7] Fearful of a government conspiracy and lack of reliable information on the affairs of state in the Near East, Detzer urged Stimson to end the secret diplomacy and demanded that the United States observe the international acts. Discouraged by the administration's lack of real action, WILPF drafted a bill to limit U.S. munitions sales and sought out support from individual congressmen. Between 1931 and 1934, Detzer worked the chambers of Congress to promote adoption of WILPF's bill to prohibit the sale of munitions to any country that violated the Kellogg-Briand Pact of 1928 that outlawed acts of war. Detzer then worked with

Congressman Howard Fish to promote a resolution that would address all of their concerns, while the State Department worked in concert with the Senate Foreign Relations Committee to kill the bill. By 1933, the mood in this committee shifted some, and through a series of letters and personal exchanges, Detzer found favor with newly elected Senator Gerald P. Nye, of North Dakota. By 1934, the Senate authorized an investigation, due in large part to the lobbying efforts of Detzer and other peace organizations. For her efforts, Detzer earned the reputation as the most famous lobbyist of the 1920s and 1930s.[8]

EMERGENCY PEACE CAMPAIGN

A growing body of peace organizations formed in response to U.S. foreign policy and global politics. The horrors of World War I and the sanctions that came out of the Treaty of Versailles fostered a growing peace movement that included internationalist and liberal pacifists that shared similarities in promoting peace, but their programs and philosophies varied by organization. The invasion of Manchuria by Japan in 1931 highlighted the inability of the League of Nations to enforce peace and sparked the formation of the Emergency Peace Campaign (EPC) in the 1930s. The EPC brought together a diverse array of peace organizations that included the NCPW, the WILPF, the League of Nations Association (LNA), the Fellowship of Reconciliation (FOR), the American Friends Service Committee (AFSC), and many other groups.

The EPC campaign relied on regional organizations to disseminate educational information through conferences, lectures, petitions, and civil protest. As Charles Chatfield noted in his seminal study on American peace movements, the EPC, despite its failure to "foster international cooperation and avoid war," succeeded in producing a large-scale movement of peace activists, albeit fractured by ideology and goals. Detzer played an important role in the EPC, working with male and female leaders, while providing leadership for building grassroots support of the campaign. WILPF and other organizations depended on each other to lobby Congress and the president. Indeed, this campaign depended on the ordinary activism of local peace activists. A good example is the Connecticut branch of the LNA—a liberal internationalist organization committed to building U.S. support for the League of Nations and promoting neutrality legislation. Florence Kitchelt served as the local chapter's director, where she worked collaboratively with peace organizations and civic/political organizations to establish educational programs for high school students through various state peace conferences, publications and curriculum, parades, peace plays and radio broadcasts, in addition to the formation of a speaker's bureau. Between the years 1918 and 1929, Kitchelt delivered more than 180 speeches. Kitchelt helped organize and scheduled a variety of conferences and model assemblies. Model assemblies offered students the opportunity to dramatize their own assemblies or produce verbatim assemblies using the original speeches from Geneva.[9]

Between 1930 and 1931, the LNA sponsored over 45 model assemblies in 24 states, with approximately 7,200 student participants. On the East coast, Connecticut, Massachusetts, and New York LNA branches organized several model assemblies. In 1928 Yale University hosted a number of these assemblies in the state. According to the 1928 pamphlet "Model Assemblies of the League of Nations, what they are and how to give," students learned to study for themselves the "new method of conducting world affairs." Aside from its value visualizing the League's work, it served to illustrate the broader idea that nations may solve their problems by conference instead of conflict.[10]

AMERICANIZATION PROGRAMS—EDUCATION

Industrialization resulted in tremendous expansion, which as we have seen stimulated unprecedented population growth and increase of immigrant populations across the United States. Progressive social reform was a direct outcome of this expansion. Between 1890 and 1920, education reform became an important piece of the Progressive Era reform. California serves as an excellent case study on the implementation of educational reform with the adoption and implementation of a set of policies referred to collectively as the California Americanization Programs (CAP). California women had the advantage of suffrage in 1911, which enabled them to play an important role in building a legislative framework for reform that included child welfare, public health, prohibition of alcohol, protection of female chastity, age of consent laws, and changes to educational programs. CAP designed programs to facilitate the assimilation of new immigrants into mainstream society and focused on the cultural uplift of immigrant women by modeling white middle-class values. Similar to the experience of women in the Midwest and East, California women created their own female dominion as policymakers and as progressive leaders.

California faced a tremendous population growth as a result of immigration to the United States. The CAP was created in response to the population explosion and the need to assimilate new immigrants into mainstream culture. In 1900, the state population consisted of 1.5 million people, and in 1920, it more than doubled to 3.4 million people. This growth fueled the expansion of the state, which was undergirded by the Southern Pacific Railroad and the extension of the rail lines to the Midwest. Families from across the United States steadily entered the Golden State, hoping to establish new agricultural roots. Immigrants from England, Germany, Ireland, and China arrived as well. The largest immigrant group came from Mexico, with approximately 88,771, while the Italians trailed close behind with 88,504. These newcomers flocked from San Diego to San Francisco in search of new economic opportunities. Los Angeles became home to diverse immigrant groups, but the size of the Mexican population would make Los Angles the second largest community of Mexicans outside of Mexico City. The population boom and the hysteria brought on by World War I gave a new boost to education programs aimed at the immigrant population. The Compulsory School Act of 1903 forced progressive educators into action as the population boom created concerns over rising juvenile delinquency and school truancy. This new social and political climate created a new imperative to address immigrant education. Educated in the settlement house movement, California women hoped to replicate neighborhood services that would result in acceptance from the various communities and allow them to educate women and children in American civics and middle-class values. Los Angeles became the center for education reform. The impact of overcrowded foreign quarters and the mix of languages provided new and more forceful programs. Albert Sheils, the newly appointed superintendent of schools, helped launch English-language programs for adults. While the basis of the adult education program was ostensibly designed to teach reading and writing, the program also focused on U.S. loyalty and patriotism.

In 1913, Mary S. Gibson, a well-connected suffragist and reformer, was appointed to serve on the newly formed California Commission of Immigration and Housing (CCIH). The education division's mission was to provide immigrants, children as well as adults, with educational and citizenship opportunities. Gibson believed that assimilation lay at the heart of the immigrant problem and that immigrant mothers offered the key for building good American citizens.

Through the CCIH, she designed a program to bring education to immigrant women, through a home teaching program that focused on English language education, civics, and home economics. In 1915, legislators formed the California Homes Teachers Act (CHTA) to focus on the Mexican community. The curriculum was designed to provide Mexican women with the proper American housekeeping skills while at the same time reinforcing the importance of work productivity and civic loyalty to the United States. This domestic education provided the basis to reinforce a cookie-cutter approach to homemaking, helped secure domestic stability, and created a training ground for potential employment outside of the home as maids, seamstresses, and laundresses. Los Angeles served as the test case for the program because it had a large immigrant population base and had both citizenship and adult education programs already in place. Amanda Matthews Chase, a university-trained teacher with experience in Mexico and fluent in Spanish, became the first teacher of the program. Part of her job was to build support from the local school districts, but primarily she spent her time visiting families and immigrant neighborhoods. Chase succeeded in producing some results from her initial pilot program, and by 1918, the Los Angeles School District employed 44 home teachers, and this number rose to 63 by 1927.

Class attendance and dropout rates were high for all immigrants attending night classes—out of the 122,131 immigrants living in Los Angeles, only 3,448 actually attended, and only 322 finished the program. Insensitivity to the Mexican culture limited the success of these programs, and while some of the goals to provide English and teach American civics were beneficial, the reformers believed they were racially superior—a common view held my most progressive reformers. For example, Chase and Gibson shared the view that Mexicans lacked industry and ambition. Americanization programs were designed to make immigrants 100 percent American, by eliminating their cultural language, customs, and identity. In another example, Pearl Ellis, reformer and author of *Americanization through Homemaking,* instructed home teachers to conduct lessons on changing cultural diets, by replacing beans and tortillas for lettuce and white bread. New cooking and housekeeping methods were also encouraged.

While part of the rationale behind the program was clearly racially insensitive, the reform had practical public health benefits. U.S. Immigration Commission studies of seven major cities documented the problem of freshwater supply and sanitation systems that serviced the growing tenement housing projects and the barrios in urban cities. Sanitation problems, insufficient indoor and outdoor plumbing, and the lack of sanitary water created a public health crisis. Many of the tenements and barrios lacked adequate plumbing or water to sustain the community. Several households shared one toilet or had to share outhouses. In Chicago, for example, 80 percent of one Slovak district shared common toilets located in commonly shared cellars and yards, and under sidewalks. One investigator reported that in one example 5 families consisting of 28 people shared one yard toilet. One of the goals of the Home Teachers Program was to teach proper American housekeeping skills, while training immigrant women to become the housekeepers for middle-class and elite families.

The success of the program is difficult to gage. Gibson estimated that 50,000 families were reached by the program, yet the small numbers of adult education graduates highlights the limited success of the Americanization programs in the state. Indeed, as historians Vicki Ruiz and George Gonzales have shown, the message of the reformers never assembled an optimistic ideology, and their insensitivity to Mexican culture and to Catholicism, combined with a lack of commitment from the Mexican community to assimilate, guaranteed failure. Moreover, the rapid expansion of the Mexican barrio and the increase in migrant labor created a self-sufficient community away from the white mainstream. Despite the failings of the CHTA, Gibson received recognition from Richard Campbell, U.S. commissioner of education, for her work. To be sure, this program like other progressive experiments had its flaws, and the real measure of success resulted in the building of a female dominion in education and development of ideals of citizenship.[11]

WORLD WAR I FACTORY WORK

During World War I, many women contributed to the war effort through their labor. As the war industries ramped up, widespread opportunities for new factory work, in fields previously not open to women and to African Americans, increased dramatically. Consumer culture helped to build female support through their labor. The government utilized war posters to remind women of their patriotic responsibilities. Through the CPI, the government hired well-known magazine illustrators to produce more than 2,500 different posters and distributed over 20 million copies throughout the United States. These posters were designed to connect women to the war effort through their labor, food conservation, knitting socks for soldiers, supporting the Red Cross, the YWCA, and the Land Army—women who worked in agriculture. Land Army women were depicted as daughter's of liberty, as icons of democratic virtue, as saucy new women, as homemakers, war workers, and as agricultural workers. The objective was to enlist the support of all American women, and even if women opted not to work in dangerous factories, they were encouraged to support the war effort through household conservation of natural resources and agricultural labor. The Red Cross and YWCA sponsored many of the posters and advertisements. The CPI program succeeded in reaching women across the United States to participate in the war effort, and more than 1 million women entered the workforce.

The World War I generation of female war workers has been largely overshadowed by the iconic imagery of Rosie the Riveter—the symbolic female war worker of World War II. More than 1 million women traded their long skirts for bloomers and overalls. For the first time in U.S. history, women were asked to take on the job responsibilities of men. These women built fabric-covered planes, hauled scrap metal, welded, produced copper bullets, filled grenades, managed public transportation, maintained the train and shipping industries, and worked as meatpackers and in many other heavy industries. For immigrant and working-class women, working in a factory environment was old school, but for the masses of married women and middle-class workers, noisy factories, vibrating machines, and handling dangerous chemicals was an eye-opening experience. Munitions work, while more dangerous, was mechanized, and the work process was subdivided so as to allow unskilled and semiskilled immigrant men and women to perform a wide variety of jobs. Immigrant and working-class women's work in the needle trades was similarly mechanized and subdivided to increase production rates. As several historians have noted, women exchanged traditional forms of female labor such as sewing to work on metal machines. The business of stamping out buttons easily transferred to drawing out brass cartridges, in the same way that cutting a dress pattern transferred to cutting the linen coverings for airplanes.

The employment of women in the munitions industries in Connecticut highlights the impact that the wartime economy had on women's employability, while showing how employers capitalized on their labor because of the shortage of a male labor force. In Connecticut, undergarment companies, also called "white goods," transformed from making corsets, bras, and underwear to become leaders in the production of munitions, guns, and machine tools. The state became a center for World War I munitions contracts. The Remington Arms–Union Metallic Cartridge received government contracts for more than $168 million to produce small arms and munitions. These contracts lead to large numbers of newcomers to the state seeking employment. Bridgeport and neighboring New Haven were unprepared to provide the housing needed for 25,000 new workers, and because of the lack of local services, women began to fill the gap in the labor force. At Remington alone, some 5,000 women found jobs.

Several strike actions took place during this time period, and both male and female munitions workers walked off their jobs seeking contract provisions for an 8-hour workday, higher wages, and over-time compensation. The Warner Brothers corset factory granted its workers an 8-hour workday and reported that they were at 95 per-cent of the output they had under the 10-hour workday. The shortage of labor and the demand for war products created an environment more favorable to the workers, and companies ran advertisements in the local newspaper to encourage women to consider employ-ment. Some of these ads described the work environment as clear, well lit, and ventilated, while others mentioned good pay and working hours (48-hour week). The Union Metallic Cartridge plant targeting young women advertised as an 8-hour shop with good pay. Professor of economics and war industries investigator Amy Hewes came to Bridgeport to report on the working conditions of the women. A longtime advocate and social reformer for labor and minimum hours laws, she visited the women at their homes and got to know their families. Her final report described a city in serious distress, and she detailed the work environments. She de-scribed the production process to produce metallic cartridges, the problems with the machines, and the dangers of handling fulmi-nate of mercury, which caused eye irritation and sores on the skin. While sinks were installed in the plant, the workers were not al-lowed to wash their hands after handling the mercury until the end of their shift, and they had no protective gear like aprons or gloves. The rate of injury on the job was not recorded, but she found that one woman per week was injured badly enough to require several days off. Crushed fingers, burn accidents from handling chemicals and from serving overheated machines and parts, and gunpowder explosions were common injuries.

As part of the domestic war program, President Wilson estab-lished the Council on National Defense and appointed Samuel

A 1918 YWCA poster showing a parade of women workers wearing uniforms appropriate for specific jobs. (Library of Congress)

Gompers, the president of the American Federation of Labor. Initially, Gompers ignored the role of women in labor and appointed an all-male committee. The women of the Women's Trade Union League (WTUL) used a massive letter-writing campaign to demand female representation on the council. Gompers eventually appointed Mary Anderson, a former boot maker and paid organizer of the WTUL, to the committee. Anderson had a long-term connection to working women and was an advocate for protective labor legislation for women. Prior to the war, she had helped institute legislation to protect mothers from hazardous chemicals, night work, and excessive hours. Anderson and Mary Van Kleeck of the Russell Sage Foundation would lead the Committee on Women in Industry (CWI). Van Kleeck had specific experience working as a consultant to the Ordnance Department—a division that provided all of the supplies to the army, from basic supplies to medical supplies, uniforms, and guns and ammunition. As a consultant, she investigated government-contracted factories where she reported on the working conditions and use of female employment. In the textile industry, she found major violations in use of tenement home workers and of children. This practice was commonplace, yet the factory foremen frequently denied it. Investigator Mary Hewes confirmed the violations in the textile trades. In one example, she reported that more than 21,000 black and white women between Indiana and Kentucky were employed to work in their homes, while the factories were laying off their workforce. Using cheap household labor for the production of clothing was common practice. Van Kleeck recommended that new government standards regulating contract standards and government codes would end the abuses of tenement labor. She further recommended that the War Department create a Women's Bureau to investigate actual factory practices and to serve as the principle advisor for employment of women in war industries. The Ordnance Department created the Woman's Branch, which would later become the U.S. Women's Bureau. Van Kleeck and Anderson would lead this wartime department. The Department of Ordnance established the standards that included reasonable hours, healthy work environments, equal pay for equal work, and the right to organize. Oversight of the chemical industries became an important purview of the Women's Industry in Service (WIS), and the agency pointed to the investigations in Niagara Falls that illustrated the hazards of working with lead and other minerals. This region had a serious employment shortage long before the war, which had to do with the unhealthful working conditions. Women working in this industry did not directly handle lead, but they worked in other processing areas and were exposed to lead poisoning through poor air ventilation, porous flooring, and limited access to clean water and soap. Niagara Falls had a long history of burning out its workforce through direct and indirect exposure to harmful chemicals. The locals joked that the workforce changed faster than the tourist population, due in part to the unhealthful working conditions and severe environmental pollution. Van Kleeck successfully argued that immediate wartime action was needed to address the public health issues before women should be recruited to work in these industries. Factory improvements required new air filtration, installation of nonporous floors, basic facilities for cleanup, and separate lunch rooms. Van Kleeck hoped that new labor standards granted to women would eventually apply to all workers.

THE GREAT MIGRATION

For the black population, the war served as a monumental turning point for migration to the North. In this era, known as the "Great Migration," more than 500,000 blacks made their way to northern cities in pursuit of employment and a chance for a better life away from the ramped racism of the South. The significant increase of the populations in Chicago and Detroit best illustrate the degree of black flight from the South. For example, Chicago's black population increased 150 percent, whereas Detroit expanded by 600 percent. For a brief moment in time, black women escaped the drudgery of domestic and agricultural work and joined the factory workforce. Popular newspapers and magazines provide a brief glimpse of their ordinary experience. Individuals wrote newspapers advice columns seeking information on how to migrate north, possible job opportunities, and housing assistance. The African American paper the *Chicago Defender* published many of the letters. In one letter, from McCoy, Louisiana, dated April 16, 1917, a reader asked for help finding free rail for herself and her husband and daughter. Another writer from Biloxi, Mississippi (April 27, 1917), asked for similar advice. Social organizations like the YWCA and the National Association of Colored Women (NACW) also provided some assistance in helping new migrants find housing and jobs. Wartime job opportunities provided incentives for black families to migrate north, but the newspaper letters highlight the violence and discrimination African Americans felt under Jim Crow, and they raised awareness of the plight of lynchings in the South. Once they reached Chicago and other cities, they did not find the land of milk and honey, but wages were dramatically better. In the North, a black woman could earn more in one day than she could in a week of domestic work in the South. The racial climate was generally better, yet the number of urban race riots during this period make it very clear that the Northern life offered new sets of problems for segregation issues. While migrants earned better salaries and lived outside of Jim Crow laws, the cost of living, substandard housing, and poverty prevailed in Northern cities and is reflected in the number of race riots in urban cities of the era. *The Chicago Commission on Race Relations Report* (1922) recorded the experience of blacks following the 1919 race riot. In one interview, the respondent felt that the North offered great freedoms, the ability to vote, better overall treatment, and better working conditions. In contrast to the South, higher income rates paid the bills and allowed for some extra pleasures. Black and white women served a variety of industries, but as noted by a popular author of the time, Alice Dunbar-Nelson, in her article "Come out of the Kitchen Mary" (1919), black women were encouraged to enter war production as munitions workers. They performed a variety of jobs including the production work of building airplanes, serving as elevator operators and subway porters, driving trucks, packing and unloading freight cars, digging ditches, and working in shipyards and meatpacking houses. In these jobs, black women were hired to work at the lowest level and were used for the heaviest, dirtiest, and most dangerous work. When the war ended, they were the first to loose their jobs. Despite the grim reality of war work, black women embraced the independence of factory work, in contrast to domestic and agricultural work.[12]

Women worked in all segments of wartime industries. The variety of jobs performed and the hard labor this work required is astounding. World War II Rosies learned from their mothers and grandmothers that they could assemble airplanes, make bullets, fill grenades, make gas masks, weld heavy iron and steel, operate trains and trucks, build ships, and work in the meatpacking and cannery industries. When the armistice agreement ending the war was signed, layoffs for women came quickly. Remington announced they would release half of their employees. Munitions workers were the first to be laid off, while workers in lighter industries in food production and textiles would have a two-year or so reprieve before facing unemployment. The Paris Peace Treaty sealed the fate of all female war workers, and the U.S. economy eventually spiraled into a serious depression. Nevertheless, women learned that they could perform jobs that were designated for men, and they developed new confidence as leaders and as workers. More importantly, World War I women workers raised the next generation of women who would serve in World War II.

The devastation of the Great Depression on middle-class American families was extreme, but minorities of working-class status and rural families were hit the hardest. Mexican cannery and migrant farm workers returned to subsistence jobs, and African American women lost their economic foothold as they returned to low-paid domestic and agricultural work. White rural families suffering from the environmental disaster of the Dust Bowl in Oklahoma, Texas, Kansas, and Colorado migrated en masse to California in hopes of finding work. These "Okies" and "Arkies" as they were called flooded the agricultural labor positions normally held by Mexicans and African Americans. The suffering and devastation was well documented by Dorothea Lange's photography, through John Steinbeck's *The Grapes of Wrath*, and the music of Woody Guthrie. President Hoover failed on all accounts to address this misery and poverty and lost the confidence of American voters. As a result, in 1932 Franklin D. Roosevelt took 57.4 percent of the poplar vote and 472 electoral votes for a landslide victory over Republicans.

REBUILDING NETWORK OF WOMEN

The Great Depression and the election of Franklin Roosevelt in 1932 would lead to a second revival of women's influence in politics. Despite the failure of Sheppard-Towner, it laid the foundation for large-scale national reform from 1932 to 1938. FDR took office in 1933 promising a New Deal with government control over banking, support for agriculture, and social welfare. He created new agencies to implement his New Deal, and several prominent women who had experiences in government as social reformers were appointed to work on social welfare policies as part of a Women's Cabinet. Molly Dewson became the director of the Women's Division of the Democratic National Committee, Francis Perkins became secretary of labor, Mary Anderson ran the Women's Bureau, Rose Schneiderman became a member of the Labor Advisory Board, Julia Lathrop continued on as the director of the Children's Bureau, and Mary McLeod Bethune served as the head of the Office of Minority Affairs—the only African American to serve in the Women's Cabinet. These women and several others influenced the direction of the National Recovery Administration (NRA) to provide labor and social security legislation. Government jobs for women increased from 15.8 percent to 18.8 percent, representing 90,000 new jobs.[13]

As historian Susan Ware has shown, the rise of women's employment in high-level government positions and in independent agencies correlates to job increases brought on by economic and wartime emergencies. For the bulk of the women employed in high-level jobs, they brought specific skills as social scientists and as welfare reformers, but they only represented a small margin of working women.

The program priorities that came out of FDR's first 100 days included restoring confidence in the banking system, assisting agriculture, and addressing unemployment and industrial recovery. The creation of the National Industrial Recovery Act (NIRA) became the centerpiece to the programs, and the NIRA created the NRA to oversee the regulation of the economy. The NRA emerged as a partnership between business and the government to set product prices and wage standards. These programs encouraged social reformers to push for deeper welfare reform. New Deal women's work managed under the leadership of Francis Perkins through the Labor Department focused on the passage of the Social Security Act (1935), the National Labor Relations Act (NLRA), and the Fair Labor Standards Act (1938). The Labor Advisory Board included the appointment of Rose Schneiderman of the WTUL to represent the interests of women, on the otherwise all-male board that was charged with the task of developing different industry codes based upon collected data and designed to improve working conditions, average earnings, and safety standards. The Women's and Children's Bureaus, both under the Department of labor, supported this research effort. For example, the Women's Bureau compiled data on 120 different industries in 1934 alone. Other labor reform groups like the WTUL and the National Consumer League (NCL) provided support at the various NRA hearings. Both groups also focused on codes related to child labor. Clearly, these organizations built a strong reputation in research and policy development—an outcome of earlier Progressive Era social science activities. At the end of the day, the final labor codes failed to encompass equal pay for women, but overall these women were happy with the increased wages for women.[14]

Meanwhile, the Supreme Court ruled that the new industrial codes were unconstitutional, resulting in dismantling of the NRA and other New Deal programs. Perkins then refocused her work at the Labor Department toward securing passage of the Social Security Act and establishing permanent new wages and hours legislation. Women had long struggled to implement social welfare policies that included social security, child and maternal welfare, widows pension, health insurance, and minimum wage and hours laws. Finally, the New Deal gave them the opportunity to see the fruits of their labor with the exception of universal health insurance. On August 14, 1935, FDR signed the Social Security Act into law. An important feature of the act resulted in the creation of the Aid to Dependent Children program that helped to increase the visibility and importance of the Children's Bureau as an advisory agency. The Children's Bureau took on the responsibility for the supervision and administration of state welfare programs and for foster care and other children's institutions. Moreover, the National Labor Relations Board (NLRB) secured laws prohibiting child labor under the age of 16 and revived wages and hours standards.

Looking at the process of policy making, we see how women's social movement networks transformed between 1900 and the 1940s. Their work had direct impact on the average lives of female industrial workers, and specifically for women of color. In one case study of Puerto Rican needle trade workers, the female labor force went on strike demanding better wages, factory safety, the right to unionize, and the enforcement of labor codes that aligned with the regulations produced from the NRA. While new codes were eventually established, the women faced difficulty enforcing the set 25 percent minimum wage increases. The outcome of the strike, and the creation of new codes, illustrates the continued struggles that women faced in the labor market, particularly in the colonial environment of Puerto Rico. Collective action, however, was an important feature of this particular struggle and provides a sense of how federal programs attempted to equalize wages and hours to the benefit of the employee.

In the United States, women across industries struggled to sustain their families on subsistence wages. In another example, Mexican women working in San Antonio, Texas, experienced severe discrimination in the workforce. The Mexican population worked at the bottom of the labor ladder, they experienced frequent unemployment, and most worked in the pecan-shelling industry. The workforce constituted anywhere from 10,000 to 15,000 workers who on the average earned less than $3 for a 55-hour workweek. The work environment was primitive, resembling the sweatshops in New York at the turn of the century. The shelling workrooms were crowded and had poor lighting and ventilation, and crude toilet facilities. The owners of the industry similarly opposed the enforcement of the NRA minimum wages. One employer had the audacity to tell officials at an NRA hearing that "Mexicans don't want much money." He argued that the shelleries were in better condition than their homes and warmer in the winter, and that they had a free supply of pecans to eat. In contrast to this employer's view, the workers wanted higher wages and tried to unionize several times, and they went on strike in 1933 and 1937. In the later example, some 5,000 female picketers were arrested for peacefully demonstrating. The Texas Civil Liberties

Union intervened by publicizing the harassment of women. When the governor got involved, the owner eventually was forced into a binding arbitration agreement to settle the strike. Sadly, the owners shut down the plants to install new equipment, eliminating the need to pay a large force at the government rate of $0.25 per hour. Though the strike failed to secure long-term job stability and wages within this industry, Mexican women became visible members of the community, and they played an important role in breaking the impact of the Depression and forced business leaders to reform the city.[15]

DATING, MARRIAGE, FAMILY

On the surface, the Roaring Twenties appeared to be a decade of unprecedented progress and prosperity. Economic expansion began the transformation of America from a producer economy to a consumer economy. The 1920s became popularly known as the Roaring Twenties or the Jazz Age, which referred to the sexual and cultural revolution that gave rise to a new youth culture and the abandonment of traditional values and clothing. The flapper defined the new features of the postwar generation. Hollywood helped to create the era, while new popular forms of entertainment portrayed in movies transformed drinking and sexual expression for women. The flapper—characterized by her short bobbed hair, knee-length dresses, dancing wildly to the Charleston, flirting, petting, and drinking—epitomized the dramatic social changes and new views on dating, marriage, and family life during the Roaring Twenties. This new female sexual revolution represented a rejection of Victorian values as many young urban workingwomen peeled off the sexual constraints placed on them by family and society. As historian Kathy Peiss has shown, the rise of amusement parks, speakeasy bars, and the movies created an unregulated opportunity for women to pursue their sexuality. The growing availability of birth control devices advanced the sexual revolution, while consumer culture glamorized female independence and mild forms of sexual expression. Young women read the glossy magazines of the day that featured advice columns, movie reviews, new fashion trends, and interviews with movie stars. *Photoplay* columnist Carolyn Van Wyck gave young women advice on dating, marriage, and divorce. Several of her columns addressed the question of wives working outside the home. One young woman of 18 expressed her desire to work and explained that her husband was not receptive to the idea. She asked Van Wyck what she thought about women working outside the home, and Van Wyck responded that she supported women's right to work but concluded that harmony in the marriage was more important. Van Wyck received a number of questions about romantic love and dating expectations. In an example of this type, a single woman asked if it was okay for a young woman to be a gold digger and to accept gifts for minor sexual favors. Van Wyck made it clear in her response that gold digging was not a virtue. Advice columns of this kind illustrate the tension between new codes and old forms of dating and marital behaviors. In contrast to the image of the flapper, many young women struggled with sexual propriety.

Romantic love and a belief in a more equal marriage relationship took firm root in this era, partially from the influences of popular culture, but also because of the increase in female labor and the previous suffrage victories that empowered women to rethink their status in society. Indeed, the image of the new woman opened the door to a sexual revolution of a kind. However, the ideology of dating and marriage had not completely eliminated a traditional belief in marriage, nor did it challenge the gender stereotypes of women's contributions in marriage. This proved to be the case following the Great Depression. More and more American couples embraced marriage as a partnership, connected by similar social values, and a vibrant sex life, but the economic crisis created an environment whereby shared breadwinning was a necessity.

The overemphasis on entertainment and consumer culture in the 1920s, strengthened by new prosperity and progress, seemed overwhelming to many as they tried to live up to the standards offered by new urban amusements and pastimes. From actress Joan Crawford to baseball legend Babe Ruth, boxer Jack Dempsey, and aeronautical celebrity Charles Lindbergh, the American obsession of the rich and famous flourished. Despite the glitter of popular culture, millions of Americans still lived in poverty and had limited opportunity to purchase new cars, radios, and household appliances, especially citizens in the urban ghettos and rural environments. Moreover, the expansion of consumer credit began to replace traditional savings practices while the rise and fall of the stock market gravely impacted family life.

As Elaine Tyler May wrote in *Homeward Bound*, the Depression created a system that involved government intervention to repair the economy, and families across America had to make significant adjustments in their attitudes about family hierarchy and gender relationships. Couples had no choice but to embrace new gender roles in the labor force and at home. In many cases, families experienced role reversals, where women's paychecks paid the bills, while men stayed home. President Roosevelt through his New Deal policies brought the government directly into the everyday lives of American families. Despite the New Deal progress by 1941, 40 percent of Americans still lived below the poverty line, and nearly 8 million workers earned less than minimum wage. These economic realities put stress on many marriages as can be seen by the decline in marriage rates. Young people delayed marriage to help support their families, and some opted not to marry at all.

The downhill marriage trend of the 1930s produced alarm from pundits, politicians, and clergy alike. Many writers of the day feared that delaying marriage would lead to sexual promiscuity and that female independence needed to be curbed. Yet, these wartime experiences gave women new opportunities to work outside the home and gave them a taste of a good paycheck. One young woman from Rhode Island commented in a magazine survey that she wanted to get married some day but enjoyed having her own money and didn't see marriage as an immediate need. Another women commented that she felt obligated to support her family. Meanwhile, Hollywood glamorized the image of the workingwoman as independent, strong, career oriented, and sensual. Hollywood movies also had a hand in projecting the concept of *equality between the sexes* in labor and love, but in marriage, women remained subordinate. The movie *Gone With the Wind* is a good example of this imagery. The heroine, Scarlett O'Hara, was an independent shrewd businesswoman, and a gold digger, but failed as a mother and wife. The message behind the movie implied that women needed men to support them. Sustainable marriage was directly linked to traditional gender roles in marriage, and female independence threatened the stability of marriage.

While romantic love and an emerging sense of sexual equality depicted in magazines, books, and movies influenced sexual expectations in dating and marriage, the New Deal programs highlight the grim reality that the economy had on working families. Married women faced federal and local job discrimination, even when families were dependent on married women's incomes. For example, where two employees worked in the same household in a federal agency, the woman was the first fired. The Economy Act of 1932 reinforced the gendered social structure of men as providers and women as homemakers. Local state agencies followed the suit of the federal government, and many women lost their jobs as a result. The severity of the unemployment of the time cannot be understated. Between the years 1933 and 1935, one out of five male workers were unemployed, or on the dole, meaning that they were dependent on charity and government assistance to sustain their families. Many social and economic factors including high male unemployment rates, destitute poverty, and changes in traditional gender relationships brought on by the depression increased interpersonal and family tensions.

The national economic failures of the Great Depression created tension between traditional gender roles and basic family survival. Making matters worse was the media's tendency to build up the supremacy of the male as breadwinner and portray the female as the homemaker. Several polls during the period illustrate the attitudes toward married women working outside of the home. One 1936 poll found that 82 percent of women believed that wives should not work if they had employed husbands, and a 1939 poll reported that 90 percent of people believed women should not work outside of the home at all. These polls confirmed the views of the traditionalists of the period that only when the family was economically in need should women enter the workforce. Notwithstanding these views, real gains were made in moving marital relationships forward. A *Ladies Home Journal* poll showed that women had higher expectations that marriage should be more equal, and many objected to the word *obey* in marital vows.

Of the women in the poll, 75 percent believed in joint decision making, and 80 percent expressed the view that unemployed men should be responsible for housework. Few marriages likely resembled these views, though some couples did express a belief in a shared union. Overall, the Depression created a unique situation that pushed and pulled between new ideas on equality and traditional gender roles, and new marriage expectations based on romantic love and equality.[16]

CONCLUSION

From World War I through the period of the New Deal, ordinary American women confronted a range of social, economic, and political challenges. While World War I, or the Great War, as it became known, offered a new world order that opened new avenues for women to pursue equal rights, to promote world peace, and to fight for legislation and new policies that addressed the diversity of American life. The suffrage victories of the era provided the opportunity for women to expand the base of their social networks and taught women to diversify their interests, sometimes as pacifists, as labor activists, as social reformers, or as politicians and policy makers. The diversity of women's experience following the suffrage victory illustrates the difficulty in working toward a single objective as a group, but also helps us understand the importance of social, political, and economic agency. It is also clear that not all women identified as feminists, though the work of these women rested on the belief that women deserved equal treatment in the workforce, under the law, and in their personal lives.

At the conclusion of World War I, the formation of the League of Nations encouraged many peace activists to be hopeful, but the following world depression and the entanglements of a bad peace treaty ensured that a second war would follow. In the United States, the wars and the Depression created new expectations from citizens that the government was responsible for providing services that supported the needs of the people. The earlier work of social progressives laid the groundwork for the New Deal, and as we have seen, women played a large role in demanding democratic policies that addressed the welfare of women and children. The next two decades were marked by a second world war and a postwar world that would be defined by an arms buildup that would produce decades of international conflict. On the domestic front, American women would continue to face employment discrimination, fight for new equal rights legislation, and begin to play a significant role in addressing civil rights for African Americans and other minorities.

NOTES

1. John Mack Faragher, ed., *Out of Many: A History of the American People*, sixth ed.(Pearson, Prentice Hall, 2009), pp. 631–33.

2. Danelle Moon, "Feminists Politicians," in *Icons of the American West*, ed. Gordon M. Bakken (Greenwood Press, 2008), p. 415.

3. Moon, "Feminists Politicians," p. 418.

4. Moon, "Feminists Politicians," pp. 404–5.

5. Carrie A. Foster, *The Women and the Warriors: The U.S. Section of the Women's International League for Peace and Freedom, 1915–1946* (Syracuse University Press, 1995), p. 10.

6. Jo Freemen, "The Spider Web Chart," http://www.jofreeman.com/polhistory/spiderweb.htm.

7. Carrie A. Foster, *The Women and the Warriors; The U.S. Section of the Women's International League for Peace and Freedom, 1915–1946* (Syracuse University Press, 1995), pp. 194–96.

8. Foster, *The Women and the Warriors,* pp. 194–96.

9. Foster, *The Women and the Warriors,* p. 13.

10. Florence Ledyard Cross Papers, MS 315, Manuscripts and Archives, Yale University Library, New Haven, Connecticut.

11. Danelle Moon, "Educational Housekeepers: Female Reformers and the California Americanization Program, 1900–1927," in *California History: A Topical Approach,* ed. Gordon Morris Bakken, pp. 108–24 (Harlan Davidson, Inc., 2003).

12. Ellen Carol Dubois and Lynn Dumenil, *Through the Eyes of Women; An American History* (Bedford/ St. Martin's, 2005), pp. 443–44, 466–72.

13. Susan Ware, *Beyond Suffrage: Women in the New Deal* (Harvard University Press, 1981), p. 61.

14. Ware, *Beyond Suffrage,* pp. 90–91.

15. Ivette Rivera-Guisti and Thomas Dublin, "How Did Women Needleworkers Influence New Deal Labor Policies in Puerto Rico?," in *Women and Social Movements in the U.S., 1600–2000 Scholar Edition,* eds., Kathryn Kish Sklar and Thomas Dublin, pp. 1–3 (State University of New York, 2007).

16. Elaine Tyler May, *Homeward Bound: American Families in the Cold War Era* (Basic Books, 1988), pp. 37–56.

4

WORLD WAR II
TO THE COLD WAR

This chapter will focus on the period between World War II and the Cold War, 1942–1952. As we have seen in the earlier chapters, wartime experience shaped American culture in a variety of ways. Building the war machine required an organized home front that provided the labor for agricultural production, industrial expansion in munitions, shipbuilding, and aerospace. War contracts opened up new labor opportunities for single and married women across the board, represented by the iconic image of Rosie the Riveter. For women of color, labor demands built a new sense of entitlement to compete for jobs held by white women and to work in positions previously held by men. We shall also see how different ethnic groups faired during the war and after, specifically the suspension of basic civil rights for Japanese Americans and the continued struggle for civil rights for African Americans and Hispanics.

Following the end of World War II, the U.S. economy transformed from war to a consumer-based society. At the same time, global uncertainty created by tensions of nuclear war, and the fear that the Soviet Union intended to dominate world politics and their aggression in creating a bloc of Communist run nations, created a new Red scare in the United States that targeted groups that failed to live according to the tenets of *containment*. This theory reflected the international commitment of the United States and

Great Britain to contain Communism by uniting military, economic, and diplomatic strategies. On the political-domestic front,
containment ideology created heightened social and political fears
that Communists were ever present and undermining government. The House Committee on Un-American Activities (HUAC)
formed in 1945 to investigate subversive Americans, creating a
new Red scare that targeted specific groups and individuals. On
the home front, containment translated to social conformity undergirded by strong nuclear families. The postwar prosperity that
followed transformed the middle class and produced a baby boom
(1946–1965). Despite the hyperbole of the period, many groups refused to conform to the traditional ideology of domesticity, while
others took to the courts to contest civil rights violations. The perception of the 1950s as the golden era of the family was far from
ideal, and as we shall see, women played a significant role as social
activists and feminists. Thus, this era established the foundation
for the protest movements of the civil rights era.

WORLD WAR II

World War II set in motion a series of new patterns of social, economic, and political behavior for Americans and the world that dramatically improved the working lives of women. Just as the World
War I generation collectively supported the war effort, women
of all ages and backgrounds entered the workforce once again to
fight against Fascist aggression in Europe and Asia. The home front
image of Rosie the Riveter dominated the war era and encouraged
many women to don overalls for jobs building ships and aircraft,
manufacturing munitions, producing food, and so on. Like their
mothers before them, women of this new generation became the
backbone to the home front mobilization effort. Women from all
classes, ethnic origins, and races dedicated their lives to service
and sacrifice. While the biases against women and continuation of
racism remained strong, Americans of different creeds, colors, and
economic positions embraced their patriotic duty, with the expectation and hope that in the postwar years they would benefit from the
American promise of democracy and equal rights.

World War II opened untold job opportunities for women and
promised increased pay and the ability to join labor unions. Overall,
workers' earnings increased by 70 percent, and farm income doubled.
Labor organizing grew by 50 percent, and despite union agreements
with the government to suspend all strike actions during war, the

United Mine Workers went on strike in 1943. Their action resulted in the passage of the Smith-Connally Act (1945), granting the government the ability to seize control of plants involved in wartime production. Nevertheless, women and minorities joined unions in large numbers and in some cases organized their own unions. The war ushered in a new era of unprecedented gains for women in the workforce and in their personal lives. The laws that barred black women from working in defense industries were lifted, married women entered the workforce in large numbers, and for the first time married women out numbered single women in the labor force. The government and war industries actively recruited married women into the labor for the first time in U.S. history. For example, advertisements from the War Manpower Agency used propaganda to encourage women to join the war effort and specifically targeted married women. In contrast to the era of the Great Depression, where 80 percent of Americans believed that women should not work outside the home, World War II social attitudes shifted to supporting married women who worked outside the home. Prior to the war, women worked in mostly low-paying light industrial jobs that lacked unions.

During World War II, factory jobs doubled women's wages, and more than 300,000 women took jobs in aircraft production. In one example, a San Diego women developed skills as a draftsman in the Convair Aircraft Company, and by the end of the war, she contributed to wing designs for B-24 aircraft. Indeed, war work exposed women to new skills as welders, riveters, and designers. The war also invited a new corps of women to volunteer in the military, and for the first time in U.S. history, women were actively recruited. Some 100,000 women volunteered to become navy WAVES, and 140,000 joined the Women's Army Corps (WACs). Other branches included the Marine Corp Women's Reserve and the Coast Guard Women's Reserve, representing 36,000 additional women. Just as impressive is the fact that 76,000 women served as nurses in the army and navy. Despite their entry into the armed services, these women remained in gender-segregated positions as clerks, telephone operators, and in other nonindustrial work, while others worked in skilled jobs as welders and mechanics. Nursing had long provided women with the opportunity of service, as was true in World War I.

Initially, the military avoided bringing in female physicians, but because of shortages in 1943 they lifted the ban on commissioning female doctors. The Nursing Corps worked closely behind the lines of combat and faced the same dangers as enlisted men.

Black women also served in the military, but they did so under the onus of additional racial segregation. The military refused to include black women in the corps until 1944, and like black male soldiers, they were segregated into all-black volunteer units and were only assigned to serving African American soldiers and prisoners of war. Native American women and men also served, and some 800 women functioned as WACs; mostly in noncombat roles. More than 300 Japanese American women served in the WACs and in the Army Cadet Nursing Corp.[1]

SUSPENDING CIVIL RIGHTS— AFTER PEARL HARBOR

The tensions of the World War II era can be traced back to the Treaty of Versailles, which created weak economies in Europe and Asia and increased Fascist aggression by Germany, Spain, and Japan. U.S. diplomacy with Japan was strained in the early 1930s, but with the formation of the Axis pact between Germany, Spain, and Japan, tensions rose to an all-time high. A series of events led to the Japanese occupation of Manchuria (a large Chinese province), the installation of a Japanese-run puppet government, and declaration of war on China that led the United States to break all diplomatic ties with Japan. Amid the early crisis of World War II, the U.S. Congress passed three neutrality acts outlawing the sales of arms to nations at war and prohibiting loans. In 1937, the German invasion of France and England, and FDR's support of China, poised the United States to act. FDR hoped that through a strong military presence in the South Pacific he could forestall Japanese aggression, but this was not to be so. Instead, the Japanese started planning an attack on Pearl Harbor, and on that fateful day of December 7, 1941, the surprise attack left Hawaii in flames and destroyed much of the U.S. Pacific naval fleet. A similar attack followed at the U.S. base in the Philippines, destroying half of the U.S. Air Force in the Pacific. The impact of the loss of life and destruction of the U.S. Navy was staggering. In response, Congress declared war on Japan, and three days later, Germany and Italy declared war on the United States.

JAPANESE INTERNMENT/ DISCRIMINATION/CIVIL RIGHTS

Anti-Asian sentiments in the United States ran high long before Pearl Harbor, and in California, agribusiness longed to eradicate the Japanese from the farming industry. Military leaders reinforced

Five female Japanese American women boarding a special electric train at the Long Beach Train Station, bound for the Santa Anita Relocation Center, 1942. Flaherty Collection: Japanese Internment Records, San Jose State University Library Special Collections and Archives. (Courtesy of San Jose State University, Special Collections and Archives)

undocumented concerns of Japanese American loyalty to the United States. General John L. DeWitt, chief of the Western Command and an extreme racist, convinced FDR that the internal Japanese community posed a security risk. In February 1942, FDR issued Executive Order 9066 suspending the civil rights of all Japanese Americans living on the West Coast and forcing more than 110,000 to leave their homes to live out the war behind the barbed-wire fences of internment camps. Because the Hawaiian Japanese represented 90 percent of the population of Hawaii, they were spared from removal. In local regions of California, Oregon, and Washington, whole communities of Japanese were forcefully relocated to centers and from there were sent to internment camps located in isolated regions like Heart Mountain, Wyoming, and as far south as Texas and Arkansas. Despite the violation of constitutional rights, some 33,000 Japanese Americans joined the armed forces and worked in the war production industries. While many Americans shared the racist sentiments of DeWitt and California business, many groups opposed the internment, and amongst these were various women's organizations such as the YWCA and Quaker relief organizations. Many high level officials similarly objected, including J. Edgar Hoover, director of the FBI.

Correspondence between the interned and relief organizations confirms the hardships of the rudimentary barracks, lack of heat and insulation, filth created by dusty desert climates, lack of running water, inadequate food supplies, and family separations and difficulty maintaining family unity. One woman arriving at the Poston, Arizona, facility complained about the dust, inside temperatures of 102–103 degrees Fahrenheit, and the lack of clean water. In her case, her two girls had the measles, and many of the residents suffered from dysentery. As she recalled, "when we got here we were quite disgusted to see everyone's hair all writhe with dust, clothes so dirty."[2]

The YWCA, Catholic nuns, and other Quaker relief organizations brought needed supplies to the evacuation centers. The San Jose YWCA worked closely with their neighbors to provide physical and emotional support. In one example, one woman writing to the YWCA described the journey from the Santa Anita Evacuation Center to Heart Mountain, Wyoming, where many of the San Jose community lived out their lives for the duration of war. She explained that the barracks were large enough to house 11,000 people. She didn't complain about the surroundings but wished for a quick end to the war so that she could return to California. The YWCA also worked to assist young single Japanese women to relocate to the Owens Valley to work, which allowed Japanese single women the opportunity to live outside of the camps.

Despite the challenges of camp life, each facility functioned as a self-sustaining city, with markets, schools, community programs, gardens, hospitals, and other needed routine services. Family life and separation from family members and friends was a common problem, especially for those who faced internment at the high-security facility at Tule Lake. One young man asked the project director, R.R. Best, for help in locating his fiancée, who did not speak or read English well, so that he could explain that he was being detained.[3] In another example, the elderly and the sick were separated from their families because of fragile or contagious health conditions. One woman writing to a Pasadena American Friends Service Committee (AFSC) relief worker reported that a Mrs. Takao was too old and frail to be sent to the camp and was placed in a local sanitarium, and that others, diagnosed with tuberculosis, were hospitalized in California. Elizabeth Page Harris, a member of the Pasadena AFSC, worked to provide some assistance in sending luggage that could not be carried in the trains to the camps. In one example, she wrote that they had someone who could drive the luggage to the Arizona facility, but that government officials would not allow the AFSC to take possession of the property without a letter of authorization from the owner.[4]

Young people had more mobility if they agreed to serve in the military and war production work. For Nisei (first-generation Japanese American) young women, they had new opportunities to work as clerks and as teachers for very low wages, but for the first time, many experienced independence as new members of the workforce. Some even attended college or worked in manufacturing and domestic service in the Midwest and East, while others served as WACs or as military nurses.[5] Despite the suspension of basic civil rights and the loss of property rights, the Japanese demonstrated loyalty to the United States through their military and war service and behind the barbed wire of internment camps.

The anti-Japanese sentiments created a number of challenges, yet not all Americans abandoned their fellow citizens as can be seen in the case of the Mineta family. Norman Mineta's (former secretary of transportation under Presidents Bill Clinton and George Bush, Jr.) family was able to rent out their home during the course of the war, largely due to the oversight of a white neighbor. They resumed their family insurance business and became prominent members of the San Jose community. The injustice of internment was not lost on the younger Mineta, who would later run for local office and subsequently provided important congressional leadership roles for recognizing racial prejudice and retribution for the 110,000 interned Americans who suffered more than $500 million in property loss. Mineta succeeded in creating the Asian American Caucus, and in 1988, Congress finally authorized the 60,000 survivors restitution payments of $20,000.

ROSIE THE RIVETER—WOMEN'S LABOR

At the early onset of the war, women were not initially courted by industry to work, but the shortage of male workers brought on by military service forced employers to hire women to complete jobs that had previously been defined as male. By the end of 1942, a massive propaganda campaign targeted women to do their part for war production. The iconic image of Rosie the Riveter appeared in posters, magazines, newspaper advertisements, and government newsreels. Women enthusiastically entered the labor force in all labor sectors.

Between 1940 and 1945, 5 million women entered the workforce, and by 1944, married women represented 37 percent of the labor force. As male labor shortage increased due to the draft, women were recruited to work in every sector from defense to agriculture. The war produced new attitudes about women's labor, and for the first time, women were trained to work in previously male-dominated jobs such as welders, riveters, and electricians. Taking on such masculine jobs took some convincing by the government and from business. The depiction of Rosie the Riveter memorialized by the *Saturday Evening Post* portrayed a strong, muscular, rosy-cheeked defense worker. This imagery combined with advertisements that appealed to femininity, sacrifice, winning the war against Fascism, and Hollywood movie stars emulating Rosie on the silver screen succeeded. These images blended messages of femininity, women's self-sacrificing nature, and the nurturing role as mothers and wives, and the messages reminded women that they played a role in securing democracy and the American way of life on the home front.

Prior to World War II women, represented less than 10 percent of the defense workforce, but they made higher wages than did women in other industries. By 1944, women's employment increased by 50 percent and in manufacturing jobs by 140 percent. Auto and electrical work offered women unprecedented opportunities to work in male-dominated industries. The transition in electrical manufacturing was smoother than the auto industry, because there were larger numbers of women workers (32.2% in 1940, versus auto employment rates of 6.7%). Both industries were retooled to produce aircraft, tanks, and ordnance needed to support the military campaign. For a short period of time, the sexual division of labor diminished in some industries during the war years. Following the war, most women lost their positions, but many were rehired during the subsequent postwar prosperity.[6]

DEFENSE INDUSTRY

One of the most important gains made during the era was the gradual breakdown of sex segregation in defense industries. Historians writing about gender in the workforce remind us that the initial gains made by women in male-dominated fields were short lived. In

some industries, such as the auto industry, sex segregation continued, and even in areas where women picked up new skills, women
worked in female-dominated departments. For a short while, sex
segregation boundaries shifted but were not entirely eliminated.
The auto industry in Detroit, for example, struggled with how to
classify temporary jobs. Instead of defining jobs as male or female,
terms like *heavy* and *light* were used to determine female classifications. Other problems surfaced with the new female workers
when male workers contested rated classifications that conflicted
with their union system of seniority. Female members of the United
Auto Workers (UAW) union did not contest job classifications;
rather they supported a systematic classification system to protect
them from heavy labor jobs. Newly employed women had limited
experience with unions and management and had little time to consider the impact of sex typing in the industry. In the case of UAW,
women openly supported the job classification system.

While World War II brought in a new class of married workers,
the reality was that the majority of women had been in the workforce as part of their daily life. Woman of color and working-class
women toiled as domestics and agricultural workers, and in food-
processing plants, light manufacturing, and the needle trade. Rosie
the Riveter advertisements and Hollywood films falsely projected
the workforce as white middle class, consisting of single and married women. In reality, women had long supported the workforce,
and many women were single, divorced, or widowed; only 8 percent of those working were married to servicemen. Prior to Pearl
Harbor, 12 million women were in the workforce, representing one-
fourth of the U.S. workforce.

GENDER DISCRIMINATION AND RACISM

The auto industry maintained the lion's share of wartime production. Detroit employed 48 percent of the autoworkers in the nation,
and with the conversion to war industries, Detroit held 10 percent
of all war contracts. This rapid expansion required a new labor
force, and many companies actively recruited in Southern states,
but the lack of housing prevented many new emigrants from moving northward. As we have seen, the hiring practices of most industries at this time period were based on gender and race preferences.
White men were on the top of the ladder, and white women were
at the bottom, just above people of color. The hiring practices in
auto and electrical manufacturing followed this pattern, and white

women and blacks were hired when the supply of white males disappeared. In this environment, black men felt the burden of racial discrimination and were given jobs as janitors. Black women's employment rose from 4 percent in 1940 to 15 percent by 1945, and while they were initially only hired for menial jobs, labor shortages improved their job opportunities in the auto industry.

BUILDING THE LABOR FORCE
FOR MILITARY EXPANSION

World War II set in motion major changes that provided the base for transforming American society, from the emergence of a vibrant civil rights movement, unprecedented growth of the West, the birth of a large middle class, and rapid buildup of the military complex, among other things. The aircraft, shipbuilding, and engineering boom in California set in motion the infrastructure for the high-tech movement that followed later in the century. Federal and military funds built the industrial infrastructure in San Diego, Los Angeles, San Jose, and San Francisco. In San Jose, Moffett Field, Lockheed Aircraft, and the Food Machinery Corporation received large government contracts in the 1940s to produce arms and later helped rebuild Europe under the Marshall Plan. Cities like Oakland, San Diego, San Francisco, and Los Angeles housed military bases and ports and shipyards. Richmond, California, dominated the shipbuilding industry, while San Diego and Los Angeles dominated the aircraft industry.

This military expansion required a large labor force of married and single women. The growth of the industries in California encouraged women from across the United States to head west to earn a better living in shipbuilding, ironworks, aerospace, and food processing. Whites, African Americans, Japanese Americans, and Native Americans undergirded this expansion through their work in these industries. Women of color faced many challenges as they entered the industrial workforce in California.

In the San Francisco Bay area, shipbuilding employed large numbers of men and women to support the production of warships. The Richmond Kaiser Shipyard female labor force consisted of African American, Asian, white, and Native Americans representing 27 percent of the total population of workers. War production dramatically increased the population that had stood at 20,000 before the war, and within a few years following Pearl Harbor, the population swelled to 100,000 people.

While the war economy created new jobs at higher wages, the impact on local community resources was severe, and newcomers faced horrible housing shortages. Despite some of the positive changes in labor practices, the work environment remained segregated; blacks worked in specific units, and they faced daily discrimination from management and other white coworkers. The lack of adequate housing for the ballooning population brought on by the military complex created serious challenges for all workers, but for African Americans and other ethnic groups, people were forced to find living space in cars, railroad boxcars, and tents. Others were lucky enough to find overcrowded housing. The Rosie the Riveter history project in San Francisco highlights the challenges of the war years. Through oral history, many of the workers described the hardships and discrimination they faced as shipyard workers and in their daily lives.

The imagery of Rosie the Riveter paints a false image of the diversity of the women working in the defense industry. Black women were basically ignored as contributors to the workforce, and at least of half of the working population of black women were married. By the end of the war, black women represented 50 percent of women working in the war plants. Historian Sherna Gluck documented some of the experiences of black women during this time period. Through firsthand accounts, we can begin to piece together the diverse experiences of individuals and see how the war transformed black women's lives by freeing them from the drudgery and low pay of domestic work to manufacturing jobs and improving their living conditions. For example, Texas-born Fanny Christina Hill came to Los Angeles to find better opportunities. She initially took work as a domestic, but as the aircraft industry ramped up, she found permanent employment at North American Aircraft. She took some time off while on maternity leave and was forced to leave during the massive layoffs as the war ended, but by 1946, she returned to North American where she remained until her retirement in 1980.

Hill's experience is a good example of how the war industry helped to improve women's opportunity in manufacturing in the postwar period. Active in the Los Angeles Negro Victory Committee (LANVC), Hill benefited from the local protest against the U.S. Employment Office that resulted in new job training opportunities for blacks. The LANVC had a long-term purpose to secure permanent employment for black women. Other organizations similarly focused on job retention after the war. For example, the National Council of Negro Women initiated the "Hold Your Job Campaign."

Female cannery workers pitting peaches. Richmond Chase Company Photo Album. San Jose State University Library Special Collections and Archives. (Courtesy of San Jose State University, Special Collections and Archives)

Hill's postwar experiences illustrate some of the slow gains made in providing better employment access. A combination of civil rights activism and support of the union made Los Angeles more conducive to building black work units specifically in the North American Aviation Company.

Just as Oakland and Richmond expanded, the South Bay similarly transformed from an agricultural economy to a defense-based economy. Military contracts for weapons and engines shaped the employment opportunities for women in Santa Clara County. The Hendy Iron Works located in Sunnyvale produced engines and weapon parts. By late 1945, the workforce had increased and more than doubled when Hendy built 754 engines for the Liberty ships being assembled by Rosie the Riveters in the Richmond shipyards

Prior to the war, employment opportunities for women living in Santa Clara County were limited to agriculture and low-paid domestic service. Hendy thus provided cannery workers new opportunities to work as machine operators at much higher pay. For example, Lola Vaughn left Nevada for California and found work as an engraving machine operator. She and her coworkers thus escaped working in the canneries and became new union members. As one group moved into heavy manufacturing industries, others took jobs in agriculture and food processing. San Jose is a good example of this process. As one group climbed the ladder, new ethnic groups took over vacated jobs in food processing. As a result, the region witnessed a tremendous transformation in the ethnic composition of its workforce. As white cannery workers entered defense plants, Mexican Americans soon dominated farm labor and food-processing work. Like black women in the aircraft and shipbuilding industries, Mexican American women were paid low wages and worked long hours, but both groups benefited overall in terms of better wages and working conditions.[7]

RACE RIOTS AND CIVIL PROTEST

The wartime military-industrial complex clearly led to certain advantages for all groups of American women, but everyday life was not as rosy as government propaganda would have us believe. Indeed, American cities were rife with racial tension and strife. The call to fight for democracy and the American way of life severely contradicted the realities of life for minorities and women. African American leader W.E.B. Du Bois noted that the war marked the beginning for racial equality in the United States and that the struggle for democracy was not just for white people but for "...yellow, brown, and black."[8] Yet, racial tensions abounded, especially for blacks, Mexican Americans, and Japanese Americans. Facing consistent exclusion from higher-paying defense jobs, black civil rights activists took direct action through grassroots organizing and social protest. For example, A. Philip Randolph, leader of the Brotherhood of Sleeping Porters, secured a union contract with the railroad in 1937 by organizing a nationwide strike. This first strike provided a base for Randolph to fight against all aspects of Jim Crow in the defense and military during the war years. He organized the March on Washington Movement (MOWM) in the early 1940s, which provided a new social vehicle for black men and women to protest against employment discrimination. In 1941, Randolph promised FDR he would organize a massive march on Washington if he failed to act to end employment discrimination in the defense industry and the military. FDR responded by issuing Executive Order 8802, which created the Fair Employment Practices Commission (FEPC). The march was canceled, but the work of the MOWM continued throughout the war years.

The grassroots nature of the MOWM highlights the role that women played in different social movements to force social, political, and legal change. Pauli Murray, an attorney and social activist, joined forces with the MOWM to combat racial and gender discrimination. She became very aware of the double bind that black women faced under the system of Jim Crow and as female civil rights activists. A graduate of Howard University Law School, she quickly realized that she would never be treated as an equal among black civil rights leaders, despite her credentials. This combined with the highly segregated society of Washington, D.C., compelled her to join the MOWM and to spend her life fighting for racial and sexual equality. Murray and other women of her generation and later generations would feel the burden of what Murray referred to as "Jane Crow."

The MOWM provided and important outlet for grassroots organizing. Powered by 24 branches in different cities, and highly successful chapters in New York, Chicago, and St. Louis, they organized major conferences in Detroit and Chicago that brought together a forceful group of speakers and large crowds. This group inspired black communities to question the meaning of democracy, in the face of German and Japanese aggression, and to demand full civil rights as Americans. One flyer printed in June of 1942 began with the statement "Wake Up Negro America." First circulated in Chicago during a June rally, it reinforced the demand for equal rights, equal opportunity, and racial equality in the United States. Indeed, MOWM called on 50,000 blacks to "storm the coliseum" to condemn and denounce all Jim Crow policies in the military, the Red Cross, and employment.

The grassroots activism of the MOWM highlights the race and class tensions that marked the home front. Riots and strikes of every kind erupted across U.S. cities. Racial tension ran especially high in cities where all-white-male labor forces were rapidly replaced with women and minorities. Competition for work created an explosive setting in cities like Detroit and Butte, Montana. In California, the racial tensions between U.S. soldiers and the Mexican American community created a month-long crisis known as the Zoot-Suit Riots. The death of a Mexican American youth and the prosecution of 22 Mexican American men sparked by Anti-Mexican sentiments amongst the police and the white community created a powder-keg environment. Racism undergirded the tensions, but the popularity of a new dress code—the zoot suit—worn by rebellious teenagers as social/cultural protest against mainstream culture, fueled the violence. The Pachucos, a Mexican American gang, contested the social boundaries in their community and mainstream American culture through a new flamboyant dress known as the zoot suit—

baggy pants, long jackets, and large hats—and those donning the zoot suit became known as *zooters*. The Pachucas—zooter girls similarly dressed in zoot-suit attire—gained the attention of the police and community. The Zoot-Suit Riots highlight the rebellious youth subculture of second- and third-generation Mexican Americans. Through their dress, hairstyles, and makeup, they flaunted their ethnic identity and rebelliousness in a period of intense nationalism and amid wartime shortages.

Reaction to this youth culture reached the breaking point in June of 1943 when a group of white servicemen took to the streets looking for the zooters, sometimes pulling them from bars and even from private homes, shearing them of their hair, striping them of their distinctive clothing, and beating them. At the end of the riots, some 600 Mexican men and women were arrested, and the War Department was forced to limit military personnel access to the city. President Roosevelt expressed concern that the riots would impact diplomacy efforts with Mexico and soon after federal funds were allocated for job training and education for Spanish-speaking Americans. The

Woman in jail after the Zoot-Suit Riots, June 9, 1943. (Bettmann/CORBIS)

impact of these riots on the Mexican American community would resonate for the World War II generation, and some of these zooters became the future leaders of the Chicano movement. For example, Cesar Chavez, the leader of the United Farm Workers, and a zooter during the war, recalled that it took a lot of guts to wear the baggy pants, knowing that their rebelliousness would draw attention and criticism from the police and older people within the Mexican community.

Historian Catherine Ramirez in *The Woman in the Zoot Suit; Gender, Nationalism, and the Cultural Politics of Memory* illustrates how these women were negatively portrayed as too masculine and lesbian, but through their appearance and dress, they contested the social boundaries of traditional family life and mainstream American culture. One could place the zooter girls into the same context with the feminist extreme of the flappers of the 1920s decade. The zooters stood squarely against the mainstream culture through their behavior and dress, which serves to illustrate the racial tensions of the period but also shows how one specific group of young people contested the social norms of mainstream society.[9]

FEMINISM AND HUMAN RIGHTS

The war and postwar years created several unintended consequences that would improve the lives of women and lead to a more cohesive feminist movement in the 1960s. As we have explored earlier, the postsuffrage era resulted in a schism between mainstream social feminists and the more radical National Woman's Party (NWP) over the Equal Rights Amendment (ERA). Quickly following the first introduction of the ERA to Congress in 1923, mainstream women's organizations mobilized an anti-ERA opposition on the basis that the amendment would nullify sex-based protective legislation mandating working conditions, hours, and wages. The leaders of the opposition included Florence Kelly of the National Consumers League; Maud Wood Park, president of the national League of Women Voters (LWV); Carrie Chapman Catt; Mary Anderson of the Children's Bureau; and Dr. Alice Hamilton, champion of industrial medicine and labor advocate, backed by major women's groups from the national Women's Trade Union League (WTUL), Women's Christian Temperance Union (WCTU), and General Federation of Women's Clubs (GFWC). In contrast to the opposition, Alice Paul never wavered in her commitment to the ERA, and through the NWP, she consistently maintained that sex-based legislation reinforced women's economic dependence, and that through a constitutional amendment, women would be guaranteed the same rights as men in the labor force and would raise their status and economic opportunity.

Given the domestic focus on war production, World War II surprisingly provided a unique environment to build new support for the ERA. The small elite band of women who made up the NWP recognized the need to build a larger coalition of women to succeed, and growing support from different groups steered the debate over the right method to pursue complete equality in the United States. Between 1940 and 1946, support for the ERA reached an all-time high. A series of events influenced the momentum including the endorsement of ERA by key organizations and the political parties. The NWP with important assistance from regional organizations and local NWP chapters wore down some of resistance from many social feminists and mainstream women's groups. Educating women about the ERA required a multipronged approach, one that depended on the support of local women to lobby at the regional level. Moreover, the Depression and World War II highlighted gender employment discrimination and confirmed that protective legislation prohibited women from competing in the workforce. By 1944, the National Federation of Business and Professional Women's Club (BPW), and the GFWC endorsed the ERA, and the formation of the Women's Joint Legislative Committee (WJLC), which served as a clearing-house for the campaign, exponentially expanded the constituency to approximately 6 million women. Meanwhile, the Republican and Democratic parties endorsed the amendment. These events combined with the favorable reports on the bill between the House and Senate boosted the NWP's confidence that the amendment would pass in the next few years, though sadly it did not.

Protective legislation dominated the debate between feminist factions, yet it became increasingly clear that the protections that been hard won created a double standard in labor organizing and kept women in the lowest-paid jobs. The NWP argued that the ERA would abolish the need for protective legislation because it would grant full equality not defined by gender. In contrast, women connected to the National Women's Bureau (NWB) and other organizations argued that the amendment would result in legal and social chaos by negatively affecting the Social Security system, force female military conscription, and challenge the laws mandating male support of their families. The Women's Bureau and other supporting organizations firmly believed that ERA would adversely impact women as mothers and wives and believed that the statutes should be changed at the state level. Concerned by the growing support for the ERA, they responded with an aggressive and very negative counterattack. It continued to support protective legislation, but in the face of continued labor discrimination, its argument against the ERA wore thin. In an effort to offer a different alternative, it formed the National Committee to Defeat the Unequal Rights Amendment (NCDURA). When this organization proved too negative, it followed the advice of Eleanor Roosevelt and introduced the "Status Bill," also known as the Taft-Wadsworth Bill, and changed its name to the National Committee on the Status of Women (NCSW). The Status Bill sought to balance the responsibilities of family life and gender discrimination. Holding true to the ideology of protective legislation, the bill prohibited sex discrimination except where justified based on "…physical structure, [and] biological and social function." While they hoped this bill would serve as a compromise to the ERA, it never received full backing from Congress or from the ERA supporters. The success of the UN charter recognizing the equal rights of men and women fueled more debate at the congressional level, and in 1948, the NCSW maintained its opposition to the ERA and argued that its opposition to ERA at home did not conflict with the UN charter.

Both ERA supporters and opponents lobbied individual congressmen and government officials to promote their position. During the height of the NWB's attempt to promote the Status Bill, it worked closely with Secretary of State Dean Acheson to confirm its position against the ERA. Acheson testified during a congressional hearing that a constitutional amendment would only confuse rights and responsibilities between the sexes and that state laws should be modified to address equality issues. He also refused to apply the principle of the UN charter supporting basic equal rights for women of all nations to the U.S. political environment. Ironically, Eleanor Roosevelt encouraged the NWB to promote the Status Bill, while providing U.S. leadership on the UN Charter for Human Rights.

Even with international support for equal human rights for women, the NCSW continued to oppose the ERA in the United States, while ironically endorsing the tenets of the Human Rights Declaration. The conflict between women's organizations over the ERA continued during the 1950s. The opposition helped to undo the progress made in Congress, when the NWB convinced Senator Carl Hayden to tack a rider on the amendment, during the 81st Congress (1950), to protect women's natural rights and labor protection based on gender. The rider caught the ERA supporters by surprise, and they launched an anti–Hayden Rider campaign, but lack of support from Congress and an absence of a strong grass-roots movement to support ERA derailed the lobbying activities of ERA supporters. While the trends in the labor environment clearly showed the limits of protective labor legislation for women workers, the NCSW, NWB, and the LWV continued to support a state-by-state approach to winning equality, and it would take another decade with a younger generation of feminists to transform the political divide between feminists groups.

The ERA schism fractured the postsuffrage movement, yet the degree of political activism on both sides illustrates the diversity of women's views on equal rights legislation. The increased support for the ERA during World War II sparked a short-lived feminist revival, which in turn encouraged some women to reverse their opposition. Endorsement by key women's groups like the BPW and the GFWC, and most importantly movement in the Republican and Democratic parties' platforms to endorse the ERA, influenced congressional activism on both sides. It is easy to conclude that ERA severed postsuffrage unity, yet the years between 1923 and the end of World War II illustrate the changing forces in employment opportunity, new employment legislation, unionization, international diplomacy, and specifically the impact that the UN Charter for Human Rights had on social movements and the struggle for civil rights. The Cold War years would create a political and social climate that embraced traditional family values and had little use for the aging population of feminists. It would take a younger and more radical group of social activists to push the ERA forward.[10]

LABOR FEMINISM

Much of the history detailing the feminist movement in the 1940s and 1950s has been dominated by histories focused on the divide between social feminist and equal rights feminists over the ERA. However, average working women never identified themselves as feminists. The NWP was really the only branch that embraced the feminist label. It is important to point out that diverse women's groups worked toward the same goal to achieve gender equality, but they didn't all fit neatly into the historical categories of *social feminist* or *equal rights feminists*. These terms are nonetheless helpful in describing some of these differences. *Labor feminism* is a term that historians use to identify the role of women labor activists in pursuing gender equality but through the labor movement, rather than through other mainstream women's organizations.

In contrast to middle-class feminists, labor feminists were working class, poor, and racially diverse. Many of the leaders were African American, Hispanic, and Jewish. Some prime examples include African American Dorothy Lowther Robinson of the Amalgamated Clothing Workers and the U.S. Women's Bureau; Mexican American Dolores Huerta of United Farm Workers; and Rose Schneiderman, a Jewish leader in the WTUL, the International Ladies Garment Workers Union, and member of the Labor Advisory Board (National Recovery Administration during World War II). Labor feminists also played a prominent role in emergence of the Presidential Commission on the Status of Women (PCSW), as well as serving as members on the commission. They also identified collectively, and their values were shaped by class loyalties and community. They valued justice and equality, but they were grounded in a class consciousness versus individual right.

Historian Dorothy Sue Cobble documented the history of labor feminists during this time period, and she shows how different branches of the female labor movement responded to social justice and wage justice during and after World War II. Women feminized the postwar workforce and labor unions following the war. The primary female sector jobs were in food service, department stores, telecommunications, and manufacturing. While most of these women did not identify as feminists, they used labor unions to promote gender equality in the workplace and other social justice issues that would improve women's place in society.

Labor studies have tended to focus on male unions and male domination over female workers. More recent studies like Cobble's unravel and complicate the revisions of labor history. The image of Rosie and the image of women's postwar unemployment does not accurately represent women's contributions in manufacturing or in the pink-collar labor force. For example, women joined unions in large numbers during World War II and after the war. Women may have lost their manufacturing jobs at the end of the war, but they returned to previous employment in what Cobble describes as the "pink-collar ghetto." What she means by this is that women left the auto plants and shipyards to work in food service, the telephone company, and in sales. Unionization in these industries steadily increased in the 1950s. For example, more than 200,000 female service industry workers unionized, representing 45 percent of the labor force, doubling the wartime membership among female workers. Clearly, the experiences of wartime work and labor union activism empowered women to join unions in the postwar years. The earlier perceptions of the male union leadership in the American Federation of Labor for example, maintained the early 20th century argument that women would not organize collectively, and that they only worked temporarily as single women.

More recent studies make clear that women labor represented the fastest-growing labor group in the United States. Apparently 40 percent of members in the telephone company, department stores, and other food-based industries were women. While wartime unemployment of women was drastic—the percentage of women working in the postwar period continued to increase significantly. Cobble refers to this process of union activism as "pink-collar" labor feminism. During World War II, female telephone operators and food service workers demanded better wages, hours, and union recognition. As represented by the telephone and restaurant strikes, pink-collar activists used collective action to improve working conditions for all. For example, in 1947, the largest nationwide walkout of women telephone operators in U.S. history took place. Women represented 230,000 of the 350,000 telephone workers. Major strikes took place in department stores and in food service where women represented the majority of strikers. In Oakland, California, female department store clerks walked off the job demanding union recognition. In the aftermath of this 1946 strike, pro-labor union city council members were appointed. Oakland highlights the role that local women played in demanding recognition and better contracts from store owners, and how their collective action influenced local politics. Similarly hotel and restaurant strikes in San Francisco, Detroit, and New York resulted in better wages, hours, and working conditions.

The variety of postwar female labor activism represents another strand of feminism during this era. Moreover, these women led the movement to close the wage gap among working-class women. Economic equity and social justice were central to this strand of feminism, and the labor movement served as the vehicle for achieving gender equality in the workforce. Laboring women worked closely with the NWB to address state and federal equal pay laws.

Thus, the creation of the 1961 Presidential Commission on the Status of Women (PCSW) can be directly tied to the lobbying work of labor union feminists and the Women's Bureau prior to and during World War II. During the 1920s and 1930s, feminists worldwide began pushing for commissions on the status of women. The international movement was mired by conflict between U.S. feminists over the promotion of the "Equal Rights Treaty," proposed by the NWB.

NWB bureau chief Mary Anderson argued against the treaty based on the fear that it would override protective labor legislation. Labor feminists agreed with Anderson on protective labor legislation, yet they also supported the creation of an international women's commission committed to promote equal treatment of the sexes in laws and politics for all nations. Labor feminists believed that studies were needed to address the economic and social status of women worldwide, as well as women's political and civil rights. The years between the wars thus provided a foundation to pursue labor equity in the United States, and despite some of the international and national disagreements among feminist groups, labor feminists and the NWB believed in women's equality but disagreed over the ERA.

As previously described, the NWB and labor feminists countered the ERA with the women's Status Bill, which they hoped would protect hard-won labor legislation for women and provide an alternative solution to the ERA. Encouraged by international support through the creation of the UN Commission on the Status of Women in 1946, the NWB argued that the 1945 UN charter promoting human rights and the creation of the UN Commission on the Status of Women, supported the creation of a similar commission to address women's status in the United States. They argued that a U.S. commission was a necessary component to the UN. In addition to international recognition, the women modeled the Women's Status Bill legislation around the President's Commission on Civil Rights, which President Harry Truman established in 1946. The women blended the concepts for human rights and equal status with Truman's 1947 report entitled *To Secure these Rights*. While the Status Bill failed in Congress, the original legislation provided the framework for the creation of the PCSW.[11]

POSTWAR TRANSITIONS

World War II resulted in unprecedented worldwide devastation. The scale of death, disease, and destruction is hard to comprehend. Sixty million people lost their lives. The Holocaust destroyed the Jewish communities in Eastern Europe with more than 1 million lives lost in Nazi gas chambers. The United States ended the war by dropping two atomic bombs on the civilian population in Japan, ushering in a new period of uncertainty for all. U.S. casualties at some 400,000 were low compared to the losses of other nations, and by the end of the war, the United States emerged as the most powerful nation in the world. Yet, the conclusion of peace following the war created a precipice between nations and growing tensions between the United States and Soviet Union that resulted in a Cold War power struggle that would last almost one-half of a century. The global tensions impacted political relationships from the East to the West and would dramatically influence domestic policies and behaviors in the United States.

HOUSING

In comparison to the death tolls in Europe, American casualties were low. Nonetheless, American families faced untold grief from these losses, and the return of millions of traumatized veterans brought new challenges to postwar family life. Unlike other nations, the U.S. economy was not totally broken by the war because the war had not taken place on our soil. The U.S. government quickly took steps to eliminate a postwar depression through a series of congressional acts. The Servicemen's Readjustment Act (GI bill) of 1944 provided $14.5 billion in financial aid for low-cost mortgages, college tuition, and the creation of veterans' hospitals and health care. The GI bill also created unprecedented opportunity for Americans to move up the social ladder and to move into the growing middle class. Housing shortages abounded during the war, but the GI bill gave birth to new suburbs across the United States and promoted the building of the interstate highway system. In Long Island, for example, the Levittown developers sold 1,400 homes in 1949. Between the years 1944 and 1950, home building expanded from 14,000 new homes to 1.7 million homes. The growth of the suburbs cannot be understated. Between 1950 and 1970, the population of expanded from 36 million to 74 million, creating a large middle class that included second- and third-generation European immigrants. However, it should be noted that this growth excluded Jews and racial minorities from purchasing homes in white neighborhoods. Despite federal laws outlawing segregation, private banks and developers placed racial covenants making it impossible to resell property to Jews and people of color. The Federal Housing Authority (FHA) and other banks used a system of *redlining* to eliminate racial minorities from obtaining mortgage loans in specific geographic areas. In effect, redlining reinforced Jim Crow laws that denied minorities access to the American dream. Most racial minorities lived in urban and rural areas and, in some cases, in segregated suburbs. It would take another two decades and a full-blown civil rights movement before minorities were granted full equality as American citizens.

CIVIL RIGHTS LEGISLATION

Race relations and the movement toward more just and humane laws for people of color came slowly. While fighting for democracy abroad, minorities now had to return to prewar Jim Crow laws and racism. In one example, a black soldier said that he entered the army as a "nigger but came out as man." His sentiments reflect well the barriers that blacks faced in general society while demonstrating the importance of military service for black men. Fighting against the Nazis and Communism to preserve American democracy empowered and radicalized black soldiers to fight for basic civil rights after they returned from the war. The National Association for the Advancement of Colored People (NAACP) provided the organizing body to pursue justice for black Americans. Through a calculated legal strategy, the NAACP slowly stripped away Jim Crow laws through a case-by-case approach. Some of the early cases included *Smith v. Allwright* (1944), which outlawed segregation in voting primaries; *Morgan v. Virginia* (1946), which challenged interstate transportation segregation; *Shelley v. Kraemer* (1948), which contested racial covenants in house sales; and *Sweatt v. Painter* and *McLaurin v. Oklahoma*, both in 1950, which contested the "separate but equal" doctrine of the earlier *Plessy v. Ferguson* (1896) case and the graduate education cases in Texas and Oklahoma. The latter two cases challenged the concept of separate but equal and most importantly built on case precedent arguing that this doctrine violated Fourteenth Amendment rights of equal protection. NAACP attorney and future supreme court justice, Thurgood Marshall represented many of the plaintiffs in these cases.

The NAACP legal strategies provided the model for other disadvantaged groups to pursue racial and gender justice through the court system. For example, the Hispanic community followed the lead of the NAACP to challenge discrimination through the court system. The League of United Latin American Citizens provided the leadership and succeeded in outlawing segregation in California through *Mendez v. Westminster* (1947), and several laws would follow that addressed discrimination in public accommodations. The key to all of the legislation that resulted from individual lawsuits was anchored on new interpretations of the Fourteenth Amendment that provided equal protection to all Americans. Throughout the civil rights era, different groups used the "equal protection clause" to fight for a variety of injustices, including domestic violence in the 1990s and most recently in the same-sex marriage movement.

COMMUNISM AND CONTAINMENT

National security dominated American politics during the postwar era. International conflicts in Greece, Turkey, and later in Korea, reinforced Prime Minister Winston Churchill's prediction that an Iron Curtain separated the East from the West. Thus, American politicians and diplomats articulated a new policy of containment directed at home and abroad. U.S. diplomat George Kennan in a 1946 speech defined the next half century when he stated that the United States needed to contain Soviet aggression and expansion. The so-called Iron Curtain represented repression under Communism in contrast to the liberation of democracy in the West.[12]

What did this all mean for average American families and ordinary life? Historians have labeled this period the era of the "warm hearth," which idealized the nuclear family and domesticity. As the atomic age unfolded, Americans embraced the idea that the family and home would provide a refuge against the threats of a nuclear disaster and Communism and provide security in a very insecure world. The fears of nuclear fallout created a new industry for prefabricated above- and below-ground fallout shelters. Several magazines ran stories highlighting different features of the shelters, which included ample storage space for consumer goods and supplies, and room for furniture. One honeymooning couple was photographed kissing as they descended into their bomb shelter, while other images made popular by *Life Magazine* depicted a nuclear family in their shelter with all their supplies on display. Various manufacturing companies sold prefab shelters that could be quickly assembled. One advertisement made clear that nuclear fallout and family survival depended on the purchase of such structures. The *Life Magazine* headline on January 12, 1952, read: "New Facts You Must Know about Fallout: The Drive for Mass Shelters."[13]

The hearth and home symbolized a new social construction of domesticity—one that ironically fostered materialism, consumerism, and social conformity. Consumerism and fears of subversive behaviors undergirded these developments. Through popular culture, the media, movies, and government propaganda, the postwar ideal reinforced the image of then nuclear family, steeped in the belief that separate spheres of influence, men in the workplace and women in the domestic sphere as wives and mothers, would somehow insulate Americans from the threats of the atomic age and from potential Communist subversives. The mushrooming of new suburbs across the United States provided new havens of domesticity, away from urban centers. The massive expansion of the economy between the years 1947 and 1961, the unprecedented increase in the number of families, the increase in the gross national product, and increases in personal income provided a ripe landscape to create an image of conformity. These postwar developments represent a reversal of the Depression era, where delayed marriage, small families, and frugality were the norm. In contrast, the postwar generation spent beyond its means to fabricate the American dream. Home ownership, domestic appliances, televisions, cars, and family vacations produced the first "buy now, pay later" generation. Indeed, between the years 1950 and 1970, the suburban home population increased from 36 million to 74 million, while 20 percent of the population remained poor and outside of the greenbelt track homes of the middle class.

Middle-class families centered their lives on their homes and community, embracing new pursuits of leisure that included visiting new theme parks that were designed to cater to family entertainment. Disneyland opened in 1955 specifically to support family-centered entertainment, replacing older amusement parks that catered to the working poor and immigrants. Disneyland offered a pure family entertainment compared to the wild rides and mixing of classes and ethnic groups such as Coney Island offered. Religion played a key role in rebuilding the traditional family, as all religious affiliations experienced unprecedented growth in their memberships. The home and suburban family life became the ideal, and it provided a refuge away from large cities, and away from subversive behaviors. The Cold War also played a significant role in the development of an interstate highway system. Policymakers argued in favor of decentralizing urban centers, while the evolving American Road Builders' Association lobbied Congress to pass the 1956 Interstate Highway Act to connect all the new communities. Politicians who touted the American dream reinforced these efforts. A primary example is the debate that took place between Vice President Richard Nixon and the Soviet Primer Nikita Khrushchev during an American Exhibition at the Sokolniki Park in Moscow in 1959. Dubbed the "Kitchen Debate," both leaders touted the virtues of their systems. Using the model American kitchen as the setting for the debate, Nixon connected American women's happiness to capitalistic-based domesticity that included a modern kitchen with new appliances. The "Kitchen Debate" became a metaphor for technological advancement and American capitalism.[14]

SEXUAL CONTAINMENT

It is hard to fathom the degree to which Cold War sentiments influenced the supremacy of the family. The family represented the economic stability of the nation, and women were targeted as the chief purchasing agents in the home. National magazines, newspapers, advertisers, and policymakers zeroed in on the role of women in building the economy while still remaining subordinate members of society. Childbearing and childrearing became the central role of married women. The fertility rates of the era confirm a renewed enthusiasm for family life, with a significant baby boom. Between the years 1948 and 1953, more babies were born than had been in the last 30 years—couples married in large numbers and at younger ages than had been the pattern during the Depression.

UNWED MOTHERS

In the 1940s and 1950s, social workers and those in other academic fields became concerned over the problem of unwed mothers. Working-class women, lesbians, and African Americans were targeted for reform, though the approach to understanding the causes of single motherhood varied by class and race. As historian Rickie Solinger has documented, race and class played an important role in how reformers addressed the problem of unwed mothers. In the 1940s, the percentage of unwed mothers increased, causing overcrowding in the maternity homes, but the increase of unwed mothers from the middle class created much alarm. In years earlier, the clientele was made up of work class and ethnic minorities.

The increase in middle-class women led social workers to reevaluate the causes of out-of-wedlock pregnancy. Aided by new psychiatric theory, social workers determined that pregnancy was a neurotic symptom caused by social repression. The rise of psychotherapy reinforced by cultural belief in a nuclear family ideal thus created a social environment where single pregnancy was an abnormal behavior, and young women of all races, ethnic groups, and classes were socially stigmatized. The failure to conform to the sexual social standards that held sexual purity and marriage as the ideal created a severe social backlash. Young women who found themselves pregnant faced social rejection and were isolated during the stages of their pregnancies. As one oral-history project details, most of these young women were forced to give up their children for adoption. During and after the 1940s, there was a strong chance that young people would have premarital sex before age 20. Despite the changes in dating patterns, young people had limited access to birth control or sex education. Educators, clergy, and other believed that sex education would promote rather than deter premarital sex. While sexual norms were changing, the shame assigned to single mothers remained in place. This was especially true in white middle-class families, where social standing meant everything. Many of these young girls were sent them away to special maternity homes and religious halfway houses and forced to give up their children for adoption. Between the years 1943 and 1973, 1.5 million babies were adopted by nonfamily members. As Ann Fesslor writes, almost everyone who lived during this period had someone in their family, neighborhood, or school, who disappeared. The sexual double standards of the time treated young women as social outcasts, and young men were not held accountable. One of the cultural myths of the time was that young women were having sex with multiple partners, but Fesslor found that most women got pregnant the first time they had sex, and they did not choose to give their babies up for adoption but were forced by their parents and social service providers.[15]

LESBIANS

Sexual conformity in this era translated to heterosexual marriage and the creation of a nuclear family. Lesbians were similarly vilified, as were prostitutes and unwed mothers. In earlier decades, the mannish woman was associated with unmarried career women like Jane Addams, who lived with other women, and who formed intimate relationships with women. By the 1920s, lesbians were vilified for defying sexual norms and for failing to embrace marriage and maternity. By the 1940s and 1950, the increase in the visibility of lesbians sparked a national crusade that projected lesbians as sexual deviants and sexually depraved, aligning them with prostitutes. According to one historian, Hollywood films projected the imagery of lesbians and prostitutes as the model for uncontained female sexuality—thus sexually depraved and dangerous to society. Pointing to the dangerous side of female sexuality, social, religious, and political commentators hoped to reinforce the boundaries of normal behavior and to force sexual conformity. The political environment reinforced the Cold War ideology that danger was lurking behind the Iron Curtain, and the only means to curb the dangers of Communism was through secure sexual boundaries within the context of heterosexual marriage. Psychiatry played an important role in defining deviancy, and after World War II, psychiatrists were accepted as authorities on sexuality and sexual deviancy. The fears created by Communism and the Cold War reinforced the dangers of nonconformity.

Yet, despite the increased surveillance of homosexuals, a vibrant gay community emerged in the 1950s. A growing national and international movement was underfoot in the early 1950s. For example, the publication *Homosexual Today* was first published in 1956. This book consisted of essays written by gay and lesbians, which originated from a conference that brought together different homophile organizations that included One Inc. (Los Angeles), the National Association for Sexual Research, the Mattachine Society, and the Daughters of Bilitis (DOB; San Francisco).

Historians refer to this early movement as the American homophile movement, which formed in California in the 1950s. The goal of this movement was to create new community networks that would improve their lives. The gay male Mattachine Society and the lesbian DOB persisted throughout the 1960s. These groups provided the foundation for a larger gay movement that radicalized in the 1970s.One of the primary goals of Mattachine and the DOB was to develop communication networks between geographic regions. These early groups maintained the goals to foster self-esteem, promote equal rights, and build group consciousness long before the civil rights movement took hold.

The DOB was formed in 1955 by a small group of lesbian couples. Del Martin and Phyllis Lyon, the primary leaders of DOB, organized to provide a lesbian communication network as a means to end the feelings of isolation and to distribute educational information about sexuality and the movement. The Supreme Court decision *Brown v. Board of Education* case influenced Martin and Lyon to pursue a path of integration rather than maintain a path of isolation. Following the early formation, they produced the newsletter *The Ladder,* which they distributed across the lesbian networks.

Thus, through disparate regional networks, the gay community worked toward ending the secrecy of their lives and challenged social norms that defined homosexuals as depraved and sexual deviants. Gay and lesbian organizations also faced constant harassment from law enforcement and particularly from anti-vice crusades that were organized around obscenity laws. In one example, the lesbian bar known as Tommy's Place was raided in 1954. The *San Francisco Chronicle* ran the headline "Sex Deviant Ring Here," which purported that underage girls were being seduced to lesbianism, prostitution, and drug abuse. These kinds of raids and news reports were repeated in cities across the United States in the 1950s era.[16]

ACCESS TO BIRTH CONTROL

Where single unwed mothers, lesbians, and prostitutes were defined as sexual deviants, most young women conformed to the social-sexual norms. Married women were expected to produce large families and to play a secondary role as mothers and wives. Women who wished to control the size of their family had very few options. In several states, married women were prohibited from accessing any birth control, and abortion was illegal until 1972. Connecticut was one of the states that prohibited married women from obtaining birth control. In the landmark case *Griswold v. Connecticut* (1965), Estelle Griswold, executive director of Planned Parenthood League of Connecticut, was arrested for distributing birth control to married women. Her case relied on the due process clause under the Fourteenth Amendment, and in 1968, the court struck down the state statute that prohibited access to birth control. Thus, Griswold opened the constitutional gateway to overturn state laws that criminalized abortion through the famous case *Roe v. Wade* (1973).

The belief in the sexual double standard of female sexual purity remained firmly in place, but as Dr. Alfred Kinsey revealed in his famous study on American sexual behavior, premarital intercourse, homosexuality, and prostitution were widespread during the era. Kinsey's report was one of first scientific studies in the 1950s to challenge long-held assumptions of sexual purity in American society. The imagery of sexually contained Americans in the "nifty-fifties" era needs to be reassessed, given the number of unwed mothers, adopted babies, the growth of gay and lesbian activism, and the demand for birth control and sex education. At the same time, it should be clear that the prevailing attitude among mental health professionals that lesbians were sexual deviants and colloquially referred to as "sicko" highlights the hardships that different groups of women faced who lived outside of mainstream norms. Women who failed to preserve their virginity or identified as lesbians and prostitutes were defined as hypersexual and pathologically neurotic. Psychiatry reinvented the Progressive Era impulse to regulate sexual conformity, and by defining as deviant any form of sexual expression outside of marriage, whether through lesbianism, prostitution, or through illegitimate pregnancy, mental health professionals reinforced a culture of secrecy and isolation.

THE SILENT GENERATION

Historians have studied with great interest the social environment of the 1950s, and many concluded that parents of the 1950s became the silent generation. More recent studies, drawing from longitudinal research and more comprehensive review of magazines, newspapers, and other forms of advertising, confirm Kinsey's findings that Americans did not always stay true to their ideals. The work of Joanne Meyerowitz, Jessica Weiss, and Stepahine Coontz are examples. Weiss reminds us that the 1950s generation nurtured the next generation of children who would contest the political, social, and cultural boundaries. Furthermore, not all Americans lived in these greenbelt communities, and even those who appeared to live like June and Ward Clever—characters from the popular television show *Leave It to Beaver*—raised the generation that transformed gender and family life in the next several decades. Indeed, the process of change started much earlier than what we think of as the sexual revolution of the 1960s and 1970s. From the 1920s forward, family and gender relationships were slowly changing, and by World War II, many of the seeds for racial equality, equal pay, and even equal rights for women were taking firm root, though it would clearly take a fresh generation of grassroots activists to create the explosion of social protest that shook the next two decades.[17]

How Silent Were They Really?

We can point to a variety of social movement activism amid the era of the so-called silent generation. Despite the shallowness of separate spheres, middle-class families' demand for clothes, appliances, and other luxury goods required some female wage-earning support. Most middle-class women worked part time while their children attended school, and those who did not work served their community through civil organizations. Many more volunteered for the Parent Teacher Association (PTA). Others joined the LWV and the GFWC, but perhaps the most symbolic grassroots activism emerged from the new environmental movement.

In the 1960s, social concerns over the nuclear arms race, the use of harmful chemicals in manufacturing, and the use of insecticides, especially DDT, sparked a new feminist-based environmental movement. The work of Rachel Carson, author of the famous book *Silent Spring*, gave birth to the green movement. Similarly, peace activists opposed to the testing and proliferation of nuclear weapons challenged the status quo of the Cold War. The Women Strike for Peace (WSP) organized and staged a national protest in more than 60 communities, demanding the government to "End the Arms Race—Not the Human Race." Some 50,000 suburban housewives took to the streets to protest U.S. policies. The FBI kept them under surveillance, and in 1962, the leaders of the WSP were called before the House Un-American Activities Committee (HUAC). The women entered the hearing with their babies, using motherhood as their badge of courage, and refused to be intimidated by the congressional investigators. The photographs of the era portray average American women with their children in toe in baby strollers, holding WSP signs, while striking in their local communities.[18]

Meanwhile, for women of color, the middle-class ideal was more tenuous, yet many Hispanic women, for example, entered pink-collar employment as hairdressers and as waitresses, a step above field and cannery work. The prosperity of the era transcended a variety of ethnic groups, though the era did not end racial discrimination or Jim Crow. However, black women for the first time had new opportunities to stay home with their children. In 1949, the popular black magazine *Ebony* ran the headline "Goodbye Mammy, Hello Mom," highlighting a new era of family life for African Americans. Ethnic groups and the laboring classes that lived outside of suburbs relied on grassroots coalition building to improve their lot in American society on a variety of fronts, including improvement societies, mutual aid, and labor protest, and through the legal system. These groups and even the more affluent middle-class women engaged in national political life through different organizations.

FEMININE MYSTIQUE—POPULAR CULTURE AND FEMINISM

Domesticity and suburbia reinforced by movies, television shows, politicians, writers, and pundits created the mythic ideal of the middle-class family. Behind the white picket fences and red-and-white-checked aprons, there were undercurrents of discontent for many middling women. The book *Feminine Mystique,* written by Betty Friedan, acclaimed author and feminist, articulated a new feminist manifesto to conquer what she called the "problem that had no name"—that is to say freedom from the chains of domesticity. *Feminine Mystique* opened the eyes of many white middle-class women to work toward social change. Selling more than 3 million copies, Friedan tapped into the many frustrations that married women felt over their domestic roles and the isolation they felt as housewives and mothers. Friedan's book, while significant in kick-starting a feminist revival, did not accurately characterize the experiences of American women. Based on her research of magazine articles, advertisements, and select interviews with women, she concluded that American culture promoted only one version of womanhood focused entirely on marriage, motherhood, and parenting. Historians since that time have more carefully studied the cultural literature of the period and have rightly pointed out that Friedan's conclusion represented only a small subset of women's experiences. Joanne Meyerowitz, for example, found that many magazines of the era featured articles on individual women's achievements, political activism, voting trends, environmental activism, activism in trade unions, and civil rights.[19]

Students need to question the standard assumptions of history, and the recent work on the myth that American women were stuck in the doldrums of domesticity as articulated by Betty Friedan in her best-selling book *Feminine Mystique* is a good example of new analysis that has widened the historical narrative. We should remember that not all women embraced her feminist manifesto, including African Americans who finally had the means to cultivate a nuclear family, and many white middle-class women were already active in the LWV and other civic organizations that provided a basis to engage in national and international politics and community affairs. Women's lives were not totally absorbed by housework and motherhood, and the 3 million readers of *Feminine Mystique* were not all fans of her thesis. The fan mail that Friedan received after publishing this important book provides a snapshot view of how individuals related to the political and social culture of the era, and to Friedan's book. In several letters, young women expressed their gratitude, while other readers debated the fine points of family and gender relations. Both male and female readers sent her letters, and she received many letters from women living in other countries. Postwar historians embraced the *Feminine Mystique* because it reinforced the cultural and gender assumptions that women were whisked from employment in World War II to become suburban housewives. This conventional perception oversimplified the reality of women's lives in the postwar years and totally ignores the agency of individual women from different classes and ethnic groups. Ironically, Friedan's book contributed significantly to the stereotypes of the era and failed to account for the diverse experiences of American women, including suburban women. Yet, her influence on modern feminism cannot be understated. Nor can the influence of popular magazines, movies, and literature.

CONCLUSION

The postwar era embraced the nuclear family, built large families, and created a new military-industrial complex that supported the massive expansion of the U.S. economy. The atomic explosion is an apt metaphor for the social, political, and economic transformation that galvanized the younger generation to enter multiple arenas of social protest—civil rights protest, the sexual revolution, drugs, sex, rock 'n' roll, and antiwar protests that shaped the decades of the 1960s and 1970s. The sheer magnitude of the baby boom generation and the activism that began with the civil rights movement had a transformative impact on American life.

It should be remembered that the process of social change, whether in the form of civil rights or gender roles, did not happen in a vacuum but took place over generations, was incremental, and at times slowed by the Red-baiting hysteria of the postwar years, and was hampered by political, religious, and cultural identity to the mythic traditional family. The belief in so-called traditional values proved to be an unreachable ideal, as evidenced by the concern to encourage early marriage and eliminate premarital sex and the production of illegitimate children. The theories of conformity and containment during the 1950s and 1960s provide a starting point for a better historical understanding of the past, present, and future. Historical analysis of this era provides a framework from which we can enhance our understanding of the diversity of the American experience. Sexual containment fostered a new generation of revolutionaries, as well shall see in the next several chapters.

NOTES

1. Ellen Carol Dubois and Lynn Dumenil, *Through the Eyes of Women: An American History with Documents* (Bedford/St. Martin Press, 2004), pp. 507–5.

2. Letter to Elizabeth Page Harris, June 9, 1942, in Elizabeth Page Harris Collection, MS 771, Manuscripts and Archives, Yale University Library (b. 79, folder 1726, June 9, 1942).

3. Willard Schmidt Papers, MSS-2007-08-01, San Jose State University Library, Special Collections & Archives.

4. Elizabeth Page to Mrs. Richard Nishimoto, May 29, 1942, Elizabeth Page Harris Collection, MS 771, Manuscripts and Archives, Yale University Library.

5. Dubois and Dumenil, *Through the Eyes of Women*, p. 515.

6. Ruth Milkman, *Gender at Work: The Dynamics of Job Segregation by Sex during World War II* (University of Illinois Press, 1987), pp. 50–55.

7. Sherna Berger Gluck, *Rosie the Riveter Revisited: Women, The War, and Social Change* (Twayne Publishers, 1987), pp. 11–12.

8. Jacqueline Jones, Peter Wood, Thomas Borstelmann, Elaine Tyler May, and Vicki L. Ruiz, eds., *Created Equal: A History of the United States*, 3rd ed. (Pearson and Longman, 2009), p. 735.

9. Catherine Ramirez, *The Woman in the Zoot Suit; Gender, Nationalism, and the Cultural Politics of Memory* (Duke University Press, 2009), pp. 18–19.

10. Cynthia Harrison, *On Account of Sex: The Politics of Women's Issues, 1945–1968* (University of California Press, Berkeley, 1988), pp. 39–65.

11. Dorothy Sue Cobble, "Labor Feminists and President Kennedy's Commission on Women," in *No Permanent Waves: Recasting Histories of U.S. Feminism*, ed., Nancy A. Hewitt, pp. 154–57 (Rutgers University Press, 2010).

12. Jacqueline Jones, ed., *Created Equal: A History of the United State*, 3rd ed. (Pearson Longman, 2009), pp. 744–60.

13. Elaine Tyler May, *Homeward Bound: American Families in the Cold War Era* (Basic Books, New York, 1999), pp. 4–5.

14. Jacqueline Jones, Peter H. Wood, Thomas Borstelmann, Elaine Tyler May, and Vicki L. Ruiz, eds., *Created Equal: A History of the United States*, 3rd ed. (Pearson Longman, 2009), pp. 778–81.

15. Ann Fessler, *The Girls Who Went Away: The Hidden History of Women Who Surrendered Children for Adoption in the Decades Before* Roe v. Wade (Penguin Books, 2006).

16. Martin Meeker, *Contacts Desired: Gay and Lesbian Communications and Community, 1940s–1970* (Chicago University Press, 2007), pp. 77–99.

17. Jessica Weiss, *To Have and To Hold: Marriage, the Baby Boom, and Social Change* (University of Chicago Press, 2000), pp. 2–6.

18. Jones, Wood, Borstelmann, May, and Ruiz, eds., *Created Equal*, pp. 786–87.

19. Joanne Meyerowitz, "Beyond the Feminist Mystique: A Reassessment of Postwar Mass Culture, 1946–1958," in *Not Just June Cleaver; Women and Gender in Postwar America, 1945–1960*, ed. Joanne Meyerowitz (Temple University Press, 1994) pp. 229–62.

5

CIVIL RIGHTS

As we have seen in the previous chapter, the decade of the 1950s was not as contained or as conservative as popular culture and memory had previously conveyed. Indeed, underneath the false calm of secure American suburbs, many Americans actively contested the boundaries of domestic and sexual containment. As a result, many different forms of social protest and activism took root in the postwar years. Pockets of resistance occurred through grassroots activism, which collectively led to a more organized civil rights movement that included labor activists, feminists, politicians, radicals, peace activists, and community activists. Despite the very conservative political environment and the so-called family ideals of the 1950s, many important social changes firmly took hold. The television imagery of *Leave It to Beaver* replete with Ward and June Clever as the American family icons created a false understanding of the complexity of society during these years. Moreover, the civil rights movement had begun long before Richard Nixon's famous "Kitchen Debate" glorified the American family and newborn consumerism.

The overarching theme of this chapter will focus on various grassroots movements that relate to the history of the long-term struggle for civil rights for African Americans, and from there expand to the widening circle of civil rights activism among different communities such as Chicano/Chicana, Native Americans, Lesbian, Gay,

Bisexual, Transgender, Queer (LGBTQ), and feminists. The widening circle represented a new trend toward identity politics, where different groups of women combined racial and sexual identity as a focus of their political struggles. For women of color, identity politics provided a base to focus on their own oppression, which included race and gender identity and equity. In this way, identity politics broadened the diversity of women's political voice and created new dimensions/new voices of feminisms.

The history of the social movements during the civil rights era (1950–1980s) has largely focused on the male leadership. We are all very familiar with Dr. Martin Luther King Jr., Malcolm X, and to a lesser extent the work of Chicano labor activist Cesar Chavez. Students are even less familiar with the role of women, though some may recall the role of Rosa Parks in the Montgomery Bus Boycott. Behind the scenes and on the picket lines, women played a central role as organizers and leaders in the larger movement. We will look at a variety of these leaders and organizations, as well as reviewing the legal battles that followed. The struggle for civil rights in the 1950s and 1960s focused on African Americans who were a diverse group of men and women that fought against Jim Crow laws and extreme racism that limited their quality of life and disenfranchised people of color from exercising their constitutional rights. It should be remembered that labor unions and middle-class organizations, along with the radicalization of college students, created a dynamic environment to push for radical legal and social changes. A very good example of middle-class support can be seen through the work of the Young Women's Christian Association (YWCA), which became one the first national organizations in the United States to desegregate and to actively promote racial equality as part of its mission statement.

As we have learned, World War II helped set the stage for the civil rights political activism, with specific legislation designed to address unfair labor practices through the establishment of the Fair Employment Practices Commission in 1941, the Interstate Transportation Act of 1946, and new case law and constitutional law that redefined the court's interpretation and enforcement of the Fourteenth and Fifteenth Amendments. In the same way that the imagery of the Cold War family and the cultural stereotype of the average American housewife as a white middle-class woman living in the suburbs belied the reality of American women, the history of the civil rights movement has also tended to oversimplify the grassroots nature of the movements and the important role that ordinary women played in these movements. These women acted extraordinarily to combat racism and sexism through grassroots movements, and they deserve a place in this history.[1]

BROWN V. BOARD OF EDUCATION OF TOPEKA (1954)

Challenges to segregation began in the late 19th century with the Reconstruction amendments, but acceptance would take half a century to take root. Through the landmark Supreme Court decision in *Brown v. Board of Education of Topeka* (1954), the modern civil rights movement was born, however, preceded by 50 years of gradual case precedent and the beneficiary of a more liberalized Supreme Court.

Brown represented the first major case to begin a long process of dismantling Jim Crow segregation in the South. The National Association for the Advancement of Colored People (NAACP) formed in 1909 to promote equal rights to African Americans, eradicate race prejudice, advance the interests of African Americans, and promote justice in the courts and equal education and employment opportunities. The NAACP legal counsel provided the basis to challenge court rulings that continued to treat African Americans as second-class citizens. Their lawyers focused on undoing the previous rulings that justified Jim Crow laws based on the doctrine of "separate but equal," as defined in *Plessy v. Ferguson* (1896). Case law provided that each state could segregate whites from blacks in schools, as long as they provided equal facilities. In reality, U.S. school systems never provided equal facilities, resulting in unequal treatment. There are several examples across the South where the dollar amount spent on schools was clearly at odds with the law. For example, in one county in South Carolina, public funds provided $179 per white child and only $43 per black child—a clear violation of the "separate but equal" court ruling.

The NAACP legal council initially tried to argue under the structure of the equal protection clause. The legal defense team, led by Thurgood Marshall and Charles Hamilton Houston, spent several decades working toward undoing the "separate but equal" doctrine. During this time, other minority courts cases helped to influence new court rulings in education cases that established precedence for the *Brown* decision. Not all of these cases took place in the South. For example, in the 1947 case *Mendez v. Winchester,* four Mexican American families from Orange County, California, filed a class-action lawsuit on behalf of 5,000 families to desegregate the schools. They did not argue on "separate but equal," but argued that segregation was based solely on national origin and that this violated constitutional law. The Orange County School District justified racial segregation based on the "equal protection clause." The district reasoned that students who were not proficient in English could be segregated, as long they have had the same access to education. The court ruled that discrimination by national origin was unconstitutional. At the time, Governor Earl Warren encouraged the state legislature to repeal all state education codes that allowed segregation in the public schools. This case ruling opened a small floodgate of cases arguing against the "separate but equal" doctrine, including cases in Texas and Arizona, and finally in the *Brown v. Board* case.

The NAACP legal defense filed a lawsuit against the Topeka Kansas Board of Education on behalf of Linda Brown. Thurgood Marshall argued the case before the court, making clear that separate facilities by definition denied African Americans equal citizenship rights. The Supreme Court had the case under review for three years, and in 1953, President Eisenhower appointed Earl Warren as chief justice of the U.S. Supreme Court. Warren had a long record in government, including serving as California's attorney general and the governor, and despite his earlier position supporting the interment of Japanese Americans—a decision he later deeply regretted—he used his power and legal skills to convince the other justices to strike down segregation. On May 17, 1954, Warren delivered his most famous speech announcing that segregation in public schools was inherently unequal because to segregate children based on race generated feelings of inferiority and had far-reaching implications on the community. The Supreme Court unanimously agreed. Following this major victory, the ruling to desegregate met with swift and violent resistance from Southerners, and though the ruling did not address segregation in public transportation or facilities, it opened the door for other cases and propelled civil rights activists into action across the United States.

Brown offered a new hope and led to a multipronged movement to permanently take down segregation and racial discrimination. Desegregating public education was no simple feat, but it would eventually impact every branch of public education from grammar school to higher education. Central High School in Little Rock, Arkansas (1957–1958), became the first test case to implement the federal desegregation order. The local school board agreed to abide by the order, but because of mounting community pressure, the board instituted a registration requirement. NAACP lawyer Wiley

Branton filed the lawsuit on behalf of 33 students and their parents to speed up the process to integrate all public schools. Under the school board plan, some 400 students should have entered Central High, but social unrest and registration barriers imposed by the district resulted in registering only 25 of 75 eligible black students by the end of the summer. The school board then only allowed 9 students to enroll—the NAACP handpicked the Little Rock nine to test the law. The students and their families received important support from the NAACP and from local activists. Daisy Bates played a primary role in assisting the students by escorting them to and from school. She was a vocal leader in the community, she served as the president of the Arkansas branch of the NAACP in 1953, and she and her husband owned the local black newspaper, the *State Press*.

While the Little Rock School Board accepted the order to desegregate, Governor Oral E. Faubus refused to accept integration and promised that blood would flow in the street if the black students tried to enter the school. He mobilized the resistance movement by calling in the National Guard to bar the 9 black students from entering the school. A court order followed removing the guardsmen, but a white mob formed to block entrance to the school. President Eisenhower, much to his displeasure, then stepped in to enforce federal law. Governor Faubus refused to bargain with the president, and instead of complying with federal law to desegregate, he closed down the school for two years. The impact of Little Rock only strengthened the determination of African Americans to fight to end Jim Crow and racial discrimination. It also foreshadowed the role that television would play in ending Jim Crow. The contrasting images of the raging white racists against the very calm, but resolute black students on television challenged Northern whites to support the civil rights movement. Indeed, 90 percent of Northern whites supported the use of federal troops in Little Rock, according to a 1957 public opinion poll. Similarly, most Northern whites supported the Civil Rights Act of 1957, establishing a permanent commission to investigate civil rights violations—the first of its kind since Reconstruction. This act was a first step, but it did not guarantee voting rights or oversee black voter registration. In contrast to the pulse of the nation, Southern whites convinced themselves that black families wanted separate facilities, but the remarkable courage of these students and the personal sacrifices of their families confirm the desire of most African Americans to end segregation and racial discrimination.

Oral histories and scholarly works on the *Brown* decision have documented the experiences of the individual students and their families. The 9 black students each faced threats of violence and extreme verbal abuse. Upon their arrival at the school, they daily faced hostile crowds of white protestors. Imagine having to walk through a crowd of yelling, hateful racists, many of whom were your neighbors. Melba Portillo, one of the 6 female students, later recalled that she was taunted with potential sexual assault, but she never let her parents know how bad the situation really was; they would have pulled her from school. Little Rock set the stage for a series of clashes between nonviolent protesters and Southern racists as the battle for civil rights heated up. By all accounts, the progress of desegregation was incredibly slow—only 2 percent of black students were integrated into southern schools in 1964, a full 10 years after the *Brown* decision. Nevertheless, *Brown* provided the constitutional base to address other forms of segregation in public transportation, voter registration, and employment law.[2]

RESISTANCE MOVEMENT

Between 1950 and the 1960s, radical changes swept across America. During the immediate postwar years, the NAACP and the Congress for Racial Equality (CORE), joined by the labor movement, challenged segregation and disenfranchisement through legislation and key court victories that laid the groundwork for the Civil Rights Act of 1964. Following the *Brown* decision, a swift Southern resistance movement emerged in Congress and throughout the South. The year 1956 marked the signature of the "Southern Manifesto" by Southern congressmen denouncing *Brown* as "a clear abuse of judicial power." Southern politicians at all levels of government promised to protect the South from desegregation, and segregationists used violence and intimidation to defend their Jim Crow system.

To fully grasp the violence of the period, it is important to review the terror that African American's lived under following the failure of Reconstruction in the post–Civil War years. Despite the importance of the Thirteenth, Fourteenth, and Fifteenth Amendments, African American communities faced another half century of intimidation, terror, violence, and discrimination. Several significant events illustrate the deep roots of racism that shaped the era's politics and culture in the aftermath of the Civil War. The racial politics of the postwar years evolved from World War II African American experiences and the growth of the NAACP and other grassroots organizations determined to radicalize the modern civil rights movement.

One of most chilling, yet symbolic examples is the brutal murder of Emmett Till, a 14-year-old from south Chicago, who mistakenly stepped out of line under Jim Crow while visiting relatives in Mississippi. According to oral histories documenting the events that unfolded, on a dare, Emmett Till spoke to a white girl and called her "baby." Other historical accounts claim that he had a speech impediment that was misinterpreted as a whistle. His behavior whether innocent or not ended in violence after two white men kidnapped the boy, brutally beat him, and finally lynched him. According to the reports from his mother, Mamie Till Bradley Mobley, her son's face was unrecognizable, one eye was gouged out, and his forehead was crushed. The local sheriff's office tried to force the family to bury the body as soon as possible. The family demanded the body and had an open casket so that the world could see the truth. *Jet Magazine* and the *Chicago Defender,* one of the largest black newspapers in the country, gave front-page coverage of the funeral. Mississippi racism made headline news in white papers across the country. The story woke a sleepy nation to the reality of racism and violence against African Americans.

The NAACP investigated the killing and played an active role in the trial that followed. Medgar Evers, serving as a field secretary in the region, investigated the case. Myrlie Evers later recalled how she and her husband had cried over Till's death and the frustration they felt and the sense of hopelessness at the time. To add to these sentiments, the all-white jury found the two confessed defendants not guilty. Despite the lack of justice in Mississippi, Emmett Till's death helped spark a more organized movement, and for the first time, mainstream white Americans and the press were given a brutal snapshot of the horror that African Americans faced daily under Jim Crow justice.[3]

PUBLIC ACCOMMODATIONS AND TRANSPORTATION

Under the South's Jim Crow laws, the black population faced a full range of discrimination in public schools and public accommodations that included theaters, restaurants, hospitals, courthouses, and all forms of public transportation. African Americans were required to sit at the back of the bus, and when the white section filled up, they were expected to give up their seats and stand. African American protest against segregated travel dates back to the early 20th century, but between the years 1955 and 1956, the Montgomery Bus Boycott escalated the protest, and national coverage of the events that took place further increased national awareness of Southern racism and inequality; a nonviolent struggle thus emerged.

The leadership of the black nonviolent movement organized community ministers and other civic male leaders who in turn became the voice of the movement. Yet women played a significant role as grassroots organizers, leaders, and as rank-and-file participants. Scholars studying the role of women in social movements have applied the term *bridge leadership* to show how lesser-known activists have provided bottom-up leadership. This label is a fitting description of the role that different African American women took on in the civil rights movement. Scholar Belinda Robnett provides an interesting model for understanding the variation in leadership among large organizations and grassroots movement work, which include professional, community, indigenous, and mainstream leaders. In short, each of these categories describes the variations in building support for different movements by women, the ability to move between organizational hierarchies, to work more effectively with local communities, to use different tactics and strategies, and to promote community consensus. Despite the role of women, civil rights and social movement leadership was dominated by the public male personalities. In the NAACP and the Southern Christian Leadership Conference (SCLC), men dominated as decision makers and dealt with the media and political sphere, while women typically played secondary roles as unofficial leaders providing the backbone of community and grassroots organizing. The male leaders marginalized women and in many cases relegated them to secretarial roles or as workers on education-based projects—this was particularly true in the SCLC and in the Student Nonviolent Coordinating Committee (SNCC). Gender stereotypes played an important part in social movement hierarchies, despite the number of very qualified women. Many women felt frustrated by the gendered boundaries within specific civil-rights-based groups, and for some, the sexism they faced inspired them to become active in the modern feminist movement.[4]

BRIDGE LEADERSHIP AND ELLA BAKER (1903–1986)

Ella Baker is a primary example of a female bridge leader. Baker grew up in the South and was firmly minted in social reform activism as a young child. Her grandfather, a former slave and

Reconstruction-Era activist, and her mother, a well-known public speaker and active member in the local church and missionary society, served as her role models. Baker excelled in school, becoming the valedictorian of the 1922 class at the historically black Shaw University. She had hoped to go to graduate school, but her family lacked the financial means to support her. She left the South for New York, hoping to find stimulating work, but at that time, employment opportunities for black women were limited to domestic service, factory work, or teaching. Baker's interests were not met in these areas, but she found the city a stimulating environment for radical new thinking. Baker earned her living writing editorials for several different newspapers, and during the Depression, she became the national director of the Young Negroes' Cooperative League, an organization committed to building economic opportunities for the black community. This work brought her notice from members in the NAACP, and in 1941, she became a field secretary, where she worked to build membership, supported fundraising, and fostered black consciousness for civil rights. In 1943, she became the national director of the branches, but she never agreed with the top-down leadership style of the NAACP and described the NAACP as too "Uncle Tom," meaning that the organization catered to the white middle class and did not focus enough on grassroots organizing and the community.

She left the NAACP in 1946 to become the president of the local branch of the National Urban League in Harlem. Baker believed strongly that the community needed a voice in the movement, and she helped foster better interaction between blacks and Hispanics living in Harlem. One of her most important contributions was working to improve the quality of education for blacks and Hispanics, while fighting together against school segregation. By the mid-1950s, she helped create In Friendship, an organization committed to building a mass-based organization to end segregation. In Friendship became one of the first organizations to support the Montgomery Bus Boycott that brought together a number of groups, including the well-known SCLC, headed by the Reverend Martin Luther King Jr.[5]

BOYCOTTS AND STRIKES

Long before Rosa Parks refused to give up her seat on the bus, she and other female activists spent their lifetimes protesting transportation discrimination in Montgomery, Alabama. In 1946, Mary Fair Burks, a professor at Alabama State College, founded the Women's

Political Council (WPC) of Montgomery to provide information to the community about their constitutional rights and to encourage voter registration. Motivated by a traffic accident that led to her arrest, based on a false accusation from a white witness, Fair Burks was determined to challenge the Jim Crow status quo in Montgomery. The arrest and interrogation that followed reinforced the second-class status that blacks faced in the South. Eventually set free after the driver confirmed her story, Burk decided to do something about the system. Her experience was very common, and many of the rising stars in the civil rights movement shared similar stories of humiliation and intimidation from the legal system, and they faced constant harassment and jail time based on unsubstantiated accusations from white neighbors.

A professional women's organization, the WPC gave women important leadership opportunities to combat racism. Jo Ann Gibson Robinson, a young professor at the same college, joined the group, and she would play a significant role in community activism with the WPC and lead the organizational support for the Montgomery Bus Boycott. Between 1954 and 1955, the WPC petitioned the mayor and city bus officials to address bus services; though they did not demand desegregation at this time, they threatened to organize a bus boycott in March of 1954. The busing laws deeply impacted black women, who made up the majority of bus passengers in the city. Women thus depended on bus services to get to and from work, and they were the ones who were forced to give up their seats and stand to make room for the white passengers. In contrast to the white population, black families were less likely to own automobiles, and if they did, men usually took the car to work, while the women took the bus. Thus black women were the most impacted by transportation segregation laws. Tensions between black passengers and the bus drivers began to mount in 1954. Several black women refused to give up their seats. For example, Claudette Colvin, a regular bus user, refused to give up her seat in 1954 and was tried and found guilty. The local branch of the NAACP refused to take on the Colvin case and a few other cases that followed, based on the social standing and questionable character of the women involved, until the arrest of Rosa Parks. On December 1, 1955, Rosa Parks, a seamstress by trade and an important activist in the NAACP, refused to give up her seat to a white passenger in the "colored" section of the bus and subsequently was arrested. Out of this singular event, the Montgomery Bus Boycott was born. Rosa Parks did not suddenly wake up one day and decide to protest, rather her refusal to give up her seat was well planned and executed. Parks had long protested the segregation policies of the bus system and was a well-known activist and secretary of the Montgomery branch of the NAACP and the advisor to the NAACP Youth Council. Moreover, she had participated in the NAACP Leadership Conference, where she attended the Citizenship Education Program (CEP) workshop led by longtime NAACP activist Septima Clark.

Parks had for years protested the racial policies that forced blacks to give up their seats to white bus riders. E. D. Nixon, a Pullman car porter and leader in the black community and president of the local NAACP branch, posted bond for Parks and with the help of white lawyer Clifford Durr pursued a lawsuit to break down segregation on the buses. A yearlong bus boycott followed, and when the city leaders refused to budge in changing the laws, they took their case to the U.S. Supreme Court.[6]

Nixon joined forces with Jo Ann Robinson, and together they organized an overnight boycott. Through grassroots mobilization— that is, through the local black women's network, local churches, and support from black-owned taxi businesses—the movement was born. The black ministers used the power of the pulpit to encourage support from the community, but the WPC did the groundwork to organize the boycott by distributing flyers to their communities and making the female networks aware of the boycott prior to congregational announcements from the ministers, and they organized car pools and taxi rides. Bridge leadership between women's organizations, their communities, and with the SCLC fostered the support needed to sustain a long-term boycott. The protest lasted for 381 days, with close to 90 percent of the black community refusing to ride the bus.

Martin Luther King Jr., pastor of the Dexter Avenue Baptist Church and a relative newcomer to area, quickly embraced the boycott and through his charismatic leadership became the most important leader of the movement. The impact of this protest influenced the Supreme Court to strike down segregation of the buses in Montgomery, and it galvanized the movement and led to the creation of the SCLC, which united black religious leaders to fight for civil rights. It should be noted that the NAACP and the SCLC have been credited for the organization of the boycott, but it is clear that the WPC and the work of bridge leaders like Ella Baker raised awareness and increased the grassroots support. The ministers of SCLC maintained a traditional view of gender roles in the movement and believed that women's natural role was as wives and mothers, and not as community activists. In the preface to Septima Clark's autobiography, *Echo in My Soul,* King wrote that this book epitomized the struggle of Southern black women to "realize her role as mother while fulfilling her forced position as community teacher." King's reflections demonstrate the sexual divide within the civil rights movement, and the difficulty that women faced as bridge leaders, while recognizing that women's activism was the backbone to civil rights movement.[7]

The yearlong boycott is a testament to the role of grassroots activism in forcing legal change, while illustrating the degree to which racism in the state of Alabama was firmly institutionalized. As the African American population organized car pools as an alternative boycott strategy, the local law enforcement officials and state politicians embraced Jim Crow. For example, on November 16, 1956, the state court of Alabama outlawed car pools, but on the same day, the U.S. Supreme Court ruled that the public transportation policies in Montgomery violated the Constitution. The court ruling was a monumental victory, and the sustainability of transportation boycotts for the black community impacted their ability to earn a living. Clearly, the Montgomery Bus Boycott built upon the awareness of local African Americans in other states and planted the seeds of change for federal legal reform. It would take several more cases like this boycott before the high-tide of the movement fully washed against institutional racism at all levels. The Civil Rights Act of 1957 provided the legal justification to end Jim Crow laws, led to a mass demonstration for voter registration throughout the South, and opened the door to more dramatic legal reform with the Civil Rights Act of 1964 and Voting Rights Act of 1965.

President Eisenhower signed the Civil Rights Act of 1957 into law on September 9, 1957. It was the first civil rights legislation passed by Congress since the Reconstruction amendments and was designed to ensure that all African Americans could exercise their right to vote. At the time, less than 20 percent of the black population had registered to vote. The battle in Congress against the act was fierce, and as a result, the enforcement powers were weak and largely ineffective. It eventually led to an effective voting rights act, ended segregation, and introduced housing rights. This first substantial civil rights act became a stepping stone toward social justice and emboldened the building of a mass movement in the 1950s against the tidal wave of extreme racist sentiments and diluted federal support.

Living in the South as an African American was both challenging and dangerous. The South had a long history of violence against the black population, and the struggle for civil rights fostered the rage of the Ku Klux Klan (KKK) and other whites opposed to integration of any kind. Ruby Hurley, the Southern regional director of the NAACP, fully described her experiences investigating racial murders in Alabama. Hurley's story of murders and lynching of African Americans, derived from her experiences as a field investigator, tell this horrific story. Her first assignment was to investigate the murder of Reverend Lee; Lee was gunned down on Mother's Day in 1955 for trying to register black voters. Hurley also investigated the murder of Emmett Till with Medgar Evers. They blended in by dressing in "cotton-picking" clothes as they visited different plantation locations to get eyewitness accounts of the murder. According Hurley's report, Till had infantile paralysis and could not speak clearly but whistled as part of his speech pattern. Mistakenly, he whistled at the wife of a white storekeeper, and he lost his life. These early NAACP field investigators put their lives on the line, facing constant death threats, drive-by shootings, and house bombings. It is well known that Martin Luther King Jr.'s house was bombed in 1956, but church and house bombings were common place. These activists and their families witnessed one murder after the other. In 1963, Medgar Evers was killed by a white sniper in front of his home after returning home from an NAACP meeting, and by 1968, King was struck down by an assassin's bullet.

FREEDOM RIDES AND SIT-INS

The Montgomery Bus Boycott provided an important model for other community activists to follow. During the 1950s and 1960s, a series of sit-ins and boycotts occurred in several Southern cities that included Baltimore, St. Louis, Tallahassee, Miami, and Oklahoma City. These local campaigns used direct action to derail public segregation in amusement parks, restaurants, public swimming pools, and theaters. Ordinary citizens encouraged by the work of Martin Luther King Jr. used similar nonviolent strategies to force legal and social change. Incrementally, these smaller, local movements built the momentum for a mass movement. Individuals like Clara Luper, high school teacher and local leader of the NAACP Youth Council, fought against local segregation laws by leading a group of students to desegregate a local food counter in Oklahoma City—a struggle that lasted six years.

A group of college student freedom riders catching a nap in the Birmingham, Alabama, bus station after trying unsuccessfully to board a bus to Montgomery, May 20, 1961. (AP Photo/Horace Cort)

VOTER REGISTRATION

The SCLC and CORE provided the mobilization leadership for the voter registration drives in the Deep South. The leadership of both organizations was male dominated, but women played significant roles in these movements, and through bridge leadership, they navigated the male hierarchy of organization, while building community connections with rural blacks. Ella Baker, as we have seen, played a significant role in the mass mobilization efforts. As the temporary director of SCLC, she took on the Crusade for Citizenship project, which involved organizing simultaneous meetings in 21 cities. Voter registration education and awareness of civil rights became the primary objective. Baker spent a great deal of time typing correspondence, writing letters, and duplicating flyers—common tasks performed by a secretary, even though she held the position as director. King and the other male leaders basically ignored her and treated her as a secretary rather than as an equal.

As a result, she had limited interaction with the male hierarchy of the SCLC, and despite the subordinate treatment, she refused to defer to the authority of the ministers. Most women in the movement faced similar disrespect from the male leaders.

Women activists resented the gender dynamics of the male leadership, but they continued to serve as bridge leaders between communities and the primary organizations. Septima Clark's experience working with Myles Horton (SCLC) in the Crusade for Citizenship Program (CCP) illustrates this point. Clark directed the well-known CEP at Highlander Park School in Monteagle, Tennessee. This program helped train activists in mobilization strategies, and she was particularly successful in building networks and connections with rural small-town communities. Part of her success was building the trust of the local community and providing a literacy program that prepared illiterate voters to read and sign their names.

The SCLC leadership expressed frustration over the lack of interest among rural blacks to vote. In 1959, at the suggestion of Baker, King, and Myles Horton, one of the founders of the CCP program, the SCLC established a facility where Clark could train local activists. Clark and Horton worked together, but they frequently disagreed over strategies. Clark had a better pulse on community bridge building than did Horton, who thought they could go into neighborhoods and just get people registered to vote. Clark understood that they needed to first establish the trust of the community, but she also knew that the illiteracy rate created a barrier in their mobilization efforts. Clark focused on teaching the community how to read and write (the illiteracy rates in the South numbered 12 million), which was the first step toward exercising voting rights. Literacy proved to be critical to one's ability to vote. If you could not read or sign your name, you could not register to vote. With the help of her cousin Bernice Robinson, she initiated an education program to teach reading and writing. The CCP focused on teaching literacy, self-respect, cultural pride, entitlement as American citizens and built awareness of civil rights in rural communities. As Clark explained, registration was the goal, but they first had to address the needs of community. Clark later recalled that she and Horton had many yelling matches over registration strategies. In her words, Horton thought she had new-fangled ideas, which at the time, she wasn't sure would work, but in the end succeeded in building literacy rates among rural blacks, which increased the SCLC voter registration drives. While Clark played a key development role in the formation of the CCP, she has not received much historical credit for her contributions, whereas Horton and Esau Jenkins, a community bridge leader, have been credited for the creation of the CCP.[8]

STUDENT MOVEMENT—FREEDOM
RIDES AND SIT-INS

A series of protests took place throughout the South from 1957 to 1964. These include lunch-counter sit-ins, freedom rides, voter registration drives, and the Montgomery Bus Boycott. The movement inspired the student population in the North and South to take direct action through nonviolent peaceful protest. One of the more famous sit-ins took place in Greensboro, North Carolina, in 1960, when four African American college students sat down at the all-white lunch counter at the local Woolworths. When they were asked to leave, they refused and were forcibly removed by the staff. They returned the next day with 23 more students, and by the end of the week, another 1,000 students joined the protest.

The sit-ins inspired college students to respond to the civil rights violations against African Americans in the South. Freedom rides protested interstate segregation on the buses and demanded that the 1946 federal law that prohibited segregation on interstate buses be enforced. In 1961, the CORE organized the first freedom rides where black and white civil rights workers challenged the segregation policies from Washington, D.C., to New Orleans. It began as a peaceful demonstration, but at one of the stops in South Carolina, a black rider was beaten for entering the white-only restrooms. Violence against the freedom riders rippled across the South. The riders faced severe beatings, the tires of the buses were slashed, they were fire bombed, and the protesters faced arrests and jail. At every Southern stop, the freedom riders faced large groups of hostile white racists. In Anniston, Alabama, a group of Klansmen boarded the bus and physically threw the black riders to the back of the bus. White riders bravely tried to intercept the Klansmen but were beaten up. One young man was injured so badly that he had a stroke and was permanently paralyzed. As they neared Birmingham, the violence escalated, when a mob of 20 men with pipes brutally beat the riders. The police were conveniently absent. Federal troops were eventually called in, and President Kennedy finally petitioned the Interstate Commerce Commission to implement regulations that would enforce the legislation. Following the beatings in South Carolina, SNCC students joined the protest traveling to Jackson, Mississippi, where some 300 students were arrested and jailed in August of 1961.

SNCC originated as a civil rights student network. Ella Baker recommended this idea to SCLC and began the work of bridging students to the larger civil rights movement. While SCLC wanted to form a separate student chapter, Baker supported a separate organization, run by students, but guided by SCLC advisors that included Baker, King, and Reverend Lawson. SNCC became a decentralized organization with rotating chairs and an executive committee. The students embraced Baker's suggestion for a more democratic structure and implemented a group-centered (consensus driven) leadership for making decisions. However, SNCC still maintained a gender ratio imbalance when it came to leadership positions and remained a male-dominated organization. Only a few women actually held leadership roles. Diane Nash, the president of the Nashville student movement, was one of the female figures that helped form SNCC. She became a formidable leader and helped develop the tactics and strategies of the organization. In one example, she and Peggy Alexander, another fellow student, wrote a paper, "Non-Violence Speaks to the Movement." SNCC's main objective was to serve as a clearinghouse of information for the other groups and to establish education programs that included 31 Freedom Schools across Mississippi.

While SNCC originated as a clearinghouse for other groups, the students were compelled to participate following the freedom ride violence in South Carolina where at their final destination of Birmingham, the chief of police and public safety commissioner Eugene "Bull" O'Connor, famously attacked the protesters with fire hoses and attack dogs. This spectacle was broadcast on national television for all of Americans to witness. An extreme racist, O'Connor's actions horrified the nation, and his tactics served as a catalyst for sweeping social and legal changes in the South and influenced the passage of the Voting Rights Act in 1965.

The students were incredibly brave given the brutality of Southern officials and the KKK. Diane Nash was asked by an SCLC minister if she was aware of the dangers and potential death, and she responded, "Yes, that's exactly why the rides must not be stopped. If they stop us with violence we are dead."[9] Nash organized a group of students form Nashville to ride to Birmingham. The students bravely boarded the bus knowing that they might be killed; several wrote out wills and had sealed letters for their families. They were jailed overnight and escorted out of the city to the Tennessee border by Bull Connor. The freedom riders continued to press forward, and many of them faced prison, including black and white

A policeman leans over to question two black women who kneel on the steps of City Hall during racial demonstrations in Birmingham, Alabama, May 4, 1963. They were taken to jail. (AP Photo/Bill Hudson)

women. Diane Nash risked her life and the life of her unborn child when she was brought to trial for teaching workshops on nonviolence to young black children. She was tried for "contributing to the delinquency of minors" and sentenced to a two-year prison term, though she only served 10 days.

Violence was a fact of life for African Americans living in the South. As we have seen previously, Southern blacks faced the constant threat of death without cause or due process. The victims included men, women, and children. This form of violence continued during the civil rights era but escalated with legislative mandates to desegregate the South and with the growth of the mass movement for civil rights. White racists incensed by civil rights activists used every form of violence to intimidate black and white activists including bombs, threats, beating, and murders.

Fannie Lou Hammer of Sunflower County, Mississippi, joined SNCC to stand up for freedom through the voter registration drive. A cotton plantation worker with a sixth-grade education, she became a charismatic organizer, despite losing her job and experiencing constant threats of violence. A force to be reckoned with, Hammer is an iconic representation of the role of rural Southern women who became the pillars of their communities and of the civil rights movement. They did so at great personal sacrifice. Hammer, for example, suffered emotionally and physically as a result of a brutal beating she received in 1964 following a voter registration drive. She never fully recovered from her injuries and suffered until her death in 1977. The entrenchment of Jim Crow and the violence and racism created by this system showed little mercy to the black community and Northern white participants. By June 1964, the violence against the student volunteers escalated with 4 deaths, 80 beatings, and thousands of arrests. The impact on the local black community was much more dramatic, and their sacrifice to challenge racism in their community was more than brave. The 37 black churches that were bombed or burned down illustrate the bravery of the community.

SEXISM IN THE MOVEMENT

There are many personal accounts that describe the sexism within the various social movements. Ella Baker's work with the SCLC is a good example. The SCLC faced a leadership shortage following the Montgomery Boycott, and in 1957, Baker became the executive director, and she worked with other community members to organize voter registration and citizenship classes. Baker stayed on as director for a couple of years but quickly recognized that her leadership style and gender limited her ability to create change. She remarked that she knew all along that her role would be limited to a subordinate status. The male leaders expected women to serve as secretaries and to take orders, rather than treating them as equals as activists and as leaders. As was the case for Baker, the male ministers of SCLC did not share the leadership with female bridge leaders and relegated them to work as secretaries, to fundraising, and as educational workers. Baker worked in all three areas, and while she enjoyed her work, she was clearly frustrated by the sexist attitudes of the ministers and left the SCLC to work with college students.[10]

Despite the difficulties within the structure of SCLC, Baker's work with local college students opened the next chapter of her career as a major player in the formation of the SNCC. Baker promoted the idea of SNCC remaining a student-run organization, a contrary position to the SCLC and CORE. By 1961, SNCC became the independent organization that she hoped for, and it adopted a group-centered leadership model. Baker worked throughout the period of the 1960s with a variety of organizations, and most importantly, she helped organize the Mississippi Freedom Democratic Party, which influenced some of the early leaders of Students for a Democratic Society (SDS). Baker sold the idea of group-centered leadership over the traditional leader-centered ideology present in many national organizations. She believed that teaching self-sufficiency in orga- nizing rallies and other events was more important that focusing on one charismatic leader to carry the movement forward. She de- scribed the reliance on one great leader as a handicap because the leader becomes too focused on fame and publicity and less on the actual grassroots organizing. Moreover, the growth of organizations tends to weaken the community decision-making structure creating serious conflicts and factions within the organization. SNCC faced this very problem by 1964, and some historians have suggested this rapid growth became its demise, but the changes in the organiza- tion's philosophy toward more violent strategies, coupled with the emergence of modern feminism, influenced the decline of SNCC as a student organization.

As SNCC moved from a largely black grassroots base to become a more integrated organization, tensions between white and black members emerged. In particular, the formation of the Freedom Schools opened new opportunities for women as field-workers and supervisors, while promotion to the executive board and as key representatives remained a male privilege. Most of the members of SNCC, and particularly in leadership positions and as bridge lead- ers, were primarily black and white women who were never domi- nant leaders but remained active in the organization. Scholars have frequently pointed to the sexism within SNCC based on a paper written by white members Casey Hayden and Mary King that ad- dressed sexism in the movement. In an oral-history project, both women later described the empowerment they felt from their work in SNCC, but they also agreed that the questions they raised about sexism and equality within SNCC in their article was badly timed. However sexist the male structure may have been, the women were also influenced by new feminists ideas, including Betty Friedan's book *Feminine Mystique*. The women objected to the patriarchy and hierarchical structure of SNCC and the move away from nonvio- lence as the organizational philosophy. The experiences of Hayden and King highlight the changes that took place in the freedom movement. By 1964, Northern white volunteers flooded the South creating tensions and resentments from the indigenous civil rights groups. The participation of young college women in the freedom rides added to the violence and to the tensions within SNCC. White women represented one-third to one-half of the new volunteers, and any interaction between black and white women increased the hostility from white racists. The presence of white women also created tension with black men and women in the movement. Hayden and King, reflecting on the often-repeated joke from Stokely Carmichael that "the only position for women is prone," reflected his frustration with the sexual liaisons between white women and black men.[11]

The tumult that rocked the South between 1960 and 1961 convinced civil rights activists that nonviolent mobilization could only be taken so far, and it became increasingly clear that comprehensive civil rights legislation was needed to guarantee full citizenship rights to African Americans. King and his SCLC contingent launched a new campaign to address the extreme segregation in Birmingham, Alabama. They needed a major victory to further fuel the nonviolent struggle and to raise national awareness of the extreme violence that African Americans faced daily. Birmingham, the largest segregated town in the South, proved to be the ideal target. The city had a long-term history of racial violence, and blacks were segregated in all areas of society from schools, city parks, department store dressing rooms, courthouses, hospitals, and restaurants. While the black population represented more than 40 percent of the city population, only 10,000 were registered to vote, out of a total city population of 80,000 people. King, working with the local community, organized protests and boycotts against the local department stores. The intention was to enrage Public Safety Commissioner Eugene "Bull" Connor. King launched the protests by demanding the end of racist hiring practices and segregated accommodations. King's strategy worked, leading to hundreds of arrests, and he faced several days in solitary confinement as the chief architect of the protest. During his jail time, he wrote the now famous "Letter from a Birmingham Jail," which was reprinted and distributed nationally. In this letter, he set out the moral principles at stake. After his release, the protest continued, and Connor tried to break the demonstration through excessive force using high-powered water hoses, billy clubs, and attack dogs against the protesters. The younger black community responded by fighting back. A truce was finally reached between the Justice Department and SCLC, and the local businesses agreed to desegregate and begin hiring blacks. The violence continued and eventually President Kennedy was forced to order 3,000 army troops to nationalize the state guardsmen. The unrest was quelled, but attacks against the black community continued, and in September of 1962, a bomb killed four black girls in a local Baptist church. Birmingham sparked seven long months of protest in other cities, and of the 100,000 activists, 15,000 were arrested.

Victory for King was bittersweet, but the television coverage finally woke the nation to the violence created by extreme racism. The March on Washington in 1963 represented a turning point in the nonviolent protest movement, which concluded with King's famous "I Have a Dream" speech. This march and his speech inspired the nation, but it would take the cumulative pressure of civil unrest to convince President Kennedy to support sweeping civil rights legislation. Out of this pressure, the Civil Rights Act of 1964 passed Congress, and on July 2, 1964, President Johnson signed it into law. This was the most significant piece of civil rights legislation to pass Congress since Reconstruction. It prohibited discrimination in public accommodations and banned discrimination in employment on the basis of race, color, religion, sex, and national origin; it desegregated the schools and other public facilities; it paid for desegregation assistance to the communities; and it also created the Equal Employment Opportunity Commission (EEOC) to investigate and litigate cases of job discrimination. The Voting Rights Act of 1965 similarly emerged out of the massive protest organized by SCLC, SNCC, and other organizations following the violence of the Mississippi freedom summer rides. In August of 1965, President Johnson signed the Voting Rights Act into law, authorizing federal supervision of voter registration and outlawed literacy and other discriminatory practices that barred blacks from voting. The impact in Mississippi alone was enormous—between 1964 and 1968, 59 percent of the black population registered to vote, versus 7 percent in the previous years. Across the South, the number of voting blacks grew to 3 million.

Despite these important legislative victories, 1966 represented a year of growing discontent among Northern blacks living in the ghettos of large cities. This angst resulted in a shift in the movement from the nonviolent philosophy of King to a more violent and radical black separatist movement. A good example can be seen with the disagreements within SNCC. In 1964, the freedom rides brought in skilled volunteers from Yale, Stanford, and other elite institutions, and with the increase in white female participation, the black members felt isolated and controlled by these white students. An organization once committed to nonviolence and racial integration shifted its focus to black separatism. Black activism had a long history of weaving together black separatism with elements of integration within mainstream society. As the non-violent struggle fractured, many blacks began to support black separatism and embraced *black power*. The nonviolent approach of Martin Luther King Jr., the SCLC, SNCC, CORE, and SDS gave way to a more radical movement that included the rise of the Nation of Islam, a black separatist group, spirited through the ideas of Elijah Muhammad and popularized by Malcolm X. The emerging black power movement also included the notorious Oakland, California, Black Panther Party, which formed in direct response to police brutality against the black community. Founded by Huey Newton and Bobby Seale, the Black Panther Party demanded "land, bread, housing, education, clothing, and justice." The rise of black nationalism and black power can be attributed to the problem of poverty, racism, and police brutality against the entire black community.

The Panthers dressed in all black, brandished black berets and guns, and patrolled their community monitoring the activities of the police. The Panthers also provided some community services that included free breakfast for school children and medical clinics. They were nonetheless persecuted by the police and the FBI, and between 1968 and 1969, their offices were raided more than 30 times in 11 different cities. Many of their leaders were arrested and served long jail terms. FBI surveillance successfully destroyed the Black Panther Party; however, their ideology of cultural nationalism influenced a new direction in the civil rights movement that further challenged the status quo.

A good example is the book *Black Power*, written by Stokely Carmichael and Charles V. Hamilton in 1967. In the book, they encouraged the black community to take pride in their race, history, and culture. Black power thus expanded the demand for cultural recognition and heightened identity politics. College students used this movement to expand their rights as students, and blacks students began to demand social justice on campus in athletics, student housing, employment opportunities, and access to scholarships, while they pushed for academic programs in African American studies. The field of cultural studies that focused on ethnic group identity, race, and gender led to the creation of new programs in college campuses across the nation.

Just as women were subordinate in other male-dominated organizations, Black Panther women had secondary roles in the movement. One of the exceptions was Angela Davis, a well-educated activist from Birmingham, Alabama, and a member of SNCC and the Black Panther Party. She appeared on the FBI's Most Wanted List in 1970 after being accused of supplying guns for a prison uprising in California. As a result, Davis fled the state for New York where she went underground and was later captured and sent back to California to face a criminal trial. After serving two years in prison, she was found not guilty, but an interesting international and national campaign, "Free Angela Davis," influenced the outcome. Much of the funding for the campaign came from the Communist Party and 60 local communities throughout the United States protested on her behalf. Davis became a legendary figure in the radical Left movement, as a Communist and as an outspoken activist against the policies of then governor of California Ronald Reagan. Fired at UCLA for being a member of the Communist Party, Reagan swore she would never teach again in the University of California system. She nevertheless remains a tenured faculty member at UC Santa Cruz. In contrast to some of her contemporaries, Davis was deeply influenced as a philosophy student of Marxism, and she connected black liberation to the overthrow of capitalism. Her activism did not end with her 1972 prison release. Davis ran for vice president of the United States as a candidate for the Communist Party in 1980 and 1984, and in 1995, she opposed the Million Men March, led by Louis Farrakhan, the leader of the Nation of Islam, because it promoted male chauvinism.[12]

WIDENING CIRCLE OF MOVEMENT

The black civil rights movement helped to widen the circle of the civil rights movement, providing a new momentum for liberation from diverse groups of Americans. The widening of the civil rights circle can be framed around the notion of identity politics, where different communities such as Chicano/Chicana, Native Americans, Asians, gays and lesbians, and feminists contested oppression on multiple fronts. Women from different ethnic groups combined racial/ethnic and sexual identity as a focus of their political struggles. For women of color, identity politics provided a base to focus on their own oppression within their own communities and in mainstream culture. In this way, identity politics broadened the diversity of women's political voice and created new dimensions/new voices of feminisms.

The impact of the civil rights movement on identity topics for college students cannot be understated. Feminists, gay activists, and ethnic identity groups challenged the status quo of mainstream America. The college activism brought on by the freedom rides and later the Vietnam War created a cultural revolution that would provide the legal foundation to press for basic civil and human rights, but more importantly, it would lead to new academic programs that recognized the diverse contributions of race, ethnicity, sexuality, and gender.

More directly, the civil rights movement influenced societal standards based on the concept of *cultural pluralism*. What this means is that no one culture should dominate over another. Respecting cultural differences is central to sustaining a democracy and is a right of citizenship. Understanding the diversity of experiences provides a basis to better understand the meaning of citizenship and democracy. National legislation provides the legal basis for universal human rights, but it takes a diversity of groups to push the boundaries of law and practice at the grassroots level. Social movements provide the foundation by which ordinary citizens can challenge mainstream social practice and to fight for social justice. Groups have used nonviolent and violent means to raise awareness of a variety of issues. Just as the NAACP used legal strategies to build a nonviolent arsenal of legal precedent, other groups have joined unions to force change. One of the best-known protests of this era is the Grape Workers Strike that began in the central valley of California. The leaders of movement included Cesar Chavez and Delores Huerta, who worked to build a union of Mexican American migrant farmworkers. It was through this national movement to support the boycott of table grapes and lettuce that Hispanic workers won formal union recognition from the United Farm Workers (UFW).

Building a national campaign and recognition from the UFW required a multipronged grassroots approach that not only depended on field activists from the migrant farmer's themselves, but involved working with middle-class communities to build support for a massive consumer boycott. An interesting case study in Philadelphia highlights the importance of grassroots activism among different classes and ethnic groups. The United Farm Workers Organizing Committee (UFWOC), the precursor to the UFW, depended on the role of female workers to travel to distant locations to spread the word of the boycott. Philadelphia became a center point for some of this activism. Hope Esperanza Lopez, a farmworker, mother of five, and union activist, arrived in Philadelphia in February of 1969, with two of her children in tow and two assistants.

Lopez's active role contrasts the stereotypical view of Latina women as conservative and homebound. Lopez and her staff specifically targeted middle-class housewives drawing on their roles as mothers and their awareness of feminism. They appealed to female activists who held memberships in the YWCA and LWV, as well as from college students, the Jewish Community Relations Council, and the Catholic Church. The creation of the Boycott House provided the base for a very diverse collective, and the broad-based population spread to the Spanish-speaking communities and to the black population as well. Drawing on the idea of a woman-centered movement, combined with the nonviolent protest of Cesar Chavez, Lopez blended social justice, civil rights, and civic activism to pressure local grocery stores chains to remove grapes from their stores. The diversity of the movement did not necessarily eliminate class tensions. Chicana activist's commitment to the strike was directly tied to their ethnic community and to their economic sustainability. The middle-class women who became involved in the grape boycotts joined forces as feminists and civic activists, but as many of them also did not suffer the blight of poverty or have to worry about feeding their families.

The class differences between these women influenced how they interacted. The Chicana activists were often frustrated by the lack of commitment from middle-class women. As Lopez so succinctly stated, affluent people can take a break for vacation, while those living in poverty never had such a luxury—"hunger doesn't even take a coffee break."[13]

The different realties shaped how individuals responded to each other. Despite some of the tensions between women, their efforts paid off, and grape prices fell from $0.89 to $0.29 per pound, and shipments from California to Pennsylvania by 23 percent. The nationalization of this movement resulted in collective bargaining between 27 grape growers and the farmworkers.

As we have seen, the black civil rights movement galvanized a new generation of students and activists to fight against racism and discrimination on multiple fronts. Prior to the 1960s generation, different ethnic communities contested segregation in the school system in a variety of locations, from the Southwest to California. By 1968, a series of walkouts and demonstrations highlight the empowerment that came from three decades of social activism. In Los Angeles, approximately 10,000 Hispanic students waked out of their East Los Angeles school campuses to demand changes in the curriculum that included Latino history and demanded hiring of Mexican American teachers. The Chicano movement became especially forceful on college campuses between 1965 through the 1980s, and other pride organizations followed. Similarly, Puerto Ricans represented the single largest Spanish-speaking group on the East Coast, and they experienced a similar revival in their home country's nationalism and pressed for cultural recognition. Likewise, the formation of the American Indian Movement (AIM) in 1969 brought to the fore a new radical front of Indian activist who asserted treaty rights and demanded recognition. A primary example of their expansion took place following the largest antiwar demonstration in Washington, when a group of 78 Native Americans seized Alcatraz Island in the San Francisco Bay and occupied the federal prison for a year and a half, bringing attention to continued prejudice against tribal peoples and to promote a pan-Indian tribal identity. Feminist and Native American activist Madonna Thunderhawk played an important role in the Alcatraz action and other tribal civil rights issues.

Sexual orientation represented another important protest movement of the era, which became known as the new Gay Liberation Front. In the same way that ethnic groups sought to bring recognition to their cultural traditions, the Lesbian, Gay, Bisexual, and Transgendered, and Queer (LGBTQ) community became more militant against homophobic discrimination, and they demanded to be treated with respect and tolerance. Between 1969 through the 1990s, the gay rights movement challenged laws that defined homosexuality as a mental disorder and communities in New York, San Francisco, and Los Angeles organized gay pride parades and openly took a public stand against the widespread violence and discrimination against gay people. Through the political and community activism of Harvey Milk, the gay population became a viable political force in U.S. politics. Milk's emphasis on the importance of coming out of the closet and living their lives openly, helped to galvanize gay rights, and his contribution to the movement lives on today with activism of the LGBTQ community to fight for marriage rights. While Dell Martin and Phyllis Lyon championed new communication networks for lesbians across the country through the Daughters of Bilitis.[14]

CONCLUSION

A new era of feminism grew out of the civil rights struggle. Unlike their predecessors, this second wave of feminists had diverse political perspectives and for the first time included union women, working-class women, students, middle-class women, First Nation women, lesbians, and women of color.

The civil rights movement inspired a new spirit of activism and a new national consciousness for civil and human rights. Important legal gains in the form of desegregation in public schools, public accommodations, housing, and public transportation broke down Jim Crow laws, while the Civil Rights Act of 1964 and Voting Rights Act of 1965 provided a legal basis to fight against racial, gender, religious, and sexual discrimination. As we have seen, the struggle for basic civil rights has a long history. For the African American community and other ethnic populations, the civil rights in the 1960s and 1970s provided a new political, legal, and social landscape where personal and community agency challenged the previous status quo. It opened new doors for educational opportunity, economic advancement, and legal justification to demand social justice as American citizens.

NOTES

1. Ellen Carol Dubois and Lynn Dumenil, *Through the Eyes of Women: An American History with Documents* (Bedford/St. Martin Press, 2004), pp. 571–75.

2. Henry Hampton, Steve Fayer, with Sarah Flynn, eds., *Voices of Freedom: An Oral History of the Civil Rights Movement from the 1950s through the 1980s* (Bantam Books, New York, 1990).

3. Hampton, Fayer, Flynn, eds., *Voices of Freedom*, pp. 1–15.

4. Belinda Robnett, *How Long? How Long? African American Women in the Struggle for Civil Rights* (Oxford University Press, 1997), pp. 41–43, 166–72.

5. Robnett, *How Long?*, pp. 86–97.

6. Robnett, *How Long?*, pp. 53–70.

7. Robnett, *How Long?*, p. 95.

8. Robnett, *How Long?*, pp. 53–62.

9. Robnett, *How Long?*, p. 104.

10. Robnett, *How Long?*, pp. 65–80.

11. Robnett, *How Long?*, pp. 108–9, 118–22.

12. Angela Davis, *Angela Davis: An Autobiography* (Random House, 1974).

13. Margaret Rose, "Woman Power Will Stop Those Grapes: Chicana Organizers and Middle-Class Female Supporters in the Farm Workers' Grape Boycott in Philadelphia," in *Women and Power in American History; A Reader, Vol. II from 1870,* ed. Kathryn Kish Sklar and Thomas Dublin, pp. 240–53 (Prentice Hall, New Jersey, 1991).

14. Martin Meeker, *Contacts Desired: Gay and Lesbian Communications and Community, 1940s–1970* (Chicago University Press, 2007), pp. 77–80, 113–16.

Association (PTA). Moreover, millions of American women went to work every day to sustain their families, and a growing number of middle-class women entered the workforce on a part-time basis.

Historians have used the metaphor of waves to describe the complex history of women's rights and feminist activism. The *first wave* refers to the activism that began with the Seneca Falls Convention in 1848 through 1920, when women finally were granted federal voting rights under the Nineteenth Amendment. The *second wave* includes women who were active in the postwar years and younger women who came of age during the 1950s and 1960s. The creation of the Kennedy Presidential Commission on the Status of Women (PCSW) in 1961, the formation of the National Organization for Women (NOW) in 1966, and the emergence of the women's liberation movement in the 1960s and 1970s, created a new revolution of feminism. Third- and fourth-wave movements have since followed, making clear the continuum of social movements and women's activism over time.

The modern feminist movement, or the second wave, represents a diverse movement(s) of women who struggled together and separately to rectify the subordinate status of women in society. Rather than defining this era as the second wave, it is more accurate to think about modern feminism as a series of movements. As historian Karen Offen has noted, "...many 'waves' and 'eruptions'—indeed, many 'feminisms'—can be identified."[1] By 1968, feminists used the term *first wave* to recognize the contributions of their foremothers, yet in doing so, they lumped together multiple decades dating back to the 1840s. Similarly, second-wave activists have been lumped together by the third- and fourth-generation movements. The second-wave activists believed that their approach to feminism was more diverse, inclusive, and broader in vision, while improving upon the wave that preceded them. Generationally, feminists have viewed the earlier movement goals as narrow, racist, and elitist. Third- and fourth-wave activists benefit from the social justice movements that came before them, yet they are similarly critical of second-wave movement as too elitist, and the histories tend to present the various efforts of women as a reaction to straight, white, middle-class feminists. The new waves face a similar challenge in mobilizing diverse groups of women; they also face a more diffused movement, but one that is more attentive, to race, class, sexuality, culture, and national identity. New studies on the history of women's social movements and feminism are more focused on coalitions and the diversity of women's experience in various movements. Coalition politics has come to define the modern women's movement.

This chapter will explore the emergence of the modern feminist movement in the United States in the 1960s and follow the different strands of feminisms that have directly influenced public policy and legislation to eradicate sexism in politics, culture, and society. We will see how laboring women conceptualized feminism and worked to eradicate sexual discrimination for working-class women, and see how middle-class and working-class women finally came together to promote the ERA. Similarly, we will see how women of color waged a double-pronged battle to wipe out sexism and racism, while following the social consciousness raising elements of the movement that inspired young college women from all social classes and races to find their own political and personal agency, and the role of peace activists to protest the nuclear arms race and the Vietnam War. The civil rights movement of the 1950s and 1960s built on the grassroots tradition of the Progressive Era and the women's social movements. The opportunities that emerged in the 1960s and 1970s can be tied to the Nineteenth Amendment victory in 1920, which opened the door to pursue equal rights.

Building on the legacy of the Progressive Era, several key events, leaders, and civil rights legislation created the platform for a vibrant women's movement The publication of Betty Friedan's popular book *Feminist Mystique* (1963), the establishment of the PCSW, the Equal Pay Act of 1963, the Civil Rights Act of 1964, and the formation of NOW in 1966 opened the floodgate to pursue a variety of causes and press for new legislation. The Civil Rights Act of 1964 ushered in a new approach to democracy, and women used this act and applied the principles of the equal protection clause of the Fourteenth Amendment to eradicate gender discrimination in all areas of life. The resulting outcome of the Civil Rights Act created laws that addressed women's reproductive rights and health (*Roe v. Wade*); equal opportunity in higher education as faculty, students, and for female athletes through Title I; workplace sexual harassment, rape, and marital rape laws; and the 1994 Violence Against Women Act.[2]

POPULAR CULTURE AND THE
FEMININE MYSTIQUE

Betty Friedan, in her best-selling book *Feminine Mystique,* described the inertia that many American women felt as they mopped floors, made beds, chauffeured children, fed families, and supported the careers of their spouses. In her first chapter, entitled "The Problem That Had No Name," she articulated the discontent that many women felt and provided a new forum for feminist expression by asking the question, "Is this all?" Friedan's exposé challenged the midcentury cultural glorification of housewifery and motherhood by popular magazines and consumer articles. *Feminine Mystique* sold 3 million copies, illustrating the popularity of her book and the inspirational impact it had on many of its readers. She encouraged women to remove the cultural malaise that dictated that women could only find happiness and fulfillment as wives and mothers. For the millions of middle-class women who came of age during the postwar years, *Feminine Mystique* provided a sounding board to question women's unequal status and has been cited as a major influence in building the second-wave movement.

Friedan criticized popular magazines for promoting the feminine mystique and for denying women personal autonomy and independence. She received a massive amount of fan mail suggesting that she struck an important cord for the millions of her readers. *Feminine Mystique* clearly influenced many ordinary middle-class women, while helping to spark the modern women's movement. As has been explained in chapter 4, Friedan's work fits neatly into the historical framework on studies related to the experiences of women in the Cold War era and helped create a false image of American family life, by oversimplifying the role of women as principle homemakers and mothers. Yet, her exposé had an indisputable impact on women's lives and had an unusual influence on historical analysis during the period. Historians have tended to agree with her conclusion that the postwar ideology rested on conservative traditional values of domesticity. Despite the flaws of the book, which focused on a very small subset of upper-middle-class women, she clearly had an impact on the growing second-wave movement, but at the same time, her research and analysis ignored the experiences of class, race, and ethnicity.

Moreover, Friedan was not a true victim of domesticity herself but was an accomplished professional journalist and wrote many articles in the 1950s about the sex discrimination women faced in the workplace, facts she failed to disclose in her book. While she spoke about oppression of domesticity, she also mischaracterized the level of middle-class women's involvement in civic government and as part-time workers—approximately 61 percent of the women's labor force were married women. Early historical analysis of Friedan's work accepted wholesale her conclusions, which fit nicely with postwar-era studies. A few historians have retraced and expanded on Friedan's research of popular magazines. For example, historian Joanne Meyerowitz sampled more than 498 non-fiction articles from mass distributed monthly magazines, which included the standard women's magazines like *Ladies Home Journal* and general publications like *Reader's Digest, Harper's,* and the *Atlantic Monthly,* as well as *Ebony* and *Negro Digest.*[3]

Meyerowitz has demonstrated that women's lives were not as repressive or disillusioned as originally reported by Friedan, and that the majority of women during this period had to balance going to work everyday and taking care of their families. The idea that women lost their independence to embrace domesticity exclusively is a myth. Friedan and others consistently pointed to the conservative writings of the era to demonstrate the degree of women's subordinate status. In contrast, Meyerowitz, found in her review of popular magazines that the discourse was not singularly focused on the domestic ideal but included articles that addressed nondomestic topics along side domestic issues. Her literature review provides a more complex view of women's experiences in the postwar years that included practical domestic advice, while encouraging individualism, public service, working women, and tangentially feminism. Local papers ran stories that highlighted women in politics, while national magazines such as *Ebony* (an African American popular magazine) ran stories that applauded the achievements of women as mothers and as workers. In one example, *Ebony* reported on a mother of two who worked as an airplane mechanic. For African American women, success at home and at work helped combat racism, while white magazines touted the virtues of motherhood and public service. Meyerowitz argues that the emphasis on traditional gender roles provided a framework for women's public achievements and reinforced the cultural value of hard work. Nonetheless, Friedan's book identified many of the real-life frustrations that educated middle-class women felt during the period, but her narrative glossed over the real-life experiences of women and obscured the differences in class, race, and ethnicity and failed to account for the increasing number of women entering the workforce. The complexity of women's experiences can been seen in the life of Detroit labor activist Myra Wolfgang, who had worked since the late 1930s against gender and racial discrimination in the workforce. She became well known as a labor agitator and organized the picket against the Detroit Playboy Bunny Club for failing to provide the women with real wages. The picketers donned bunny suits and carried signs that read "Don't be a bunny, work for money." Wolfgang's contributions during the Cold War era underscore the point that working-class women lacked the free time to worry about maintaining a domestic ideal. While she identified as a feminist, she attacked Friedan and other feminists for demeaning the role of women in the home and for romanticizing paid labor. Indeed, the "problem that had no name" may have resonated with some middle-class women in the suburbs, but for the majority of working women, balancing work and family was a daily struggle. Ironically, Friedan had a background in radical politics and wrote several articles on women's labor for the United Electrical, Radio, and Machine Workers Union in the 1940s and 1950s. A primary example is an anonymous 42-page pamphlet that she wrote calling for equal pay and equal treatment between men and women in this industry.[4]

POLITICAL EQUALITY

As we have learned in chapter 4, the push for the ERA in 1923 created a schism among social feminists who feared the elimination of state protective labor legislation for women. Two competing bodies, the National Woman's Party (NWP) and the National Women's Bureau (NWB), promoted and opposed a constitutional amendment. Disagreement over the right path to pursue legislation divided women who had once stood side-by-side in support of suffrage. The battle lines over the control of equal rights legislation, combined with the repressive atmosphere of containment and insistence on conformity to the feminine mystique, hampered the progression of legislation focused on women's rights. Despite these challenges, women's groups continued to lobby Congress to enact laws that addressed women's status. The most hotly contested area was clearly the battle over the ERA. The increase in support for the amendment in the late 1940s and early 1950s by key women's groups recognized that protective labor laws for women encouraged labor discrimination and limited women's economic opportunities. The National Federation of Business and Professional Women (BPW), the GFWC, and the American Association of University Women (AAUW) endorsed the ERA, and growing congressional support added to the tension between ERA supporters and opponents. The NWB, the Young Women's Christian Association (YWCA), the LWV, and laboring women continued to oppose the ERA based on Progressive Era views that women were distinctly different from men and required special protection. Disagreement over the best path to pursue equality limited coalition building among competing groups. Equal rights feminists promoted the

ERA, while social feminists from this era and working-class women focused on addressing state laws to improve working conditions and to implement equal pay laws.

Despite the failure to promote the ERA in the 1950s, the diversity of legislative lobbying by these groups provided the foundation for a more cohesive modern feminist movement, and by the early 1970s, a diverse group of women came together to promote the ERA, and laboring women no longer believed in protective labor legislation. The first-wave and early second-wave feminists became expert lobbyists; they understood the legislative process, developed relationships with congressmen and congresswomen, were well seasoned working the halls of Congress and petitioning the executive branch to eliminate the practice of gender discrimination in law, and testified in congressional hearings on both sides of the issue of ERA. Both white and black women participated in these lobbying efforts, and in the same way that the white women's groups split over the ERA, the same was true for black women. Mary Church Terrell representing the National Association of Colored Women (NACW) endorsed the amendment, while Mary McLeod Bethune of the National Council of Negro Women did not. However, the majority of black women did not support the ERA, largely because of the elitism of the NWP and the lack of interest in fighting racism by white reformers; they found the NWB more supportive. Moreover, the fight against racism trumped women's rights. There is ample evidence of the long-term process to secure equal rights. The *Congressional Record*—the primary publication documenting congressional activities—is filled with testimony from women supporting different issues, and specifically those supporting and opposing the ERA; the ERA was introduced to Congress every year beginning in 1923 through 1972.[5]

NEW FRONTIER AND KENNEDY

The 1960s political environment ushered in a new era to pursue women's rights. The election of John F. Kennedy offered the promise of a New Frontier, and women activists jumped on the opportunity to expand on civil rights legislation. While Kennedy had a less than stellar reputation promoting women's issues, his connection to labor and interaction with labor leaders led to the appointment of Esther Peterson as the new head of the NWB. Peterson established her career working on labor issues, serving in a variety of administrative positions. In 1944, she became a labor lobbyist

with the Amalgamated Clothing Workers Union, where she participated on the National Committee on Equal Pay, National Committee on the Status of Women, and the Labor Advisory Board of the
NWB. In the 1950s, she joined the Industrial Union Department of
the American Federation of Labor and Congress of Industrial Organization (AFL-CIO) serving as a legislative representative. She
joined the Kennedy campaign to help organize support from the
labor movement. Her appointment to NWB in 1961 resulted from
her long-term work for labor and her alliance with Kennedy's campaign. Under Kennedy, the NWB was given more policy control
than any previous administration, and Peterson became the high-
est-ranking female official in the Kennedy administration. In this
capacity, she had direct oversight of the Bureau Labor Standards,
employee compensation, the compensation appeals board, and for
the first time the NWB had authority over male and female workers in these areas.[6]

Peterson worked toward the implementation of equal pay legislation and to create a national commission on the status of women.
While Peterson deserves credit for convincing Kennedy to create
a presidential commission, she built on the work of earlier bureau
leaders and opponents of the ERA. In the mid-1940s, the NWB offered legislation that would address discrimination laws against
women through the Status Bill, also known as the Taft-Wadsworth
Bill (named after the congressional sponsors of the bill). The bill
consisted of two component parts, one that made a clear statement
to enhance women's autonomy and reaffirming domesticity, while
the second recommended establishing a Commission on the Status
of Women, with seven members, appointed by the president. The
bill failed in Congress, but the language of the bill provided
the foundation for a permanent commission. In the original bill,
the purpose of the commission was to study the economic, civil, social, and political status of women in the United States. The PCSW
consisted of 26 members that included 11 men and 15 women from
different sectors of labor, business, education, and politics and was
chaired by former first lady Eleanor Roosevelt. The committee also
included several subcommittees composed of a variety of women
activists. The PCSW had the charge to make recommendations to
overcome discrimination of women in all public and private employment and to help women realize their full potential as wives
and mothers and to contribute to society. The final report in 1963
made very moderate recommendations, which included a childcare tax for lower-income women, equal opportunities in private

employment, improving social security for women, enforcing the coverage under the Fair Labor Standards Act (FLSA) of 1938, and endorsement of a 40-hour workweek with overtime benefits; poor black and Hispanic women had the most to gain from the enforcement of the FLSA.

As recent studies demonstrate, new coalitions emerged from the 1940s forward, and the creation of the PCSW provided a new forum to build broad-based coalitions of equal rights, social, and labor activists. The PCSW provided a forum to address the continued inequity in state laws that limited women's ability to serve on juries and limited their property rights. Both equal rights feminists and labor feminists worked together on the PCSW investigative committees, which included Civil and Political Rights, Education, Home and Community, Private Employment, and Protective Labor Legislation. Through this diverse committee process, women worked together to make recommendations that reflected their diversity and common goals. The BPW, supporters of the ERA, took the lead in promoting the creation of state branches, which engendered new local feminist coalitions, though a few hard-line leaders from the NWP felt that the state branches would not support the ERA. Emma Guffey Miller, a life member of the NWP and close ally with the BPW expressed this view. In part, her position is reflective of the split between equal rights feminists and social feminists over equal rights, and her fears proved to be wrong, as state and local commissions later lobbied for the ERA. The BPW prevailed and played a key role in the spread of state branches. Local club women pressured local and state government to establish state and local commissions. In states where the governors refused to create commissions, club women transformed into feminist activists. The process of denying women a civic voice backfired in Maryland and Ohio.

The political environment of the civil rights movement fermented civic action by a variety of groups. This process can be seen in Ohio where the governor provoked numerous activist, labor, and church groups into action, by refusing to name a commission for the state. More than 15 organizations came together to form a citizens' advocacy group to improve the status of women in the state, and a temporary commission was named by the governor. Initially, the commission did not endorse ERA but promoted the idea that the Fourteenth Amendment implicitly protected women's equal rights. African American civil rights attorney Pauli Murray played a key role on the PCSW Subcommittee on Political and Civil Rights and made the argument that Fourteenth Amendment should protect women from "arbitrary discrimination." Murray made it clear that women's rights and racial bias were analogous. While the PCSW avoided the controversy linking racial bias to gender, by omitting discussion in the committee process, Murray moved beyond the PCSW to promote the a new legal strategy of case law focused on the Fourteenth Amendment. Murray also avoided the prickly question of the ERA, and her legal strategy was designed to build consensus among different women's groups. In this way, she clearly linked the struggle for civil rights to women's rights. The creation of state and local commissions across the United States fostered collective feminist activism among diverse groups. For the first time, grassroots activism tied to local state commissions transcended the ERA political divide. Despite some of the earlier disagreements, the PCSW helped to move the feminist agenda forward and represented the beginning in breaking down the feminist divide.[7]

EQUAL PAY ACT OF 1963

The political environment under the Kennedy administration granted the NWB the authority to effectively move equal pay legislation through Congress. Esther Peterson's experience as a labor lobbyist and her appointment to the NWB gave her a definite advantage to move the legislation forward than had her predecessors. Moreover, the rise in demand for female workers in 1950s and the dramatic increase of married women in the labor market justified the need for a federal law that barred discrimination by private employers. By 1961, 24 million women were working, and the Labor Department predicted that women workers would represent the most significant trend in employment in the United States. However, it should be remembered that while married women were entering the labor market in large numbers, women still worked in sex-typed jobs—largely in clerical and service industry jobs—and were paid the lowest wages. In order to convince Congress of the need for an equal pay bill, the NWB needed to gather statistical evidence. They relied on women's organizations and labor unions to provide the data and specific examples of wage discrimination. For the first time, the bureau succeeded in bringing together the diverse interest of women's organizations and the labor movement to support the bill. The BPW and the AAUW were instrumental in providing the research needed to support the bill.

Peterson personally traveled around the country to gather case studies that she could present to Congress. In one conversation a male manager insisted that unequal pay scales were equitable, but later admitted that the reason they paid women less was because they could.

During the congressional hearings, numerous groups endorsed the bill including the PCSW. The NWP also endorsed the bill, but the president, Emma Guffey Miller, privately referred to the bill as the "so-called equal pay act," reflecting the earlier conflict between the NWP and other women's groups over the ERA. Other supporters included Catholic, Jewish, and black women's organizations, and endorsements from high-profile women including Eleanor Roosevelt and film star Betty Davis.

One of the primary sticking points of the legislation focused on the use of the term *comparable worth.* Representative Katharine St. George suggested changing the bill to read "equal pay for equal work." Others feared that the term *equal* implied that men and women were identical and its usage would justify differences in pay. Other concerns focused on enforcement powers, while key Department of Labor officials doubted that men and women actually did equal work. Armed with supporting data from a study conducted by the National Education Association demonstrating clear double standards in pay, Peterson convinced the naysayers in the bureau and in Congress that legislation was indeed justified. The bill finally passed both houses of Congress ending 18 years of legislative lobbying, and on June 10, 1963, President Kennedy signed it into law. Several courts cases followed contesting the meaning of *equal work,* and within 10 years, more than 171,000 employees were awarded more than $84 million in back pay—thus highlighting the need for this legislation.

The Equal Pay Act of 1963 represented a significant watershed in equal rights legislation, and for the first time it forced the federal government to safeguard equal rights in employment. As historian Cynthia Harrison has stated, the law disabused the business sentiment that women only worked for "pin money"—for clothes and the like—and for the first time married women's labor contributions were acknowledged. This legislation had a powerful impact on the emerging feminist movement and would provide a foundation for other legislatives battles focused on equal rights and anti-discrimination. It also helped forge a united women's movement for the ERA.[8]

CIVIL RIGHTS ACT OF 1964

The Civil Rights Act of 1964 and the provisions of Title VII established the principle of human rights across gender, race, ethnicity, national origin, and religion but did not guarantee a positive lower court outcome; it would take several lawsuits and Supreme Court rulings to enforce the law. The congressional debates over the inclusion of sex in Title VII was controversial because for some it watered down the importance of racial discrimination, while establishing a new precedent to undo protective labor legislation based on gender differences. For example, the NWB initially opposed inserting the word *sex* because they believed that race and sex should be treated separately, and treating sex discrimination the same as race discrimination threatened protective legislation. Moreover, race held a higher claim under the proposed legislation. In the same time that the debate over the Fourteenth Amendment evolved in the 19th century, policymakers and lobbyist believed it was once again the "Negro's hour." This perspective created an immediate controversy between groups, and the support for inclusion of the word *sex* was mixed. The NWP and the Women's Division of the United Auto Workers supported the inclusion of sex, while the NWB, Department of Labor, and other business groups were less supportive. While Esther Peterson objected to the bill, Pauli Murray lobbied for inclusion based on the idea that the exclusion of sex would weaken the bill and would reinforce societal neglect of black women. The argument for inclusion won the day, and on July 2, 1964, President Johnson signed the Civil Rights Act into law.

An important part of the law dealt with enforcement, out of which, the Equal Employment Opportunity Commission was formed (EEOC). However, the EEOC did not see sexual employment discrimination as part of their charge and did not initially pursue gender bias lawsuits. In part, the concerns of the EEOC reflected the general view of the NWB and labor concerns over protective labor legislation. Some of the staff of the EEOC held the general belief that the law did not represent a mandate to pursue sex discrimination lawsuits. Even with the clear lack of interest in addressing sex cases, Congress only authorized limited powers, which included investigation of individual complaints, issuance of their findings, and seeking voluntary settlements between employees and employers.

The opinion of the EEOC can be seen in their ruling on segregated employment advertisements in newspapers and other news sources. Title VII clearly banned this type of advertising, and the agency agreed that advertisements for jobs based on race were clearly illegal, but they did not hold the same position on sex-segregated job ads. This debate forced the EEOC to issue full guidelines on sex discrimination, where they made clear that the law did not intend for the commission to disrupt the current labor law structure that protected women's labor and they placed the burden of decision making on state statues. In short, they did believe it was their job to turn over state laws, and they did not think it would result in a massive assault on sex segregated jobs. The position of the EEOC reflected their focus on race discrimination and a real lack of interest in supporting sex discrimination law suits. Esther Peterson warned the EEOC that their position to abandon enforcement of sex-segregated advertising would certainly inspire protest among women's groups. Indeed, this proved to be true, as Representative June Martha Griffith blasted the position of the EEOC on the House floor. Remarking on the choice of the EEOC to use ridiculous examples such as Playboy bunnies to argue for sex-based advertisements, Griffith blasted the EEOC for projecting hostility toward women and denying women basic human rights. A leader in the formation of the Civil Rights Act and prime mover behind the Title VII sex provision, Griffith fostered the emergence of a new feminist movement organized around sexual discrimination and with a new purpose to force the EEOC to take seriously the issues of sexual discrimination.

The imagery of the Playboy bunny and the debate that surrounded labor sex typing and equal opportunity are no small matters. Griffith's outrage on the floor of the House illustrates the challenges that women faced day-to-day in the workforce, and the traditional stereotypes of women as sex toys and property of men was serious at the time. The debates on Capitol Hill and in the press make clear the struggles of the women's movement. Following a White House conference on equal opportunity, the *New York Times* quickly picked up on the complaint that Playboy bunnies would have to employ males. The *Times* dubbed the sex amendment the "Bunny law." The editorial further suggested that Congress should have abolished sex all together and that the use of *man* should be eliminated as well (i.e., milkman, handyman, serviceman, pressman). This commentary is reflective of the fears of some, if not all, men that equality would eliminate their prerogative and power over women's lives. The editorial ended with the comment that the result would be revolution and chaos.[9]

NATIONAL ORGANIZATION OF WOMEN (NOW)

In 1966, just three years after President Kennedy authorized the PCSW, the National Organization of Women (NOW) formed as the first truly feminist organization since the suffrage movement. NOW formed in direct response to the failure of the EEOC to address the problem of sexual discrimination. A small band of Washington policy-makers that included former EEOC commissioner Richard Graham, Esther Peterson, Mary Eastwood, and Catherine East, members of the PCSW, believed that external pressure was needed to change the policies and attitudes of the EEOC. They hoped to build a large coalition of women's groups committed to fight exclusively against sex discrimination, but many of these organizations were hesitant to fight for women's rights. Graham urged Betty Friedan to lead the creation of a national organization, which she initially thought should be done through the state commissions. Friedan was invited to attend the state commission of women's conference in Washington, D.C. At this conference, Graham received word that President Johnson was not reappointing him as commissioner of the EEOC, which led Friedan to organize a small group of conference attendees to discuss the enforcement issues of the EEOC, out of which NOW was born.

The creation of NOW represented a modern watershed for women's rights. From the 1930s onward, only small steps had been taken to give women a political role in government, and the government agenda moved cautiously around traditional views of women's role in society—the NWB focused largely on marriage and children. The formation of NOW demonstrated that women were no longer willing to be dominated by government officials and that women were going to take new control over women's rights. Amid the turmoil within the EEOC in terms of commission replacements, the agency shot itself in the foot again by stating that it would not pursue any discrimination cases involving protective legislation prior to state court decisions. Not only had the EEOC enraged ERA feminists, but now labor women joined the fray. By 1965, working women flooded the commission with their complaints. For example, within the first year, 37 percent of the complaints were based on sexual discrimination, from unequal benefits, pay, hiring and firing, union equity, and state protective legislation.

Friedan was elected as the first president of the organization, and Graham and Aileen Hernandez, the only woman to serve on the EEOC, were elected to serve as vice presidents. NOW was considered by some women's group to be militant, but in reality, NOW's work paralleled the work of the PCSW. The organization membership rose dramatically in the first year, and several state branches formed. NOW became a significant organization, and while they worked in opposition of some women's groups and labor, their position against protective labor legislation influenced the EEOC to consider cases individually rather than waiting for a court judgment on issues related to protective labor. Labor unions objected to the EEOC position, but gradually labor and other groups came to agree that differential treatment of women did more harm than good, and the issue slowly died away.

NOW's early work focused on equal employment opportunity and the EEOC, and as changes were made in the EEOC policies, they were not singularly focused and they lobbied for the ERA and for abortion rights. In 1967, NOW drafted and adopted a bill of rights that pressed Congress to pass an equal rights amendment, demanded that the EEOC take seriously and fully investigate sexual discrimination cases, and identified specific laws that discriminated against women based on their sex, which the organization hoped to see repealed. Some of these included access to contraception information, maternity leave, childcare tax exemptions, and the reform of the welfare system and job training programs for poor women. An important difference between NOW and all other feminist groups that preceded them was their renunciation of biology as the determining factor for social justice. In their statement of purpose, they made clear that men and women had equal part in marriage, in childrearing, and carrying the economic responsibilities. Their program thus provided a coherent philosophy that focused on human rights of men and women and gave them an advantage in pursuing laws that extended equal treatment to all.

NOW worked collaboratively with other women's organizations in order to mount an attack against the legal system. With the help of the Women's Equity Action League (WEAL), it launched a massive campaign against sexual discrimination. By 1970, NOW filed several lawsuits and successfully used the media to raise awareness of the issues and placed pressure on the government to address pay equity and equal opportunity in the workforce. NOW joined forces with the National Women's Political Caucus (NWPC), an organization formed in 1971, to help elect women to public office at all levels. The leaders included Betty Friedan, Bella Abzug, Shirley Chisholm, and Gloria Steinem. NOW succeeded in bringing together the former factions of the earlier equal rights movement, including labor women and the members of the NWP. The pragmatic leadership of Mary Eastwood and Pauli Murray together created a legal strategy that bound Fourteenth Amendment litigation and the ERA together. This was no small feat given the degree of conflict between women's groups and legal organizations. Murray played a key role in convincing longtime American Civil Liberties Union (ACLU) board member Dorothy Kenyon to support the ERA; the ACLU had long refused to endorse the ERA from the 1940s forward on the basis that it would eliminate protective labor legislation for women. Kenyon and Murray had worked together previously to write the discrimination portion of the brief in the jury exclusion case *White v. Cook* (1965). (This case addressed the dual racial and sex discrimination against black women in jury service in Alabama—women of all races were excluded from jury service.) Both women embraced the Fourteenth Amendment litigation strategy and were committed to ending sexual and racial discrimination. Seeds of change brought on by Title VII, which invalidated sex based labor legislation and helped build consensus among former equal rights rivals, and the endorsement of the ACLU in 1970 and the LWV in 1972, signaled a new era in feminist bridge building.[10]

GRASSROOTS COALITIONS AND WOMEN'S LIBERATION

While the national organization can be characterized as a top-heavy lobbying arm for women's rights, the formation of state and local NOW branches created a more diverse opportunity for women to become involved and to effect change at the local level. The combination of local branches provided a rich membership base for the national, and by 1974, it boasted more than 40,000 members, with more than 700 branches.[11] The local branches also supported a more diverse membership base and allowed for local flexibility in the issues they pursued, while creating distinct identities as feminists. As Stephanie Gilmore argued, by looking beyond the standard labels of radical versus liberal feminism, and by studying local branch histories, we can better explore how feminist identity varies and is formed by local issues. Her study on the Memphis, Tennessee, branch of NOW highlights how grassroots activism varied in the South, and compares it against the branches in Columbus, Ohio, and in San Francisco. The Memphis branch was deeply impacted by the civil rights movement as one might expect, and especially the murder of Martin Luther King Jr. African American women in this region focused on discrimination and equality issues based on race more than on gender. With the bifurcation of race in the region and protectionists attitude of white womanhood, NOW found it difficult to attract African American members. Other local issues were more pressing and had more significant impact in building a coalition between black and white feminists in the region than did the national organizations focus on ERA. Nevertheless, black women rallied with NOW to support the ERA in Tennessee, in response to the rescission campaign "STOPERA," organized by Phyllis Schlafly. The most significant coalitions formed to address the problem of rape and domestic wife abuse. The creation the Women's Resource Center (WRC), an umbrella organization representing NOW, YWCA, LWV, Planned Parenthood, and the Church Women United, provided a range of community resources that social services agencies did not, including job training workshops, financial management, and counseling services for divorced women. The program facilitated radical and liberal approaches to feminism, and in this way, became an important coalition for the local community.[12]

Rape was a primary concern for all women's organizations in the city. Memphis had earned the reputation as "rape capital of the nation." According to one report, approximately 534 rapes were reported in 1973, with a range in age of victims from 18 months to 84 years. Thus, the rape crisis in the city shaped coalition building between organizations, and NOW through the WRC helped to create the Comprehensive Rape Crisis Center. Memphis provides an interesting view of the intersections between different women's groups to improve their community through rape crisis intervention and domestic violence support. The local issues of sexual and racial discrimination brought more diverse groups together than did ERA, and the dialog about rape was directly influenced by the women's liberation front. Memphis illustrates how local members of NOW maintained their own local autonomy, while supporting the national campaign.[13]

WOMEN'S LIBERATION

A new tier of younger feminists identified with the women's liberation movement, which can be summed up into three components: consciousness raising, theory making, and social action. The women who identified with the movement of liberation came of age during the 1960s and were influenced by the civil rights movement and were participants in the anti–Vietnam War protests. These women created a new tier of feminists, composed of younger, less-experienced, and radical female college students, who in the course of working for the civil rights movement turned to gender issues and began to actively support equal rights for women. Young people in the 1960s generally distrusted the ability of the older generation to make the social changes needed to make the world a better place, and they did not identify with NOW, which they perceived to be their mothers' movement. These young women brought a different understanding to the problems of sexual discrimination and sexual exploitation. Their ideas grew out of consciousness-raising experiences, where women talked about women's oppression and they shared intimate details about their lives. It was through this process of sharing that women came to understand that collectively they had the power to reshape themselves and society through sisterhood. Small groups of liberationists formed between 1968 and 1969, with one of the larger and more militant groups in New York, but groups popped up across the country. Some of these women identified with radical politics and some emphasized gender neutrality and supported the notion of sexual androgyny, and they questioned patriarchy in society and especially in marriage. Women's liberationist theory grew out the liberation movement, which emerged to try to understand the dynamics of male oppression. Feminist writers Kate Millett in *Sexual Politics* (1970) and Shulmith Firestone in *The Dialectic of Sex: The Case for Feminist Revolution* (1970) focused on historical patriarchy as the cause for women's oppression, and Firestone, a student of Marxism, believed that human conflicts were caused by biology and that women's maternal role created a social and biological prison. Other writers took on the charge to uproot patriarchy by empowering women to take control of their bodies. The Boston Woman's Health Book Collective published *Our Bodies, Ourselves* in 1973, providing women with information about sexuality, menopause, birth control, childbirth, sexual orientation, sexual health, and mental health. The range of ideas about oppression and empowerment was extremely diverse, yet the media tended to categorize all feminists as a coherent group of "women's libbers."[14]

The women's liberation movement, however, joined forces with NOW on a variety of protest campaigns. But for many of these young women, the litigation strategy was too slow, and the generation gap created some tension between younger and more mature women. One younger activist later recalled that she and her friends thought that NOW was an organization for their mothers and believed that it was not action-oriented or interested in building a just society, plus they never trusted anyone over the age of 30. Many of

A women's liberation movement demonstration at City Hall in New York, August 26, 1970. (AP Photo/John Rooney)

these younger women were influenced by the counterculture and
New Left ideas, a few articulated extreme positions that blamed
men for all the evils in the world. One very disturbed woman attempted to murder the artist Andy Warhol for marginalizing her
as an artist. She wrote a manifesto entitled "Society for Cutting Up
Men." The popular press latched onto the radical imagery of feminists as anti-establishment and bra-burning man haters. NOW expressed concern over the extreme views of younger feminists, and
in 1969 they organized the Congress to Unite Women in New York
City, as a means to unite diverse groups of women. A wide range of
organizations and leaders attended the congress to talk about feminist issues, though the younger more radical women dominated
the program.[15]

Consciousness raising played an important role in the emerging
women's liberation movement, representing a new form of social
action among younger women. Consciousness-raising groups pro-

vided a safe environment where small groups of women could meet to talk about their personal experiences as a means to understand female subordination in society. These sessions covered a variety of topics, from menstruation to dating, and the process rested on the notion that the "political is personal." This new form of social protest took to the streets through a variety of public demonstrations, from picketing Playboy to protesting the Miss America pageant in 1968. The latter event culminated with the participants symbolically throwing their bras into a "freedom trash can." From this event, women's libbers were labeled "bra burners," despite the fact that no burning actually took place. The protestors objected to the sexism, racism, and promotion of war. The primary agenda of the movement focused on addressing the oppression of women, and through public action, the hidden injuries that women faced daily, including rape, domestic violence, and sexual harassment were brought to the public's attention. Small groups of this kind formed across the United States, providing a forum for young women to organize protest movements around sexual violence issues. They organized public *speak-outs* to talk about rape, domestic violence, and sexual discrimination. They also challenged the male dominated medical profession, while challenging college curriculum that basically ignored women's presence in society. With the enactment of

Playboy Bunny strike, June 18, 1975. (AP Photo)

Title IX of the National Education Amendments Act of 1972, they pressured higher education to end the gender gap in hiring practices of faculty, and they pushed for women's studies centers on college campuses. Cornell University and San Diego State formed the first programs, and by 1973, several other programs formed, including the San Jose State Women's Studies Program. In reality, it took a diverse movement to push forward legal and social change. NOW and the women's liberation movement needed each other. Real tensions, conflicts, and division by generation existed, yet NOW played an important role in promoting leadership and lobby skills, as well as taking the lead on legislation, while the collective action of women's liberation groups through speak-outs raised public awareness of the sexual crimes against women.[16]

STRIKE FOR EQUALITY

The Women's Strike for Equality in 1970 is a good example of different coalitions of women coming together to make a national statement about feminism and united around core demands for equality. This event took place on the 50th anniversary of the 1920 suffrage victory. The strike was intended to serve as a symbolic reminder of women's rights, and the three central demands included the right to abortion, childcare, and equal opportunity in employment and education. Across the U.S. women went on strike, refusing to work, marched, picketed, and held teach-ins and rallies. This event sparked new interest from women who had previously not identified with feminism. According to the news coverage and the increased membership of NOW, the strike was a terrific success; NOW's membership swelled by 50 percent following the event, and the nation learned that women's liberation was not a passing fad. The second-wave movement represented a diversity of viewpoints.

The demand by radical feminists for free abortions on demand and free childcare centers illustrates the significance that reproductive freedom had on this generation. As a result of these demands, the ERA and abortion rights dominated the feminist agenda in the 1970s. These two issues pushed feminism onto the national political stage, building support from a diverse group, while fueling a minority movement that opposed both the ERA and abortion rights. As new ground was being made in Congress and later through the ratification process, a group of feminist lawyers continued to work through the courts to pursue equal rights through the equal protection clause in the Fourteenth Amendment. Among this group of activists, Ruth Bader Ginsberg, law professor and ACLU attorney (future supreme court justice), drawing upon the previous arguments made by Pauli Murray and Dorothy Kennyon in *Reed v. Reed* (1971), argued against the Idaho statute that gave preference to men in estate administration cases. In the original case, Sally Reed and her former husband both sought to become the administrator of their deceased son's estate. Under Idaho law, the court gave preference to men over women in estate administration. The Supreme Court ruling struck down the decision of the state court based on the protection provided by the Fourteenth Amendment. Reed served as the first case where classification by sex merited judicial review. This victory represented a baby step toward court rulings that applied special review based on sex. *Reed* started the process of building case precedent to liberalize laws that were gender biased. The success of equal rights legal cases created a dilemma in providing a real justification for the ERA.[17]

EQUAL RIGHTS AMENDMENT (ERA)

By the early 1970s, the rise of new organizations and growth of feminine consciousness dramatically increased the awareness of sexual discrimination, and on March 22, 1972, Congress finally passed the ERA. The Amendment guaranteed that "Equality of rights under the law shall not be denied or abridged by the United States or by any State on account of sex." The language closely resembled the original amendment introduced to Congress in 1923 by the NWP. The issue of protective legislation had resolved itself, and the ERA supporters made it clear that the amendment would not interfere in labor law reform. The one issue that remained unresolved, however, involved the application of the Fourteenth Amendment's equal protection clause to cases involving sexual discrimination. Congress passed the ERA and sent it to the states for ratification, and 21 states quickly ratified the bill. The momentum slowed, and by the year's end, battle lines began to form and the opposition to ratification succeeded in stalling the final three votes needed for a three-fourths majority necessary to ratify the amendment. By 1978, 35 states had ratified it, but that fell short by three for the requisite number of states needed to meet the three-fourths requirement to become law. A loud and organized minority opposition movement mobilized, which doomed the final ratification process. Between the years 1977 and 1979, 5 states, Nebraska, Tennessee, Idaho, Kentucky, and South Dakota, rescinded their votes. The ratification contest emerged concomitantly with the rise of the political and religious fundamentalism that took root in the 1970s and 1980s. While polls indicated wide support in favor of the amendment, ERA supporters, the birth of the new Right and its *moral majority* rallied a fierce opposition movement, and by 1982, they had successfully derailed the ratification of the amendment.[18]

RELIGIOUS FUNDAMENTALISM/ ANTI-FEMINISM

Phyllis Schlafly led the opposition based on the argument that the ERA would negatively impact traditional gender relationships and expectations. Her concerns represented a critique of feminism. In 1977, the government sponsored a National Women's Convention (NWC) in Houston to brainstorm on women's issues. The conference attendees endorsed a full program of women's rights, including the support of ERA, federally funded childcare, minors' access to contraception, federally funded abortions, and gay rights. Schlafly used the results of this conference to build a coalition of Republican activists and conservative women to support the opposition movement. Schlafly, an accomplished author, Republican activist, and a 1952 congressional candidate, had herself never embraced domesticity. She worked on the Barry Goldwater campaign and wrote *A Choice, Not an Echo*, which sold more than 600,000 copies in the first edition. Through the circulation of the *Phyllis Schlafly Report*, she made known her views that the ERA would undo family life, force women into combat, adversely impact childrearing, and eliminate financial responsibilities of men in supporting their families. She formed the organization STOP-ERA in 1972 and the *Eagle Forum* in 1975, which became an important grassroots lobbying arm to fight ERA.

Schlafly crisscrossed the country speaking against ERA, raised awareness of the issues in key states, organized local volunteers to campaign, and addressed ERA issues in 30 state legislatures. Schlafly relied on her connections to the National Federation of Republican Women, and most of the volunteers she recruited had had local experience in political campaigning. The early campaign represented a very small minority of Republican women and a few homemakers empowered by the rise of the fundamentalist (new right) movement they established a new constituency. Evangelical churches provided a strong community base to organize against the ERA, including providing meeting places and transportation, and they successfully garnered funds and energy from their members. Schlafly mobilized the fundamentalists to demonstrate against ERA, which proved to be largely successful, despite the reality that national and local polls showed a majority support for the amendment. Through the use of sophisticated lobbying and by reaching out to the religious communities of the moral majority, Schlafly succeeded in winning more than 15 states to oppose the Amendment and got 5 states to rescind their original vote in favor of it. Moreover, the Republican Party reversed its historic endorsement of the ERA.

The battle for ERA from 1923 to 1982 demonstrated the continuity of feminism following the suffrage victory in 1920. Both waves faced similar challenges in promoting a federal amendment focused on women's equality, although articulated differently. The history of the ERA reveals the complexity of social change and diversity of opinions on gender roles and responsibilities. Where the early movement faced opposition based on protective labor legislation, the modern movement opposition focused on Christian morality and preservation of traditional gender roles. Feminists of the later movement faced other challenges and opportunities. In real terms, gender relationships had just started to change, and while they did not succeed in the ratification process, their protests and lobbying efforts opened the floodgate for social justice legislation and advanced women's participation in politics. In 1982 following the failed ratification of the ERA, the National Council of Women's Organizations (NCWO) formed as a nonpartisan network of 200 organizations, representing 10 million members. In 1991, they formed the ERA Campaign Network to promote a "three-state strategy" for ratification. In March 27, 2007, two resolutions were introduced to the House and Senate. Representative Carolyn B. Maloney (D-NY) and Representative Jerrold Nadler (D-NY) introduced to the House HJ Res 40, and Senator Ted Kennedy (D-MA) and Senator Barbara Boxer (D-CA) introduced to the Senate SJ Res 10, indicating that the ERA campaign continue into the 21st century.[19]

REPRODUCTIVE RIGHTS— ABORTION—WOMEN'S HEALTH

The 1960s and 1970s represented a period in time that questioned gender roles and traditions in society and culture. The women's liberation movement played a significant role in this process, as did the sexual revolution of the era, and the introduction of the birth control pill in 1960. Activists pressed the boundaries of the birth control movement and abortion rights to the national forefront. The history of birth control and abortion has a long history, but it would take several decades before birth control and abortion laws were liberalized. In the late 1960s and early 1970s, a small group of activists challenged states laws, and by the 1970s, 11 states had liberalized their abortion laws—with New York and California taking the lead. Nonetheless, it was not until the women's liberation movement joined hands with abortion rights activist that the movement to repeal all laws that limited women's rights to abortion took hold. In 1970, it was estimated that 1 million women had illegal abortions, and many of these abortions were botched by doctors and midwives. Some states allowed for legal abortions under certain circumstances, such as rape, incest, and when the woman's life was at risk during childbirth. The demand for sexual determination and sexual freedom sparked the abortion rights movement. Abortion activists sought to liberalize the legal loopholes and pushed for the complete elimination of state laws that regulated women's bodies. Previous to this period birth control pioneers Margaret Sanger and Estelle Griswold pushed for legal

Women picket in support of abortion rights as part of a campaign to repeal Missouri's abortion laws in St. Louis, March 8, 1972. (AP Photo)

rights to distribute birth control.

Even in the postwar years, in some states married women could not legally purchase birth control. In the case *Griswold v. Connecticut* (1965), Estelle Griswold, executive director of Planned Parenthood League of Connecticut, was arrested for distributing birth control to married women. Her case relied on the due process clause, and in 1968, the court struck down the state statute that prohibited access to birth control. Griswold opened the constitutional gateway to overturn state laws that criminalized abortion through the famous case *Roe v. Wade* (1973). In this landmark decision, the court made one of the most significant rulings supporting women's rights. The ruling made clear that women had the right to make decisions about their reproductive health, which eliminated forced sterilization of poor women and women of color. For Native American women and especially Puerto Rican women, health officials pressured them to agree to sterilization—representing one-third of women of childbearing age in these communities. Most of these women lived in extreme poverty and were dependent on state welfare. State health officials encouraged sterilization under the guise of state savings programs. The high number of women sterilized in these groups amounted to racial genocide. The sterilization abuse catapulted the abortion rights movement into a larger movement about women's reproductive rights and personal health.[20]

RELIGION AND ABORTION

Just as the ERA created an anti-movement, the anti-abortion movement grew in parallel with the ERA campaign. The religious right aligned ERA and abortion together, arguing that the ERA would increase the number of abortions and would lead to women being drafted into the military. Where the religious right succeeded in derailing the ratification process of the ERA, they were not as successful in undoing *Roe v. Wade* completely. The pro-life movement began under the leadership of the Catholic Church, which formed the National Right to Life Committee, but the movement shifted quickly to Protestant fundamentalist Christians. The activists in this movement believed that abortion trampled on motherhood, and they believed that the women who made these choices were selfish or victimized by abortionist doctors. Within a few short years of *Roe,* the pro-choice movement organized an aggressive attack through consistent protests in front of Planned Parenthood Offices, clinics, and hospitals where abortions were underway.

They used intimidation tactics against doctors, nurses, and clinic personnel, leading to a severe reduction of open clinics and doctors willing to perform abortions. Some of these activists radicalized by the belief that abortion represented a holocaust against unborn babies, threatened the personnel, bombed different clinics, and murdered abortion providers. By the 1980s, Congress began to pass legislation that watered down *Roe,* by placing limits on who could get an abortion, required parental permission, and denial of public funds to support abortions, and in 2003, President Bush signed federal law banning late-term abortions. The impact of the anti-abortion movement and the ERA illustrate how minority groups can take hold of a piece of legislation and challenge the majority position; murder of clinic doctors and staff continues to this day. By the 1980s and 1990s, the power of the second-wave movement diffused as a result of the growth of the religious right and anti-feminist political landscape. Well known journalist and feminist Susan Faludi wrote about this decline and the impact that right-wing politics had on the feminist movement in her book *Backlash: The Undeclared War on American Women* (1991). The 1990s would see another feminist revival, particularly in politics and in promoting social justice for women in the workplace and eliminating sexual violence—these issues became the charge of the third and fourth waves of feminism.[21]

WORKPLACE HARASSMENT

As we have seen, women's equality rested on the activism of different groups in pursuing litigation to change state and federal laws. The work of NOW to force the EEOC to address equal opportunity for women raised the consciousness of ordinary women to file lawsuit after lawsuit. A similar process was used to address the pervasive problem of sexual harassment in the workforce. Catharine MacKinnon, a feminist legal scholar and civil rights attorney, became the legal architect of sexual harassment legislation. MacKinnon wrote several books on the topic, including *Sexual Harassment of Working Women* (1979), where she argued that sexual harassment constituted sexual discrimination under Title VII of the Civil Rights Act of 1964. MacKinnon litigated the first Supreme Court case on domestic violence in *Meritor Savings Bank v. Vinson* (1986), where the court agreed that discrimination based on sex created a hostile work environment and thus violated Title VII. This benchmark case was supported by earlier cases and similar legal strategies that

Crowd at a women's rights movement rally on August 26, 1971. (Bett-mann/CORBIS)

involved a diverse group of activists. While MacKinnon played an important role as a litigator and popular author, it is important to recognize that it took a group of ordinary women to file lawsuits against their employers and their cases provided the legal basis for *Meritor.* The filing of individual lawsuits by women in the 1970s provided the case law precedent, but it was the activism of the women's movement that challenged EEOC policies, and the creation of specific organizations to raise awareness of the problem, that challenged the male status quo in determining appropriate behavior in the workplace. The history of this movement has tended to focus on the role of middle-class white women activists, yet the early cases illustrate how women of color and blue-collar women participated as plaintiffs in lawsuits.

The first wave of activism against sexual harassment began with three lawsuits filed by black women, and the legal briefs highlighted how black women faced racial and sexual discrimination; of these early cases all of the female plaintiffs were fired for refusing the sexual advances of their employers. From 1974 to 1976, six federal district courts had issued their opinions on six cases. Out of these six cases, only one ruled that sexual harassment equated sex discrimination—the majority opined that sexual harassment was not a ubiquitous problem, but an isolated occurrence, and was not gender based or relevant to employment. The first federal case to rule in favor of the victim under Title VII took place with *Williams v. Saxbe* (1976)—an important groundbreaking decision. The groundswell of activism against sexual harassment influenced the eventual decision in *Meritor.* Two of the first organization to form around these issues included Working Women United (WWU) in Ithaca, New York, and the Alliance Against Coercion (AAC) in Cambridge, Massachusetts. These organizations used consciousness raising events to discuss the problem with different groups of women and organized speak-outs to break the silence and to build public awareness of the issues. It soon became clear that the problem was widespread. The AAC offered crisis intervention counseling services, conducted extensive research on the problems and causes of sexual harassment, and expanded from the theoretical to the practical process of helping victims. By 1977, the problem of sexual harassment was covered by the national press, when *Ms.* magazine cosponsored a speak-out with the WWU in New York. Some 200 women attended this event, and coverage from the *New York Times* and television coverage raised public awareness of the problem, resulting in new federal and state legislation to eliminate sexual harassment in the workplace. The broad-based activism against sexual harassment is an example of how different coalitions of women came together to force policy change.[22]

WOMEN IN POLITICS

One of the most significant growth areas for women between the 1960s and 1990s was in the arena of politics. The Kennedy administration opened a new door to female political appointments and the creation of the PCSW had a profound affect on the political landscape. Indeed, the second movement produced political milestones in local and national politics. In 1968, Shirley Chisholm became the first African American woman to be elected to Congress. By 1972, the Democratic National Convention had three times as many women delegates compared to 1968. In 1974 and again in 1978, Janet Gray Hayes was the first woman in the United States to be elected mayor of a city of 500,000 people. As a result, Gray Hayes received incredible local and national publicity and helped position Santa Clara County to become known as the "Feminist Capital of the World." This combined with the success of other female candidates across the United States led a number of national magazines to run stories on the role of women, feminism, and politics. *Time, People, U.S. News and World Report,* and even some international papers carried stories highlighting the success of these female candidates. Gray Hayes was featured in a number of articles, alongside Diane Feinstein of San Francisco; Jane Byrne of Chicago; Isabella Cannon of Raleigh, North Carolina; Carole McCellan of Austin, Texas; and Margaret Hance of Phoenix, Arizona. In 1979, *U.S News and World Report* ran a story highlighting the recent victories of women in politics across the United States. According to this report, 750 cities had female mayors out of 18,800 municipalities—women were making clear inroads into politics at all levels. From 1975 to 1979, the number of women in public office increased from 4.7 percent to 10.9 percent, with the largest increase at the local and state levels. For many of these women, the formation of the NWPC in 1971 provided political support and served as a fundraising arm to help women succeed in local, state, and national political campaigns.[23]

Female candidates were also motivated to enter the political fray as result of the historic NWC held in Houston in November of 1977—known as "The Spirit of Houston." This event marked a historic moment in women's political history in that Congress funded the conference, and more than 20,000 women, men, and children attended. The conference grew out of the United Nation's declaration of the International Women's Year in 1975, and the diversity of the participants represented true democratic governance. The conference took place during the height of the mobilization behind the ERA, and the conference mandate was to discuss and endorse legislation for federal, state, and local governments. Representative Bella Abzug (D-NY) authored Public Law 94–167, and she introduced the bill to Congress along with 14 other female members of the house; at this time, the Senate was composed of an all-male body. On December 10, 1975, President Ford signed the bill into law, and the National Commission on the Observance of International Women's Year (NCOIWY) was formed.

In 1977, President Carter appointed a new and more inclusive membership that included union, racial, ethnic, and lesbian appointments. Organizing the Houston conference involved forming state and territorial committees where delegates were elected and issues were recommended for the conference. The NWC was not without controversy, at the state level conferences, the right-wing opposition was fierce. Despite the conflict over specific issues, particularly related to ERA and to reproductive freedom, the meetings brought together approximately 150,000 diverse groups of women (and men), and they contributed to the National Plan of Action, which consisted of 26 planks, covering themes in the area of violence against women, economic discrimination, health issues, civil rights, education, and political representation. Some of the most important planks addressed rape, domestic, violence, child abuse, childcare, credit, welfare and poverty, reproductive freedom, and the ERA. Most all of the planks received support from 80 percent of the delegate assembly. Reproductive rights and the ERA were the most controversial issues, and openly opposed by the right-wing. Houston, nonetheless, advanced American democracy by providing diverse groups an opportunity to participate and to identify key issues of concern to women and their families. Houston also reflected the strength of feminism in the 1970s decade, but as historians have since shown, the legacy of Houston, the failure of the ratification of the ERA, and the rise of the New Right (Christian Right) and policies of the Reagan White House, shifted national support of women's issues and forced women and supportive men to focus on local coalitions. Despite the feminist backlash that took place in the 1980s, Houston stands out as a landmark event, bringing federal support and national recognition of women's contributions to society. Gloria Steinem in the conference official report *What Women Want* wrote that Houston represented an important landmark in women's history, just as Seneca Falls had been for 19th-century feminism.[24]

The history of social protest and feminism went hand in hand. For many women of this era, identity politics would influence how different groups connected to the larger and more vocal white middle-class movement. Laboring feminists, women of color, and lesbians found their political voice in a variety of formats. Laboring women rallied around wage justice issues, representing a rainbow coalition that included blue-collar and pink-collar women, race, ethnicity, and class. As the labor statistics demonstrate, most women worked in sex-typed occupations, representing the lowest-paid labor, and most were working below the poverty line. The wage labor movement in the early postwar years focused on protective labor legislation, but by the 1960s, wage justice for all became a priority. In the 1980s, the movement continued to address wage inequities and discrimination caused by gendered job descriptions through the comparable worth movement that proposed to rectify job classifications by upgrading pay scales in female dominated jobs. In San Jose, California, city public work employees' and city librarians' (pink-collar workers) local unions initiated the first comparable worth strike in the United States on April 6, 1979. San Jose had consistently discriminated against women by paying substandard wages based on segregated labor classifications. For example, a male groundskeeper made $17,521 a year, while a female clerk typist made $14,300 a year. In positions where a similar level of education was required, women were always paid less—a good comparison is the salary differentials paid to midlevel city workers and to librarians. In 1981, Local 101 composed of public works employees and pink-collar workers went on strike, and for the first time in city history, the librarians received fair wages for their level of education. Mayor Janet Gray Hayes fought strongly to address the pay inequities in the city and issued a statement confirming the importance of pay equity for women.

As we have seen previously, unions worked to address the hiring practices that discriminated against married women, particularly in blue-collar trades. By the 1950s clear progress had been made in this sector, while white-collar and pink-collar sectors still had to press for change. Marriage and motherhood was considered a liability for certain areas of white-collar employment, and particularly in teaching. School districts across the nation persisted in firing married teachers who became pregnant, on the basis that pregnancy raised the wrong questions from students on sexuality, but more importantly, school districts echoed the belief that women should be home raising their children. The sexism that embodied education took on a more severe application in the airline industry. The airline industry hiring practices focused on hiring only young and attractive women to work as airline hostesses. The industry hiring policies prohibited married women, though many were married on the sly, they could not have children, and women who did were fired. They also imposed age and weight restrictions. Despite the high level of union membership among flight attendants, protest against these policies did not emerge until the 1970s. The Association of Flight Attendants, which formed in 1973, successfully fought for contracts and new policies that eliminated weight and age requirements, marital status and childbearing, while eliminating the job title of "airline hostess" to "flight attendant."[25]

IDENTITY POLITICS

Meanwhile, identity politics and opposition to the Vietnam War shaped the emergence of racial, ethnic, and sexual politics inside the women's liberation movement. In some cases, groups formed outside of the mainstream, while there are plenty of examples of bridge politics taking place to fight for specific legislation or to raise awareness of social problems such as the ERA, rape, domestic violence, racial violence, and so on. Some of these movements or feminisms took on militant forms. The black power movement stands out as the most militant and most separatist in its organizational philosophy, which advocated black nationalism. Malcolm X became the voice of the nationalist movement working through the Nation of Islam. The formation of the Black Panther Party in Oakland, California, challenged mainstream social protest movements, by taking up arms for community defense against the police. Few women dominated as leaders, though Angela Davis became an icon of the black power movement and women's liberation. Black power had some influence on the women's liberation front, in that it inspired young women to promote agency through direct action, and it empowered them to liberate themselves from oppression. Chicana, American Indian, Asian, and lesbian women similarly engaged in identity politics, more than they engaged with mainstream feminism. In the case of lesbians, they were members of other racial or ethnic identity groups. Inside group politics, these diverse groups of women challenged the sexism and homophobia of the male family members.[26]

Activists parade up Sixth Avenue in a protest march for gay rights, June 8, 1977, New York. (AP Photo/Carlos Rene Perez)

ANTIWAR MOVEMENT

The Vietnam War inspired the formation of new student civil rights organizations like the Students for Democratic Society (SDS) to organize and protest the war. Between 1969 and 1970, SDS and other groups had taken to the streets to protest the war in Vietnam and the military draft. It has been estimated that 2 million men and women engaged in street protests of this kind, and by the spring of 1970, student protest escalated with the killing of four students by the National Guard at Kent State University, followed by another protest and killing of two African American students at Jackson State University. Antiwar protests took place on every college campus in the United States, which resulted in conflicts between law enforcement and student protestors.

Antiwar sentiments among women have a long history in the United States, and in the 20th century date back to World War I and through pacifist leaders like Jane Addams. Addams helped form the Women's International League for Peace and Freedom (WLIPF), which provided a small venue for female antiwar activism. In the modern era, the Women Strike for Peace (WSP) brought together a diverse group of women organized to protest nuclear arms race. The first strike took place on November 1, 1961, with more than 50,000 women in cities across the United States sponsored peace vigils, petition drives, and letter-writing campaigns to Congress and the president. Many of the participants were connected to Communist Party or were members of the Committee for a Sane Nuclear Policy (SANE), while others left WILPF because of its hierarchy. WSP had long embraced the argument that peace was a maternal issue, and they used motherhood as a badge to support anti-nuclear testing. When they were forced to testify before the House Committee on Un-American Activities (HUAC) in 1961, they made clear that their purpose was not subversive but directly tied to child welfare and their interests as mothers to protect and nurture their children. In January of 1968, WSP organized the Jeannette Rankin Brigade, named in honor of the first congresswoman in the United States and a lifelong peace activist. Rankin voted against World Wars I and II. The brigade gathered in Washington, D.C., with some 5,000 women in attendance, including 87-year-old honoree Jeannette Rankin. Not all of the participants shared the same ideals, but each group used the strike as a means to protest the powerlessness generated by the motherhood debate and to protest the war; women's liberationists did not endorse the maternal ideology.[27]

CONCLUSION

As historian Ruth Rosen has written, the 1960s–1980s witnessed a new surge of feminist activism that split the world open, by forcing significant legislative changes that have improved the lives of women and society. From the formation of the PCSW, the Equal Pay Act of 1963, the Civil Rights Act of 1964, feminists emerged stronger than they had in previous generations. The feminist revolution brought to the fore a new generation of women who refused to sit back and wait for government intervention. Instead, they demanded the government to enforce Title VII, protecting women from gender and sexual discrimination. Moreover, the passage of Title IX under the Education Act opened unprecedented opportunities for female faculty and student athletes. The formation of the NWPC provided the base for the increase in the number of women elected to higher office. The reproductive rights of women, from the ability to access birth control and to their ability to self-determine whether they continued a pregnancy transformed women's personal lives in untold measure. The 1977 NWC, known as "The Spirit of Houston," challenged federal and local governments to address a variety of women's issues at state and local levels, and the introduction of the Pill and *Roe v. Wade* recognized women's rights to control their bodies.

Women have come a long way since the early 20th century. The suffrage victory provided an important milestone for women to press for social, political, and economic change, and to pursue different paths toward equality. The social movements of the Progressive Era provided different gateways for women to pursue gender justice. The path to equality was rocky, yet new social movements that emerged during the civil rights era and antiwar period provided new opportunities for diverse communities of women to fight for full civil rights.

NOTES

1. Karen Offen, ed., *Globalizing Feminisms, 1789–1945* (Routledge, 2010), pp. 1–2.

2. Cynthia Harrison, *On Account of Sex: The Politics of Women's Issues 1945–1968* (UC Press, 1988), pp. 187–91; Kathryn Kish Sklar, "How Have Recent Social Movements Shaped Civil Rights Legislation for Women? The 1994 Violence Against Women Act," in *Women and Social Movements in the U.S., 1600–2000*, eds., Kathryn Kish Sklar and Thomas Dublin, pp. 1–10 (State University of New York, 2007).

3. Joanne Meyerowitz, "Beyond the Feminist Mystique: A Reassessment of Postwar Mass Culture, 1946–1958," in *Not June Clever: Women and Gender in Postwar America, 1945–1960*, ed., Joanne Meyerowitz, p. 230 (Temple University Press, 1994).

4. Meyerowitz, "Beyond the Feminine Mystique," pp. 229–46.

5. Harrison, *On Account of Sex*, pp. 7–12.

6. Harrison, *On Account of Sex*, pp. 86–87.

7. Harrison, *On Account of Sex*, pp. 182–83.

8. Harrison, *On Account of Sex*, pp. 89–105.

9. Harrison, *On Account of Sex*, pp. 28–29, 88–87, 185–91; Dorothy Sue Cobble, "Labor Feminists and President Kennedy's Commission on the Status of Women," in *No Permanent Waves: Recasting Histories of U.S. Feminism*, Nancy A. Hewitt ed., pp. 144–51 (Rutgers University Press, 2010).

10. Harrison, *On Account of Sex*, pp. 192–209; Serena Mayeri, "How and Why was Feminist Legal Strategy Transformed, 1960–1973," in *Women and Social Movements in the U.S., 1600–2000*, eds., Kathryn Kish Sklar and Thomas Dublin, pp. 1–11 (State University of New York, 2007).

11. Harrison, *On Account of Sex*, pp. 192–207.

12. Harrison, *On Account of Sex*, pp. 192–207.

13. Stephanie Gilmore, "The Dynamics of Second-Wave Feminist Activism in Memphis, 1971–1982," *NWSA* 15.1 (2003): 94–117.

14. Ellen Carol Dubois and Lynn Dumenil, *Through the Eyes of Women: An American History with Documents* (Bedford/St. Martin Press, 2004), pp. 639–40.

15. Ruth Rosen, *The World Split Open: How the Modern Women's Movement Changed America* (Viking Press, 2000), pp. 84–85.

16. Ibid.; Dubois, *Through the Eyes of Women*, pp. 639–40.

17. Rosen, *The World Spilt Open*, pp. 92–93.

18. Harrison, *On Account of Sex*, pp. 109–26; Dubois, *Through the Eyes of Women*, pp. 649–54.

19. Dubois, *Through the Eyes of Women*, pp. 649–54.

20. Dubois, *Through the Eyes of Women*, pp. 646–54.

21. Dubois, *Through the Eyes of Women*, pp. 652–54.

22. Carrie Baker, "How Did Diverse Activists in the Second Wave of the Women's Movement Shape Emerging Public Policy on Sexual Harassment?," in *Women and Social Movements in the U.S., 1600–2000*, eds., Kathryn Kish Sklar and Thomas Dublin, pp. 1–12 (State University of New York, 2007).

23. Glenna Matthews, *Silicon Valley, Women, and the California Dream: Gender, Class and Opportunity in the Twentieth Century* (Stanford University Press, 2003), pp. 183–225.

24. Kathryn Kish Sklar and Thomas Dublin, "How Did National Women's Conference in Houston in 1977 Shape an Agenda for the Future," in *Women and Social Movements in the U.S., 1600–2000*, Kathryn Kish Sklar, and Thomas Dublin, eds., pp. 1–16 (State University of New York, 2007).

25. Dorothy Sue Cobble, *The Other Women's Movement: Workplace Justice and Social Rights in Modern America* (Princeton University Press, 2004), pp. 75–77.

26. Benita Roth, *Separate Roads to Feminism; Black, Chicana, White Feminists Movements in America's Second Wave* (Cambridge University Press, 2004).

27. Andrea Estepa, "'Taking the White Gloves Off' Women Strike for Peace and 'the Movement,' 1967–1973," in *Feminist Coalitions: Historical Perspectives on Second-Wave Feminism in the United States,* ed., Stephanie Gilmore, pp. 84–112 (University of Illinois Press, 2008).

7

ANTIWAR MOVEMENT, RACE, ETHNICITY, RELIGION, AND SEXUALITY

This chapter will focus on the social movements that emerged out of the Vietnam War era. These movements emerged as a response to the Cold War era mentality of suppression and containment. Several key events led to a massive student antiwar movement, including the freedom rides; voter registration; the horror of the Birmingham protests; the murders of JFK, Martin Luther King Jr., Robert Kennedy Jr., and Malcolm X; the escalation of the Vietnam War; and the institution of the draft. The college students who came of age during this period of turbulence and violence refused to maintain the status quo of their parents, and massive student protests spread across U.S. college campuses.

Between 1965 and the early 1970s, Students for a Democratic Society (SDS) and other groups had taken to the streets to protest the war in Vietnam and the military draft. It has been estimated that 2 million men and women engaged in street protests of this kind, and by the spring of 1970, student protest escalated with the killings at Kent State and Jackson State, resulting in massive antiwar protest on more than 760 college campuses across the United States. This chapter will look at how these social protests against the war impacted higher education, and how communities, the government, and college administrations reacted to campus unrest, and the impact that some of these conflicts had on college life. As described earlier in chapter 4, groups like SDS and Student Nonviolent Co-ordinating Committee (SNCC) helped to organize campus protest, and the convergence of identity politics, feminism, antiwar sentiments, and the civil rights movement challenged the traditional values of middle-class America and the status quo that favored male white authority and power.

This chapter will explore more fully the impact of women on the antiwar act, and will specifically look at the Women's Strike for Peace (WSP) that took place in 1961 and the Women's March for Peace in 1968—also know as the Jeannette Rankin Brigade. The antiwar protest movement through specific civil rights organizations like the SNCC—1960, SDS, and the Free Speech Movement (FSM), who provided college students a new venue to organize behind antiwar protests and to demand their civil rights.

We will also look at the emergence of group identity politics, which grew out of the struggles for civil rights by African Americans and Hispanics, and extended to other ethnic groups from Native Americans, Asians, Puerto Ricans, and the gay community. Out of these diverse struggles new coalitions of social activists emerged to press for social justice and for societal recognition of the multicultural landscape and value and respect different cultural traditions and life styles. Coalition building among feminists from different racial, ethnic, religious, and sexual orientations found common ground in the sexual oppression of women and ongoing gender discrimination in the workforce. The movement to address violence against women, anti-rape campaigns, abortion rights, welfare rights, working women's rights, and the fight for national legislation to address sexual harassment and domestic violence, paint a diverse picture of the varieties of social movements and feminisms that demanded equal rights at all levels.

We will consider how identity politics and opposition to the Vietnam War shaped the emergence of racial, ethnic, and sexual politics inside the women's liberation movement. In some cases, groups formed outside of the mainstream, while there are plenty of examples of bridge politics taking place to fight for specific legislation or to raise awareness of social problems such as the Equal Rights Amendment (ERA), rape, domestic violence, racial violence, and so on. Some of these movements or *feminisms* took on militant forms. The black power movement stands out as the most militant and most separatist in its organizational philosophy, which advocated black nationalism. Malcolm X became the voice of the nationalist movement working through the Nation of Islam. The formation of the

Black Panther Party in Oakland, California, challenged mainstream social protest movements, by taking up arms for community defense against the police. Few women dominated as leaders, but Angela Davis became an icon of the black power and radical feminism. While women were frequently oppressed within male-dominated movements, their experiences on the freedom rides, voter registration drives, and as members in more militant groups influenced the growth of the women's liberation front. Young women were inspired to promote agency through direct action, and it empowered them to liberate themselves from oppression. Out of this liberation, women identified with specific communities that were shaped by race, class, ethnicity, gender, sexual orientation, and by religious affiliation. This process of social organization is known as *identity politics.* In some cases Chicana, black, Asian, Native American, and lesbians created separate organizing structures to fight against racial, ethnic, and sexual oppression and were not necessarily aligned with mainstream feminist organizations like the National Organization of Women (NOW). In some cases, there are rich examples where women formed different coalitions to address specific problems, such as rape, welfare aid, sexual abuse, and domestic violence, while maintaining specific racial, ethnic, and sexual identities. In the case of lesbians, they were members of other racial or ethnic identity groups, and inside group politics, women challenged sexism and homophobia within a diverse cultural milieu.

BABY BOOM GENERATION

The generation of children that came of age in the 1960s can be tied to the postwar-era focus on building domestic security through the family. The literature of the period emphasized the imagery of the family as the bedrock to economic and global security. Marriage rates increased dramatically following World War II, and the fertility rates and the size of the average American family went up significantly, creating a baby boom. Young couples in the 1950s married younger and had much larger families than the generations before them. The trend in the 1930s was a reduction in the size of the family, with 2.4 childbirth rate average, compared to 3.2 births in the early 1950s. This baby boom thus created the largest population of college age students in the history of the United States, which fed into the antiwar movement.[1]

This baby boom generation created the powder keg that became the 1960s experience. The presidential election of John F. Kennedy offered America a New Frontier, of foreign and domestic policies that would encouraged a new generation of young adults to flock to Washington, D.C., to participate in new agencies such as the Peace Corps. For example, in 1960, Susan Hammer and Phil Hammer left their college life at UC Berkeley behind and traveled to Washington, D.C., to work for the Kennedy presidential campaign, and both worked in positions to promote the New Frontier. Their experience provides a snap-shot view of the incredible optimism that emerged from Kennedy's election. Susan Hammer recalled the excitement that she and her husband felt as they moved across country to participate in creating change. Susan found a position working for the Peace Corps administration, while Phil Hammer worked for the Human Rights Commission. Much later Susan Hammer entered local government and became a two-term mayor for the city of San Jose from 1990 to 1998. Other young people made the same commitment working on government civil rights programs.

The death of Kennedy catapulted Lyndon Baines Johnson to the presidency and the New Frontier became the Great Society. Johnson's first two years in office brought significant social progress with the great society programs that resulted in sweeping legislative victories with the Civil Rights Act of 1964, the Voting Rights Act of 1965, and the establishment of Medicare and Medicaid, and numerous federal work programs and urban renewal projects in major U.S. cities.

The glow of what historians have named Camelot under Kennedy did not last long, and the vision of Johnson's Great Society fell apart as he focused his attention on the war in Vietnam. Following Kennedy's assassination in 1963, and the victory of the 1964 Civil Rights Act, it appeared that real changes were coming. Johnson initially promised not to send American troops to Vietnam, but following alleged attacks against the United States, he convinced Congress to send ships to the Tonkin Gulf, and Congress granted him unlimited presidential power in the region to protect American soldiers. By the end of 1965, 170,000 soldiers were sent to Vietnam, and by 1967, the number increased to 464,000. In 1968, Nixon ran on the promise that he would end the war, but in 1970, he announced his plan to invade Cambodia. Thus, from 1965 through the 1970s, antiwar student protests spread across college campuses through out the United States. In the first few years, the protests were mostly peaceful and consisted of candlelight vigils, petition drives, and lobbying Congress, as well as teach-ins, led by faculty and graduate students to educate students about the war.

Television helped to transform the antiwar movement. In contrast to World Wars I and II and the Korean War, television brought home the reality of the violence and carnage of the war. Just as the television coverage of southern opposition to desegregation raised the national consciousness of the problem of racism, the imagery of wounded soldiers and the devastation on the civilian population in Vietnam, escalated a fierce antiwar movement. The expansion of the war and the mandatory draft fueled a more violent domestic movement. Meanwhile, the increase in militancy replaced the nonviolent protest modeled by Martin Luther King Jr. The rise of the New Left, represented by the SDS and the FSM, the Black Panthers, and the domino effect of race riots in cities across the United States, challenged the status quo of white America, while attacking corporate greed, capitalism, and imperialism.

Amidst all of the unrest, a counterculture emerged with young men and women living in communes, smoking dope, and tripping on LSD. Sexual freedom and the availability of the birth control pill pushed the sexual revolution forward, and the music and drug culture offered an escape for young adults. Together these developments contributed to a growing women's liberation movement that focused on a new female consciousness and the eradication of women's sexual oppression. Young adults began to challenge the traditions and values of their parents, and they generally distrusted the ability of adults to change the world, while a growing population of activists showed contempt for law enforcement and distrusted government authorities to enforce basic civil rights. The murders of Robert Kennedy, Martin Luther King Jr., and Malcolm X reinforced these feelings of distrust in the government and law enforcement.

RISE OF COLLEGE PROTEST MOVEMENT

The political and social context of the 1960s created a ripe environment for social protest movements. Between 1968 through the early 1970s, college protests grew in number. Students objected to military presence on college campuses, protested the draft, protested ROTC recruiting, protested Dow Chemical recruiting on college campuses (Dow produced the napalm used in bombs dropped in Vietnam), and they demanded a voice in determining course programs and curriculum. ROTC buildings were burned down on several campuses across the United States. In 1970, Nixon's invasion of Cambodia led to widespread protests. At Kent State and Jackson

State, confrontation with police and state guardsmen ended in the deaths of several students and wounded protestors and innocent bystanders. As one historian noted, the decade that began as an era of hope ended in a bloodbath and a divided nation.[2]

As we have seen in chapter 2, the history of women's antiwar activism began early in the 20th century, which resulted in the creation of the Women's International League for Peace and Freedom (WILPF), an organization that continues today. In the 1960s, WILPF's top-down organizational structure appealed less to activists who were interested in bottom-up organizations that supported grassroots and local autonomy. SDS and the WSP are two good examples of bottom-up organizations.

WOMEN AND PEACE

Antiwar sentiments among women have a long history in the United States, and in the 20th century date back to before World War I, but the outcome of the Treaty of Versailles and the devastation of the war in Europe set the stage for a vibrant peace reform movement in the United States. After World War I, a growing body of peace organizations formed in response to U.S. foreign policy and global politics.

The peace movement included internationalists and liberal pacifists, who both shared many similarities in promoting peace. Some of these early organizations include: the National Council for the Prevention of War (NCPW), WILPF, the League of Nations Association (LNA), the Fellowship of Reconciliation (FOR), the American Friends Service Committee (AFSC), and many other groups. These groups came together to form the Emergency Peace Campaign prior to World War II and represent one of the first examples of student protest in the United States. Following World War II the formation of the United Nations provided a new foundation for international peacekeeping and in addressing equal rights and basic human rights. Many of the early 20th-century peace societies disbanded, but the WILPF continued on to press for peace justice, and with the growing tension between the United States and Soviet Union they protested against nuclear missile testing in the United States, and internationally.

The devastation of the nuclear holocaust brought on by the United States to end World War II, the birth of the artificial Iron Curtain of the Cold War, and the government effort to contain social and political behavior through propaganda raised concerns of ordinary women, leading to the formation of the WSP in the 1960s. This white-gloved middle-class group of women brought together a diverse group of women organized to protest nuclear arms race.

The formation of the WSP in 1961 provided an organizational base for grassroots peace activism that would continue through the 1970s. The WSP organized mainly as a white middle-class movement, composed of housewives who opposed the nuclear arms race and protested the atmospheric testing of bombs in Nevada and New Mexico. The photographs of the era depict women protesting atmospheric testing in Nevada, wearing dresses, hats, and high heels. In a New York demonstration protesting the bombing of Cambodia in 1972, a group of WSP women are shown lying down on the street, in dresses with signs that read "I am Dead." This protest targeted the International Telephone & Telegraph company for their defense contracts with the military.

On November 1, 1961, a national protest movement was organized by the WSP. Women went on the picket line to protest further testing and demanded a three-year moratorium. Approximately 50,000 women from more than 40 different communities across the United States participated in a one-day peace demonstration. Following the demonstration, they organized a variety of peace vigils, letter-writing campaigns, and lecture events to raise public awareness. At the time, these women were characterized as simple housewives, despite the fact that many of them had been involved in the peace movement for years, some had connections to the Communist Party, while others had joined with men to form the Committee for a Sane Nuclear Policy (SANE). The House on Un-American Committee (HUAC), a congressional committee organized to investigate so-called subversive behavior and to criminally prosecute them as potential enemies of the state, investigated fourteen members of the WSP on their political positions and organizational affiliations. The women refused to be intimidated by the all-male commission, and they defended their actions based on maternal interests and their love for their children. They described the impact of radiation on their children's health, pointing to the contamination of milk by the radiation testing. Major newspapers featured stories that ran headlines like "Peace Gals Make Red Hunters Look Silly," and "It's Ladies Day at Capitol: Hoots, Howls, and Charm." The WSP emphasis on child welfare and their standing as white middle-class homemakers gave them an air of respectability and they received fair treatment at the hands of law enforcement in the early 1960s.[3]

One of the House Un-American Activities Committee hearings on peace movements, in a room jammed with an audience of women, some holding babies. Most of the women were members of an anti-nuclear war group called "Women's Strike for Peace," December 11, 1962. (Bettmann/ CORBIS)

The WSP continued to influence peace activism through the 1960s, but as several scholars have pointed out, their focus on maternalism diminished, as younger women from the women's liberation movement joined. By 1964, WSP focused its energy protesting the Vietnam War. A good example highlighting the move from maternalism to become a more radical movement took place at a gathering in Washington, D.C., in September of 1967. Approximately 500 women planned to demonstrate at the Capitol in support of the anti-draft movement. A few months earlier, the Department of Interior restricted the number of people who could protest in front of the White House. The women lobbied to have the law changed, but were unsuccessful. Motivated by their cause, they ignored the ruling and converged on the sidewalk in front of the White House. The police would only allow 100 people, but several of the protestors pushed themselves through the barriers. As part of the protest they carried a black coffin with signs that read "Not My Sons, Not Your Sons, Not Their Sons." The police responded with violence resulting in several injuries and two arrests for disorderly conduct. As one historian has noted, this incident represented an important shift from the early organization's position as a mild-mannered peace organization. As Dagmar Wilson, the founder of WSP, stated after the event, their organizational goals had not changed but the conditions they faced had, and as result, they were forced to react to police brutality. Wilson's insistence that the organization was the same did not prove out. The year 1967 proved to be a turning point in the development as a middle-class women's organization, as the national organization moved in a more radical direction and included many younger women who identified with the women's liberation front.

Evidence of the WSP's radicalization can be seen in their promotion of economic and racial justice for poor women and children. Their community work with the working poor helped transform their understanding of the problems of poverty on women and children. They also looked at the disproportionate representation of black and Hispanic soldiers, and they came to the conclusion that the war was motivated by race, and the support of human rights became a core value. The WSP developed into a coalition group that worked with different groups of activists to fight against the draft, the war, and to march in solidarity with poor disenfranchised women of color to support anti-poverty and child welfare programs. One WSP member recalled that "we marched with hippies and yippies."[4] Motherhood still remained an important value of the WSP membership, but it radicalized them as they supported diverse community programs that were largely focused on poverty and child welfare. Some of the groups they coalesced with included the National Welfare Rights Organization (NWRO), the Poor People's Campaign PPC, among others. Their alignment with these groups insured that they would be treated differently than their previous white-glove campaign. Moreover, as the antiwar environment became louder, more radical, and engaged in civil disobedience, police and guardsman treatment became more repressive. One of the members, Ethel Taylor, was arrested at a Washington, D.C., sit-in, where she wore the standard white, middle-class uniform of gloves, hat, and high heels. She had to jump from a four-foot drop in heels with no assistance from the police. In her oral history she recalled that it felt like she was jumping into a new world, which from her

Participants in the Women's Strike for Peace protest nuclear bomb tests outside the Russian Mission to the United Nations in New York City, November 1, 1961. (Bettmann/CORBIS)

earlier perspective as a gloved activist, her jail experience was eye-opening—clearly law enforcement no longer treated the middle-aged activist with the same level of respect or patience.

The WSP largely was a white, middle-class organization focused on the peace movement, but by the late 1960s, they expanded the platform to address the problem of poverty among poor women of color and the lack of child welfare. They pursued economic justice in these communities, but they also tried to educate poor women and their families about the racial inequality in the draft and tried to get them see how military spending took needs funds away from social welfare. Work inside poor communities and with organizations like the PPC expanded the diversity of the WSP, and opened their eyes to the struggles of poor women. Martin Luther King Jr. had conceived of an encampment of poor people from different races and regions to gather in solidarity in Washington, D.C. King was assassinated prior to the event taking place, but in spring and summer of 1968, the PPC organized a tent city of sorts, which became known as "Resurrection City." WSP unequivocally supported this effort and took part in the fundraising efforts and worked the encampment. Following this event, it became clear to the WSP leadership that their focus had to include protecting children against hunger and neglect. On the antiwar front, they navigated between different groups and tried to serve as a moderator, while providing support to antiwar and anti-draft protestors by picketing, feeding the young people, and getting them out of jail.

As the antiwar movement escalated, the attitude of law enforcement toward middle-class female protesters became more violent. Members of the WSP were arrested, and they faced the same police brutality and harassment that younger protesters experienced. One WSPer was shocked by the level of police brutality, stating, "The extent to which some of our police (whose motto is "We Serve and Protect") seemed to enjoy their work clubbing every reachable head (newsmen, women, and bystanders included), came as a jolt to some of us...."[5] These experiences influenced an ideological shift to New Left politics and the WSP began consciously to reach out to younger more radical women.

In January of 1968, WSP organized the Jeannette Rankin Brigade, named in honor the first congresswoman in the United States, who voted against entry in both World Wars I and II and was a lifelong peace activist. The Brigade gathered in Washington, D.C., with some 5,000 women in attendance, including 87-year-old honoree Jeannette Rankin. The brigade represented a diverse coalition of women that included the WSP, Church groups, New Left organizations such as SDS, and women's liberationists. The younger women tended to identify as liberationists and were less enthralled by WSP's connection of motherhood and pacifism. They used the strike as a means to protest against powerlessness generated by the motherhood debate and to protest the war. The more radical views of the women's liberationists' isolated some of the WSP members, while others embraced the opportunity to build a stronger and more diverse antiwar movement.

One of the goals of the brigade was to confront Congress on the opening day of the January 1968 session and to demonstrate female opposition to the war. The event pamphlet illustrates the radical position of the liberationists:

TRADITIONAL WOMANHOOD IS DEAD. TRADITIONAL WERE BEAUTIFUL...BUT REALLY POWERLESS. "UPPITY" WOMEN WERE EVEN MORE BEAUTIFUL...BUT STILL POWERLESS. SISTERHOOD IS POWERFUL! HUMANHOOD THE ULTIMATE![6]

The brigade drew 500 women to the Capitol, including honoree Rankin. The event outcomes and conflict between traditional and radical tactics created a protest within a protest, in that the younger women protested against the maternalist politics. As Shulamith Firestone recounted in *Notes from the First Year,* the event underscored the generational and philosophical differences of the women present. Building consensus between women was not always smooth or did it work, though many of the leaders of WSP came to understand the need to connect with women's liberationists. For example, the national steering committee promoted moving toward a more diverse model that embraced New Left ideas, but the grassroots nature of the organization and the independence of their branches meant that local groups didn't feel obligated to follow the suggestions of the national committee.

In some cases, the New Left shift alienated some local branches, while others embraced the opportunity to expand the movement and create a more diverse group of activists. The WSPers identified with the larger women's movement, became involved with other actions including the Women's Strike for Equality, and by the late 1960s emerged as a true coalition group composed of women representing different age groups, classes, ethnicity, race, and sexual orientation. As one historian as shown, the WSP became very aware that they were a white organization, and they were determined to develop ties with women in the black ghetto. They also tended to believe that black women supported the war and the draft, because the military provided economic and educational benefits, but several studies show that black women were very antiwar. Clearly white middle-class activists had the means to support the antiwar movement, but their class position and their prejudices and assumptions about the cases of poverty and race relations sometimes got in the way of their larger goal to help poor black communities. As other coalitions demonstrated, the views of different groups varied, and within inter-racial interactions, white and women of color had specific misconceptions that sometimes got in the way of their larger goals.[7]

CAMPUS PROTEST MOVEMENTS

Free Speech Movement (FSM)—UC Berkeley

The University of California, Berkeley, campus became the national center point for the FSM, which emerged in 1964. In early October of that year, several hundred students took a police car hostage and demanded that the university address a series of grievances. Under the informal leadership of Mario Savio, Brian Turner, Bettina Aptheker, Steve Weissman, Jackie Goldberg, and others, the FSM demanded that the university lift its ban on campus political activities and recognized students' right to free speech and to academic freedom. Student activist and feminist Bettina Aptheker described her first speech, which took place from the top of the police car that she and other students had taken hostage. She was often the only woman speaking at the rallies and later recalled that she didn't think about the sexual imbalance in the FSM leadership, but her work with FSM was the first step toward her liberation as feminist.

Students organized a variety of protests, sit-ins, held a general strike, and took over campus buildings. By December mass sit-ins were organized resulting in the arrest of some 800 students. In January of 1965, the acting chancellor, Martin Meyerson, established provisional rules that permitted political activity on the campus and designated Spruill Hall as a place for student forums and discussions. FSM appealed mostly to students who identified with the

Bettina Aptheker leads a women's antiwar march in Berkeley, California, during the Vietnam War. (Ted Streshinsky/CORBIS)

New Left and students who opposed the war. The FSM had a long-term impact on the campus, but more importantly the victory to secure civil liberties had a monumental impact on higher education, and provided a model for student protest. The FSM protests galvanized a generation of college students, and provided a base for student protest across college campuses in the United States. It also led to the creation of student-centered education, resulting in the development of new disciplines that included women's studies, African American studies, Mexican American studies, and Asian studies.

Bettina Aptheker, reflecting on the impact that the FSM had on her life, wrote that at the time she was not really aware of the extent to which women were invisible in the movement and in history. As she reminds us, women have been historically unable to exercise their right to freedom of speech and "...women's freedom of speech has been particularly circumscribed when women were seeking to redress grievances against themselves. Nowhere can this be seen more clearly than in contemporary movements against sexual harassment, sexual and domestic violence, and incest and other forms of child abuse, and for women's reproductive rights."[8] Reflecting on what the FSW meant to her she reminds us that free speech and women's equality are politically connected, and to honor the meaning of equality and the practice of freedom, we need to equally bestow "...women and men of all races and ethnicities, with the same basic human rights."[9]

Freedom Summer

As we have seen in chapter 5, as the civil rights movement matured, several college-based organizations formed around the goal to assist in voter registration in the South through freedom rides. First organized by the members of the Congress for Racial Equality (CORE) in 1961, a biracial organization, the freedom riders faced mob violence from South Carolina to Alabama. Hostile southern whites slashed the bus tires, threw fire bombs into the bus windows, and violently beat the riders with their fists and with pipes. SNCC members outraged by the violence volunteered to continue the rides, where they too faced horrible beatings, and were arrested in Jackson, Mississippi. The racial violence that followed these events helped to galvanize white support for the civil rights movement, and the radicalization of college students opened a new flood-gate for social protest, directed at the Vietnam War and the draft. A series of overlapping protest movements representing the New Left, black power, the counterculture (hippies, drugs, sex, rock 'n' roll), and women's liberation challenged mainstream American society, by questioning and rejecting traditional authority. The shift from civil rights to black power in the mid-1960s illustrates the growing tension that would fuel campus protest movements across the United States. In 1966, SNCC began to question the theories of integration and began to support the idea of *black power*. In part, this shift was a direct response to police brutality, which led to the formation of the Black Panther Party in Oakland, California. In California, regular police shoot-outs with the Panthers and the Watts Riot in Los Angeles highlighted the extreme between the haves and the have-nots, and brought home the reality that many impoverished communities across the United States were untouched by the civil rights movement. The riots escalated in tandem with the Johnson administration's expansion of the war in Vietnam. Just as the black power movement demanded revolution, antiwar protesters' disgust over the carnage and death created by napalm bombs, and the military draft, fueled a more militant movement.

Face painting in Haight-Ashbury, California, during the summer of love, 1967. (Ted Streshinsky/CORBIS)

Between 1968 and 1972, college campuses became the center point for a variety of militant protests and demonstrations. Free speech or protection of speech and personal freedoms guaranteed by the First Amendment undergirded the antiwar protest movement. In some cases students protested the draft, ROTC classes and military recruitment, racial discrimination and failure to provide access to blacks and Hispanics, while other protests focused on free speech. From Columbia University in New York to San Francisco State in California, antiwar protesters and militant blacks took over buildings on various college campuses calling for a revolution against imperialism and capitalism.

At San Jose State, the black power movement included protest by black athletes, students, and faculty. Harry Edwards, a part-time professor in sociology, became the spokesman for the United Black Students for Action (UBSA), and in an interview with a student magazine, he expressed his doubt that the university could resolve the race problems on campus. A militant young professor, Edwards's statement, "We Get What's Ours or We Burn It Down," reflected the feelings of the militant black student population.[10] There was a clear frustration over the slow response to enforce civil rights legislation and a distrust that the laws would not change anything. Edwards was inspired by Malcolm X and believed that Stokely Carmichael was justified in supporting violence as means to end the race war; Edwards became a very controversial figure at the time, but he also influenced then university President Robert Clark to institute new policies that addressed racial discrimination on campus. Edwards's feelings highlight the revolutionary atmosphere on college campuses at the time.

The escalation of the war in 1971 became a turning point for campus protest movements across the country, and the revolutionary ideals of militant black students reinforced the general distrust that young people had for government. Kent State (Ohio) and Jackson State (Mississippi) campus protest took a violent turn as students were gunned down by the National Guard and law enforcement. The violence at Kent State lit the match for an explosive antiwar protest movement on more than 700 college campuses.

Kent State

In 1970 Kent State had a student population of more than 20,000 students. The university curriculum included ROTC training, and the student population included militant blacks. Some of this militancy grew out of the continued government surveillance and hostility toward the Black Panthers. Many of the students were sympathetic to the cause, and posters, newspapers, and graffiti marked the campus. The Bobby Seale trial in New Haven, Connecticut, and the Hewy P. Newton trial in California became points of contention for college students across the United States, and at Kent State, the black student population had taken on a very militant stand. The black campus newspaper, *Black Watch,* ran several articles that expressed the growing radicalization. The messages provoked black students to take up arms as the solution to their emancipation. the newspaper and other black propaganda called for the killing of authority figures and policemen. These statements mirrored the public statements of Black Panther Eldrige Clever, who supported taking up arms to fight U.S. imperialism.

The Black United Students organized a rally that took place on May 1, 1970. The rally began peacefully, with several students addressing the rally of white and black students, and the rally ended with a final demand that the "ROTC must go." Some reports estimate that 500 students were present, but the campus climate heightened with the announcement of the invasion of Cambodia by President Nixon. Anger seized the crowd, and several students watched as a graduate student burned a copy of the U.S. Constitution, while another student burned his draft card. As the night wore on, a group of young people vandalized and looted several downtown storefronts. The police force was called in to quell the unrest and the state guardsmen were called in to protect the city and campus. On May 2, a group of students burned down the ROTC building. On May 3, tensions mounted, and on May 4, some 2,000 students gathered for a planned rally.

The guardsmen were called to campus to control the crowd of students. They commanded the students to disperse, and when the students failed to follow orders, they used tear gas and advanced on the crowd. Chaos soon followed as the guardsmen fired 67 rounds over a period of 13 seconds, killing 4 students and wounding 9 others. Why they reacted in this manner is still contested today, but a 2010 audio recording analysis confirms that guards were ordered to fire into the crowd. Two of the students who were killed had been involved with the protest, while the other two were walking to class. Of the students who were wounded, Dean R. Kahler was shot in the back and was permanently paralyzed from the chest down. Jeffery Glenn Miller was killed instantly, Allison B. Krause died later that day from her chest wound, William Knox Schroeder died within an hour of being shot in the chest, and Sandra Lee Scheuer died within minutes of being shot in the neck. All of the victims were between the ages of 19 and 20. The impact of this tragedy was personal for the family members who lost their children, while the wounded lived through their own personal horrors, and the masses of college students across the United States united against police brutality, while everyday Americans were shocked and horrified by the deaths and violence.

Sadly, only 10 days after the Kent State massacre, a Jackson State student protest ended similarly as the police shot into the women's dormitory, killing 2 black students and injuring 12 others. The cause of the shooting is unknown to this day, but the FBI estimated that 140 shots were fired into the dormitory from 30 to 50 feet away. Kent State and Jackson State enraged students across the United States, resulting in more than 760 campuses closing down completely.[11]

Campus protest in California included anti-draft, anti-ROTC, antiwar, and free speech protests. At San Jose State, the campus climate represented all these factors and became internationally known as a result of the 1968 Olympic games, where track stars Tommy Smith and John Carlos raised their fists in solidarity with black militants. Prior to this event, the black student population had experienced extreme discrimination in housing and in their treatment by student organizations. Harry Edwards and the UBSA organized protests against institutional racism and housing discrimination on the campus and around the community. Edwards distrusted that university president Robert Clark would solve the race problems, and he continued to pressure the administration to address the problems by organizing student protests.

Interestingly, Clark was one of the few university/college presidents to handle the protest demonstrations in a measured way. Instead of attacking students as shiftless hippies and revolutionaries, he worked to correct the elements of racial discrimination on campus and used reason in dealing with antiwar protestors. Clark quickly addressed the student complaints by requiring a self-study of the Athletics Department, he suspended the fraternities and sororities until they could demonstrate through a written plan that they would not practice discrimination, and an ombudsman was appointed to address discrimination concerns on campus. Clark had many critics including the California Department of Education and by then Governor Ronald Reagan for canceling the first football game of the 1967 season, because of threats from the community over new campus policies against discrimination.

Other campus protests included antiwar demonstrations, protests against Dow Chemical recruitment on campus, and Chicano student protests of discrimination. Clark's mild-mannered approach created a more positive environment for student free speech, and the creation of the Education Opportunity Program provided important support for African American and Hispanic students on campus. These initiatives and programs laid the groundwork for the creation of New College, an experimental program with new curriculum that allowed students to pursue a variety of disciplines. New College (1968–1984) offered a four-year, liberal arts course of study. New College promoted the ideology of allowing students to pursue individual paths of study free of rigidly structured requirements, as well as the concept of supporting, guiding and encouraging the idealism of young people. The popularity of New College influenced the formation of new subject disciplines in African American studies, Mexican American studies, Asian studies, and Women studies.

IDENTITY POLITICS: FORMATION; BLACK, HISPANIC, RED, ASIAN; SEXUAL ORIENTATION; RELIGIOUS AFFILIATION

The history of the second wave of feminism has tended to focus on the white middle-class movement, dominated by the history of the ERA and focus on NOW. The experiences of women of color within the broader context of the second wave movement has been defined by what scholars refer to as *identity politics.* A variety of liberation fronts formed out of the civil rights movement, which included black power, red power, brown power, and gay power, which reflect the struggle for equality in mainstream American society, while also pressing for cultural recognition based on race, ethnicity, gender, and sexual orientation. Identity politics provided the first step to uncovering the invisibility of specific groups, and is useful in building a deeper understanding of the multiple layers of feminisms, and how different coalitions of women came together to fight against oppression.

Identity politics broadly refers to the actions and interests of a specific group that share experiences of real or perceived oppression. Group identity has many forms and can include one of more characteristic that include race, ethnicity, class, gender, religious, and sexual orientation. For race- and ethnic-based politics, group identity is frequently tied to cultural heritage and to nationalism.

Scholars have recently criticized the role of identity politics as a framework for research and analysis. Sociologist Todd Gitlin calls this process an "American tragedy," while feminist scholar Nira Uval-Davis argues that usage of this framework fails to account for shifting boundaries and internal differences and conflicts of interest.[12]

DIFFERENT IDENTITIES

Identity politics provides a context to understand the diverse experiences of women across time. The standard practice in women's history has tended to overstate the influence of the white women's liberation movement on other nonmainstream feminist activism. Similarly, the black civil rights movement is typically cited as the major influence on women's liberation. How did other groups of women organize, what did they organize around, and how did these experience shape ethnic, racial, or sexual identity? In using the categories of gender, race, class, ethnicity, and sexual orientation as a means to give voice to distinct groups, are we creating a multi-racial divide? How can social movements solve the economic problems, if we are only focused on differences among groups? These are important questions to consider as we look at identity politics and the role of coalitions in shaping public policy that address real community concerns and that provide a framework for true democracy and promotion of basic human rights.

The early histories of the women's movement have largely ignored the contributions and experiences of women of color, working class, and poor women. In the second wave movement, the realities of these women's lives and the struggles they faced came to light during the 1977 National Women's Conference (NWC) in Houston. The final report, *Spirit of Houston*, outlined numerous national objectives to solve a gamut of social problems that fell particularly hard on poor and working-class women, and women of color. Unlike the middle-class women, poor and working-class women were focused on community activism, versus maintaining memberships in the national organizations like NOW, League of Women Voters (LVW), Young Women's Christian Association (YWCA), and other mainstream groups. Community activism represented a variety of intended or in some cases accidental feminisms. Identity politics—how individuals relate to specific social/cultural groups, whether based on race, ethnicity, class, and sexual orientation—provides a framework to understand how community feminism has transformed social movement activism, and the role of cultural identity is central to building a new narrative that looks at specific communities and bridge coalitions.

Mainstream historical narratives have tended to lump the history of women under the umbrella of the white second-wave movement. Yet, as we have learned, the impact of the civil rights movement created different liberation fronts that included the black power movement, Chicano, Native American, Asian, and gay liberation fronts. These different fronts organized around cultural heritage and in the case of gay liberation involved cultural and sexual identity. The standard narrative has focused on the more radical groups like the Black Panthers and the United Farm Workers Union (UFW) of Mexican Americans and Filipinos. All groups deserve attention, but the lack of attention to community- and neighborhood-based organizing has created a historical hole. All the while during the policymaking that created the President's Commission on the Status of Women (PCSW) and the NWC, communities of women became agents of change at the local level. For example, in 1963 black women in Los Angeles organized a welfare-mothers organization against the backdrop of the formation of the PCSW, while Chicana feminists from Long Beach, California organized and produced one of the first femenista groups and newspaper. Similarly, Native American women formed the North American Indian Women Association (NAIWA) (1972), and as *Ms.* magazine was being launched by Gloria Steinem, radical Asian American feminists founded their community magazine, *Guidra*. All of the various struggles and work of mainstream feminists is important to our greater understanding of feminism and social movements, yet the markers of this history needs to be expanded and more inclusive of the diversity of women's experience across time.

California college campuses provided Asian, black, and Chicano students with the training to pursue identity politics through ethnic- and nationalist-based organizations. The Black Panthers and the UFW helped them organize and provided militant support to challenge racial and ethnic discrimination. Part of this process led to new curriculum focused on ethnic, black, and women's studies. Historical agency as members of these communities was grounded in having a broader understanding of their cultural heritage and national origin. For college women, consciousness-raising groups provided a format to express themselves in small groups, to talk about their personal lives, but it also informed their own sense of sexual and ethnic oppression.

For many women, this process highlighted the inconsistencies in the civil rights struggle where women were more often than not second string leaders. One young Chicana from Long Beach stated that she wanted men to be accountable and consistent in their ideology and to treat women with respect. Her sentiments were echoed by many women in the civil rights movement. Moreover, these women began to search for their own history, and through this process, they became more aware of their own culture and history. The discovery by a small group of Chicana activists in Los Angeles of an underground newspaper written by a Mexican women's organization from 1910, Revolution the Hijas de Cuauhtemoc, is an interesting example of how history is lost and later found accidentally. In this case, the name of the newspaper provided the name for their organization and their newspaper, which began in 1971. This group of women were empowered by this discovery and they reclaimed their cultural roots at the same time. Asian college students followed a similar path in making new connections to their cultural history, influenced the creation of Asian American studies programs on numerous college campuses, and were radicalized by the Vietnam War. In Los Angeles, the Asian American Political Alliance (AAPA) (1966) offered a diverse platform base for grassroots organizing that included gang members, college students, and activists who focused on drug-abuse intervention and community health. The creation of the Community Workers Collective provided communal living for the members, where they discussed politics and bonded through a collective feminist consciousness. Native American women moved more slowly in creating a separate women's organization, though they had a long tradition of women centered organizations dating back to 1920s. In the same way that other ethnic groups reclaimed their ethnic pride, the American Indian Movement (AIM) inspired women and men to take over Alcatraz Island in the 1970s. The formation of the Women of All Red Nations (WARN) took place in 1978, which became an arm of AIM. All of theses groups of women faced criticism from male community members, some claiming that separate women's groups divided their struggle, yet these women remained solid members of their communities, while developing their own cultural/feminist identity.[13]

In contrast to Chicana, Asian, and Native American women, African American women who connected with welfare rights had to confront both white and black criticism, and they were not necessarily involved with the politics of nationalism or civil rights within the scope of their community. In 1963, Johnnie Tillman helped organize the Aid to Needy Children—Mothers Anonymous (ANC) of Watts, which predated the formation of the NWRO. The ANC demanded that they receive the same access to federal welfare as others groups, and it became one of the first welfare community groups that addressed poor women's rights and one of the best examples of coalition activism. Collectively all of these identity-based groups challenged the subordination of women. Some identified as feminists, while others were more concerned about their daily existence and ability to provide for their families, but their actions spoke feminism.[14]

COALITIONS

As William Julius Wilson writes in *The Bridge Over the Racial Divide* (1999), the over-focus on racial differences limits our ability to foster the commonalities and to build political strategies to address global economic problems. Wilson is focused on present political activism and believes that in order to foster the formation of a "national, progressive, multiracial political coalition," groups need to unite and avoid the divisive trap of identity politics.[15]

The history of women's coalition politics can serve as a model for understanding group dynamics in social movements, while providing a foundation to better address grassroots, national, and global social and political interactions. One of the best means to understand the diversity of women's liberation, is to explore how different community groups came together to fight for specific issues that include rape, domestic violence, abortion rights, welfare rights, anti-poverty and public housing. As we have learned in part one of this chapter, the WSP is an example of a middle-class organization that became more focused on building broad-based coalitions with poor black women to address the problem of childhood poverty. Other community pressure groups similarly forged bridge politics, but as Stephanie Gilmore makes clear, the alliances that formed between 1960s to the present, the activists were much more diverse, some were radical feminists, others were more conservative, and many women, especially poor women did not identify as feminists at all. Moreover, some coalitions would be long lasting, others were very short term, but most came from overlapping networks, and shared common concerns.[16]

VIOLENCE AGAINST WOMEN AND
ANTI-RAPE MOVEMENT

The mainstream representation of women's equality in the modern movement has largely been dominated by the ERA campaign, labor rights, and abortion. Yet, one of the most important issues that struck a cord at the local level was the problem of violence against women and rape. The NWC in 1977 highlighted these two issues as major areas that needed government supported reform. Prior to the conference, several grassroots-based organizations made domestic violence and rape a public issues. One of the major components of the women's liberation agenda was to address the longstanding oppression of women by men. Through public speak-outs to protest sexual oppression, these women raised public awareness of the problem of sexual violence against women. Several women's organizations took on these issues, including local chapters of NOW, YWCA, LWV, Planned Parenthood, and religious groups.

Historian Stephanie Gilmore's study of second-wave activism in Memphis from 1971 to 1982 illustrates how local regional organization came together to fight for specific issues, like rape. The grassroots dynamics in Memphis illustrates the application of what Susan Freeman describes as "politics of location"—where groups used different tactics to accomplish a variety of feminist goals, to promote a variety of issues from the ERA, to policies related to rape and wife abuse. Memphis women embraced both liberal and radical "tactics, structures, and issues," and their responses to their specific regional experiences shaped how they identified as feminists and how they approached the specific cultural milieu of living in a small southern town. The grassroots organizations and the process of building coalitions in the south were steeped in the civil rights movement. Martin Luther King Jr. and the Southern Christian Leadership Conference (SCLC) were intimately involved in the grassroots activism in Memphis. King's assassination in Memphis had a profound effect on the community and his death inspired the formation of new multiracial civil rights and feminist organizations.

Southern black women were not immediately attracted to white feminism and the membership of black women in the local NOW chapter was quite small. The white members held the political clout and it took time to cultivate a strong feminist movement in Memphis. As a result of the politics of segregation and racism, black women created their own separate organizations, but worked periodically with NOW to address specific community concerns. The local NOW chapter initiated public debates on the problem of domestic violence and rape, and through this process, they created a coalition movement to create the Women's Resource Center (WRC), which provided important educational resources for women, job training programs and legal aid. The WCR represented a coalition of women's groups that supported the formation of the WRC and sought government grants to sustain the programs. The groups that participated included NOW, YWCA, Planned Parenthood, LWV, Church Women United, the Girls Club, and labor groups. Other U.S. cities created similar women's resource centers and rape crisis centered. For example, the YWCA in San Jose, California, created the rape crisis center and trained their staff to work with the police department to provide counseling to rape victims.

Because Memphis became known as the rape capital of the United States, with 534 reported rapes in 1973, Memphis NOW and the WRC confronted law enforcement treatment of rape victims and worked with the police to build a Comprehensive Rape Crisis Program. NOW also created the first rape hotline and worked on raising public awareness of the problem and to protect victim's rights, and the Memphis police department formed the Sex Crimes Squad. On the domestic violence front, the police were less receptive and NOW sponsored several public panels to address the problem, and because the police were uncooperative, they opened a wife abuse hotline, and in 1977 the Wife Abuse Crisis Service opened a women's shelter.

The anti-rape movement provided an avenue that bridged divisions between radical and liberal, and black and white feminists. The New York Radical Feminists (NYRF) led the movement. Organized around consciousness-raising sessions and speak-outs, radical feminists focused on the sexual oppression of women, which publicized the problem and led the movement to create rape crisis centers and self-defense programs. Rape education became a national issue, and in 1971, NOW added rape to their national agenda, and the Women's Legal Defense Fund supported rape law reform, and they worked to change laws and court procedures that were responsive to victim's rights.[17]

Legal reform was not without controversy among radical feminists, whom were skeptical that legal change would improve women's status. Yet, despite some of the disagreements between feminist groups over legal reform, clear successes in regional areas, including major legal reform of the rape laws in Michigan, fostered a collaborative environment for state and national reform. The formation of the Women's Anti-Rape Coalition (WARC) in New York in 1973 and the formation of New York Women Against Rape (NYWAR) lobbied to change the laws that required corroboration of every aspect of the rape charge be supported with evidence from eye witnesses. In contrast to nonsexual crimes, the victims in rape and domestic violence cases, were treated as co-defendants, and the sexual double standard prevailed in the court room. White, black, liberal, and radical feminists allied to combat the sexual abuse and oppression of women, and together they transformed the public discourse on the issue of rape, and black women helped bring a new perspective on the issue of multiple oppressions that included race, sex, and poverty.

Feminists' efforts to address the problem of sexual violence through education and legal reform were also inspired by the popular writers and scholar activists who wrote about the oppression of their sex. Susan Brownmiller, feminist, activist, and scholar gave a public face to the problem of rape in her pioneering work *Against Our Will: Men, Women, and Rape* (1975). This book helped countless women as they tried to repair their lives after being raped. Brownmiller received hundreds of letters from her readers thanking her for publishing this book. In some of these letters women told their personal stories of rape, while others talked about the rage they felt. *Against Our Will* gave voice to rape victims and it empowered women to mobilize against continued sexual oppression. Both academic and popular literature helped propel the women's liberation front forward, and the progress made through collective rape counseling centers, rape hotlines, and women's resources centers provided victims with services that they desperately needed.

A similar movement emerged to address the problem of marital rape. Prior to 1993, husbands were legally protected from prosecution for raping their wives, based on the contract of marriage, which was grounded on the principle that women were the conjugal property of men. Feminist activists worked to repeal the state statutes and to raise awareness of the oppression that married women faced. Radical feminist Laura X became one of the primary advocates to criminalize forced marital sex and she raised national awareness of the issue. She was instrumental in supporting the 1978 Rideout lawsuit, in which John Rideout became the first husband to be criminally prosecuted for raping his wife in the United States. Rideout was eventually acquitted, but the publicity surrounding the case brought national attention to the movement.

That same year, Laura X founded the National Clearinghouse on Marital and Date Rape as part of the Women's History Library at UC Berkeley. In 1979, she successfully pressed for legal change in California and worked on several other state campaigns. By 1996, 16 states repealed marital rape exemptions, and another 33 states had partially repealed marital exemptions. The activism of Laura X and others to repeal marital rape exceptions improved married women's legal rights as rape victims, yet marital rape cases have been treated less seriously than other sexually violent crimes by law enforcement and the court system.

CROSS-RACE COALITIONS, WELFARE RIGHTS

Just as white middle-class women developed different coalitions to address specific societal problems such as rape, the welfare rights movement in the 1960s and 1970s is a good example of a multiracial organization. Unlike many of the other coalitions that we have explored, the battleground for welfare rights was an alliance of poor women, largely black, but some were white, Latina, and Native Americans. As Premilla Nadasen describes, this diverse alliance of poor women was not problem-free, and at times, the cultural barriers and prejudices of different groups created feelings of distrust, resentment, and the movement was filled with diverse viewpoints and different political understandings. The movement has direct ties to the civil rights movement, and was dominated by black women. Not surprisingly, white women and women of color did not join the welfare rights movement at the same level as did black women, and there was a great deal of interracial tension that stemmed from community stereotypes and false assumptions. The campaign to address welfare reform provides an interesting look at how poor women came together to fight for basic human rights. Women in this movement came to a new understanding of their differences, but also found common ground in trying to provide basic needs of food, clothes, and housing for their families.

In the 1960s, welfare activism grew out of support groups of women who were recipients of funds from the Aid to Families with Dependent Children (AFDC), a joint program between state and federal government to provide aid to poor women and their children. Across the United States, small groups of communities formed to discuss their economic plight and served as a support network for poor women. The small group process resembled the consciousness-raising sessions used by women's liberationists to publicize a variety of issues. In the case of welfare mothers, they expressed feelings of shame and isolation, but also spoke about their hopes and dreams for their children. They came to understand that individually they had little power to address the frustrations they felt dealing with the welfare bureaucracy, and they began to embrace collective actions as a means to fight for welfare rights.

The formation of the NWRO in 1967 was organized under the leadership of George Wiley, an African American chemistry professor and head of the Poverty/Rights Action Center in Washington, D.C. The governing principles of the organization focused on integration and interracial organizing, though the membership was 85 percent black. Given the high percentage of poor black women, at 48 percent in the mid-1960s, the proportion of black members should not be too surprising. The history of black access to welfare is wedded to the racist climate of Jim Crow. The AFDC was created in 1935, but in the south racial prejudice and practice excluded black women from receiving welfare aide. Caseworkers in charge of administering the funds created barriers to women who had men in the house or employable mother-in-laws. Black women were clearly treated unfairly and received less funding. The early 1960s offered a new opportunity for poor black women to press for change, and as a result the welfare debate was framed as a black issue.

Many of the welfare activists had deep ties to civil rights organizations, including the CORE, the National Association for the Advancement of Colored People (NAACP), the SCLC, and SDS. While there was a larger representation of blacks involved in the welfare movement, the variety of civil rights organizations that looked at poverty and welfare rights was multiracial. A good example is the SDS, which initially focused on voting rights, and later formed the Economic and Research Action Project (ERAP) to address poverty and to help local communities form interracial groups to fight poverty. Religious activists and churches also played an important role in the movement; Catholic and Protestant churches provided meeting sites and they helped funnel money to welfare activists through the church. One white activist from Cleveland, Ohio got involved with the Inner City Protestant Parish (ICPP) and from that experience became involved with SDS, and for the first time she began working with black activists, which initially she found a little scary, but she soon came to the realization that they shared the same challenges whether white or black.

Other welfare activists formed organizations in New York, where Puerto Ricans, African Americans, and Jewish people collaborated on the local welfare committees, and they worked together to support the government-funded anti-delinquency program. As one welfare recipient and activist from Milwaukee explained, the problem was not being black but it was a *green* problem—meaning that they lacked the money to feed, clothe, and house their families. Regardless of race and ethnicity, poor people all shared the same problem of poverty. While the activists may not have agreed on tactics or held strong opinions on politics and other issues, they shared a common bond that allowed interracial cooperation to take place to address welfare rights in local communities.[18]

CONCLUSION

The variety and diversity of women's social movements from the early Progressive Era through the 1990s testifies to the popular belief that it takes a village to effect change. Indeed the political environment of the 1960s–1970s split the world wide open in terms of protest movements. The civil rights and antiwar movements shaped

The March for Women's Lives, April 5, 1992. Some 750,000 women, men, and children turned out for the rally in support of abortion rights. Jesse Jackson appears on the left. (AP Photo/Marcy Nighswander)

the next several generations of college students. What started initially as a movement to eliminate racial discrimination in the south, became a multiprong movement to protest sexual oppression and to change laws that were responsive to rape and domestic violence victims, to address the problem of poverty, welfare rights, housing discrimination, and discrimination in drafting disproportionately people of color to Vietnam. The civil rights movement thus shaped the development for new social justice issues, and the emergence of identity politics and interracial movements pushed the bar of democracy forward. The impact of these movements and the importance of the Fourteenth Amendment in providing the legal grounds to pursue new legislation that covered equal access to education, housing, welfare, gender discrimination in the workplace, sexual harassment, the anti-rape and anti-violence campaigns continue to transform American society.

NOTES

1. Ellen Carol Dubois and Lynn Dumenil, *Through the Eyes of Women: An American History with Documents* (Bedford/St. Martin Press, 2004), pp. 556–57.

2. Joan Morrison and Robert K. Morrison, *From Camelot to Kent State: The Sixties Experience in the Words of Those Who Live It* (Oxford University Press, 2001), pp. xviii-xxiii.

3. Amy Swerdlow, *Women Strike for Peace; Traditional Motherhood and Radical Politics* (University of Chicago Press, 1993), p. 110.

4. Andre Estepa, "Taking the White Gloves Off: Women Strike for Peace and 'the Movement,' 1967–1973," in *Feminist Coalitions: Historical Perspectives on Second-Wave Feminism in the United States,* ed. Stephanie Gilmore, pp. 86–87 (University of Illinois Press, 2008).

5. Estepa, "Taking the White Gloves Off," p. 97.

6. Shulamith Firestone, "The Jeannette Rankin Brigade: Woman Power? A Summary of Our Involvement," in *The First Year* (New York Radical Women, 1968). Found online, Duke University, On-Line Archival Collection, "Documents from the Women's Liberation Movement," http://scriptorium.lib.duke.edu/wlm/.

7. Estepa, "Taking the White Gloves Off," pp. 101–4.

8. Bettina Aptheker, "Gender Politics and the FSM: A Mediation on Women and Freedom of Speech," in *The Free Speech Movement; Reflections on Berkeley in the 1960s,* ed. Robert Cen and Reginald E. Zelnik, pp. 129–39 (University of California Press, 2002).

9. Ibid.

10. Roger Allen, "Harry Edwards: "We Get What's Ours or We Burn It Down," *Spartan Life* (Winter 1968): 7–10.

11. James A Michner, *Kent State: What Happened and Why* (Random House, 1971), pp. 8–9, 26–27.

12. Stephanie Gilmore, *Feminist Coalitions: Historical Perspectives on Second-Wave Feminism in the United States* (University of Illinois Press, 2008), pp. 2–7.

13. Sherna Gluck, "Whose Feminism, Whose History?" in *Community Activism and Feminist Politics; Organizing Across Race, Class, and Gender*, ed., Nancy A. Naples, pp. 37–43 (Routledge, 1998).

14. Gluck, "Whose Feminism, Whose History?" pp. 42–43; Permilla Nadasen, "Expanding the Boundaries of the Women's Movement: Black Feminism and the Struggle for Welfare Rights," in *No Permanent Waves: Recasting Histories of U.S. Feminism*, ed., Nancy A. Hewitt, pp. 172–73 (Rutgers University Press, 2010).

15. William Julius Wilson, *The Bridge Over the Racial Divide; Rising Inequality and Coalition Politics* (University of California Press, Berkeley, 1999), pp. 1–9.

16. Gilmore, *Feminist Coalitions*, pp. 1–19.

17. Stephanie Gilmore, "The Dynamics of Second-Wave Feminist Activism in Memphis, 1971–1982," *NWSA* 15.1 (2003): 94–117.

18. Premilla Nadasen, "Welfare's a Green Problem: Cross-Race Coalitions in the Welfare Rights Organizing," in *Feminist Coalitions: Historical Perspectives on Second-Wave Feminism in the United States*, ed., Stephanie Gilmore, pp. 178–224 (University of Illinois Press, 2008).

BIBLIOGRAPHY

GENERAL REFERENCE SOURCES

Albrecht, Lisa, and Rose M. Brewer. *Bridges of Power: Women's Multicultural Alliances.* New Society Publishers, 1990.

Alonso, Harriet Hyman. *Peace as a Women's Issue: A History of the U.S. Movement for World Peace and Women's Rights.* Syracuse University Press, 1993.

Anderson, Kristi. *After Suffrage: Women in Partisan and Electoral Politics Before the New Deal.* University of Chicago, 1996.

Armitage, Susan H., Patricia Hart, and Karen Weathermon. *Women's Oral History, The Frontier Reader.* University of Nebraska Press, 2002.

Baker, Carrie N. "How Did Diverse Activists in the Second Wave of the Women's Movement Shape Emerging Public Policy on Sexual Harassment?" In *Women and Social Movements in the U.S., 1600–2000,* eds. Kathryn Kish Sklar and Thomas Dublin. State University of New York, 2007.

Baker, Jean. *Votes for Women: The Struggle for Suffrage Revisited.* Oxford University Press, 2002.

Baker, Paula. "The Domestication of Politics: Women and American Political Society, 1780–1920." *American Historical Review* 89 (June 1984): 620–47.

Barakso, Maryann. *Governing NOW: Grassroots Activism in the National Organization for Women.* Cornell University Press, 2004.

Baxandall, Rosallyn, and Linda Gordon, eds. *America's Working Women: A Documentary History, 1600 to the Present.* W.W. Norton, 1995.

Becker, Susan D. *The Origins of the Equal Rights Amendment: American Feminism Between the Wars.* Greenwood Press, 1981.

Bevacqua, Maria. "Reconsidering Violence Against Women: Coalition Politics in the Antirape Movement." In *Feminist Coalitions: Historical Perspectives on Second-Wave Feminism in the United States*, ed. Stephanie Gilmore, pp. 163–77. University of Illinois Press, 2008.

Brecher, Jeremy, and Tim Costello, eds. *Building Bridges: The Emerging Grassroots Coalition of Labor and Community.* Monthly Review Press, New York City, 1990.

Brown, Carrie. *Rosie's Mom: Forgotten Women Workers of the First World War.* Northeastern University Press, 2002.

Brownmiller, Susan. *Against Our Will: Men, Women, and Rape.* Simon & Schuster, 1975.

Bystydzienski, Jill M., and Steven P. Schacht, eds. *Forging Radical Alliances Across Difference; Coalition Politics for the New Millennium.* Rowman & Littlefield Publishers, 2001.

Chatfield, Charles. *The American Peace Movement; Ideals and Activism.* Twayne Publishers, 1992.

Child Labor: Report of the Subcommittee on Child Labor. Ellen Nathalie Mathews, Chairman. White House Conference on Child Health and Protection. The New Century Co., New York, 1932.

Cobble, Dorothy Sue. *The Other Women's Movement: Workplace Justice and Social Rights in Modern America.* Princeton University Press, 2004.

Cobble, Dorothy Sue. "Recapturing Working-Class Feminism: Union Women in the Postwar Era." In *Not Just June Cleaver; Women and Gender in Postwar America, 1945–1960*, ed. Joanne Meyerowitz, pp. 57–83. Temple University Press, 1994.

Cohen, Lizabeth. *Making a New Deal: Industrial Workers in Chicago, 1919–1930.* Cambridge University Press, 1990.

Cohen, Robert, and Reginald E. Zelnik. *The Free Speech Movement; Reflections and Berkeley in the 1960s.* University of California Press, 2002.

Coontz, Stephanie. *The Way We Never Were: American Families and the Nostalgia Trap.* Basic Books, 1992.

Cott, Nancy. *Grounding of Modern Feminism.* Yale University Press, 1997.

Davis, Angela. *Angela Davis: An Autobiography.* Random House, 1974.

Deutsch, Sarah. *Women and the City: Gender, Space, and Power in Boston, 1870–1940.* Oxford University Press, 2000.

Deverell, William, and Tom Sitton, eds. *California Progressivism Revisited.* University of California Press, 1994.

Dubois, Ellen Carol, and Lynn Dumenil. *Through the Eyes of Women: An American History with Documents.* Bedford/St. Martin Press, 2004.

Echols, Alice. *Daring to Be Bad: Radical Feminism in America 1967–1975.* University of Minnesota Press, 1989.

Echols, Alice. *Shaky Ground: The '60s and Its Aftershocks.* Columbia University Press, 2002.

Enke, Anne. *Finding the Movement: Sexuality, Contested Space, and Feminists Activism.* Duke University Press, 2007.

Estepa, Andrea. "'Taking the White Gloves Off' Women Strike for Peace and 'the Movement,' 1967–1973." In *Feminist Coalitions: Historical Perspectives on Second-Wave Feminism in the United States*, ed. Stephanie Gilmore, pp. 84–112. University of Illinois Press, 2008.

Faragher, John Mack, ed. *Out of Many: A History of the American People*. 6th ed. Prentice Hall, Mead, 2009.

Fessler, Ann. *The Girls Who Went Away: The Hidden History of Women Who Surrendered Children for Adoption in the Decades Before* Roe v. Wade. Penguin Books, 2006.

Foster, Carrie A. *The Women and the Warriors; The U.S. Section of the Women's International League for Peace and Freedom, 1915–1946*. Syracuse University Press, 1995.

Gilbert, Marc Jason. *The Vietnam War on Campus; Other Voice, More Distant Drums*. Praeger, 2001.

Gilmore, Stephanie. "The Dynamics of Second-Wave Feminist Activism in Memphis, 1971–1982," *NWSA* 15.1 (2003): 94–117.

Gilmore, Stephanie, ed. *Feminist Coalitions: Historical Perspectives on Second-Wave Feminism in the United States*. University of Illinois Press, 2008.

Gluck, Sherna. "Whose Feminism, Whose History?" In *Community Activism and Feminist Politics; Organizing Across Race, Class, and Gender*, ed. Nancy A. Naples, pp. 31–56. Routledge, 1998.

Gluck, Sherna Berger. *Rosie the Riveter Revisited. Women, The War, and Social Change*. Twayne Publishers, 1987.

Goureia, Grace Mary. "We Also Serve: American Indian Women's Role in WWII." *Michigan Historical Review* 20, no. 2 (Fall 1994): 153–89.

Gullett, Gayle. *Becoming Citizens: The Emergence and Development of the California Women's Movement, 1880–1911*. University of Illinois Press, 2000.

Hamilton, Alice. *Exploring the Dangerous Trades: The Autobiography of Alice Hamilton, M.D.* Little Brown & Company, 1943.

Hampton, Henry, Steve Fayer, with Sarah Flynn, eds. *Voices of Freedom: An Oral History of the Civil Rights Movement from the 1950s through the 1980s*. Bantam Books, New York, 1990.

Harrison, Cynthia. *On Account of Sex: The Politics of Women's Issues, 1945–1968*. University of California Press, Berkeley, 1988.

Hartmann, Susan M. *The Home Front and Beyond: American Women in the 1940s*. Twayne Publishers, Boston, 1982.

Heirich, Max. *The Beginning: Berkeley 1964*. Columbia University Press, 1968.

Hewitt, Nancy A., ed. *No Permanent Waves: Recasting Histories of U.S. Feminism*. Rutgers University Press, New Jersey, 2010.

Hofstadter, Richard, ed. *The Progressive Movement, 1900–1915*. Prentice-Hall, New Jersey, 1963.

Jones, Jacqueline, Peter Wood, Thomas Borstelmann, Elaine Tyler May, and Vicki L. Ruiz, eds. *Created Equal: A History of the United States*. 3rd ed. Pearson and Longman, 2009.

Kemp, John R., ed. *Lewis Hine: Photographs of Child Labor in the New South.* University Press of Mississippi, Jackson, 1986.

Kunn, Madeleine, M. *Pearls, Politics & Power: How Women Can Win and Lead.* Chelsea Green Publishing Company, White River Junction, Vermont, 2008.

Kunzel, Regina G. "White Neurosis: Black Pathology; Constructing Out-of-Wedlock Pregnancy in the Wartime and Postwar United States." In *Not Just June Cleaver; Women and Gender in Postwar America, 1945–1960,* ed. Joanne Meyerowitz, pp. 304–34. Temple University Press, 1994.

Laughlin, Kathleen A. "How did State Commissions on the Status of Women Overcome Historical Antagonisms between Equal Rights and Labor Feminists to Create a New Feminist Mainstream, 1963–1973." In *Women and Social Movements in the U.S., 1600–2000,* eds. Kathryn Kish Sklar and Thomas Dublin. State University of New York, 2007.

Laura X. "Accomplishing the Impossible. An Advocate's Notes from the Successful Campaign to Make Marital and Date Rape a Crime in all 50 U.S. States and Other Countries." *Violence Against Women* 5, no. 9 (1999): 1064–81.

Matthews, Glenna. *Silicon Valley, Women, and the California Dream: Gender, Class and Opportunity in the Twentieth Century.* Stanford University Press, 2003.

May, Elaine Tyler. *Homeward Bound: American Families in the Cold War Era.* Basic Books, New York, 1999.

Mayeri, Serena. "How and Why was Feminist Legal Strategy Transformed, 1960–1973." In *Women and Social Movements in the U.S., 1600–2000,* eds. Kathryn Kish Sklar and Thomas Dublin. State University of New York, 2007.

Mead, Rebecca J. *How the Vote was Won: Woman Suffrage in the Western United States, 1868–1914.* New York University Press, 2004

Meeker, Martin. *Contacts Desired: Gay and Lesbian Communications and Community, 1940s–1970s.* Chicago University Press, 2007.

Meyer, David S. *The Politics of Protest; Social Movements in America.* Oxford University Press, 2007.

Meyerowitz, Joanne. "Beyond the Feminist Mystique: A Reassessment of Postwar Mass Culture, 1946–1958." In *Not Just June Cleaver; Women and Gender in Postwar America, 1945–1960,* ed. Joanne Meyerowitz, pp. 229–62. Temple University Press, 1994.

Meyerowitz, Joanne, ed. *Not June Cleaver: Women and Gender in Postwar America, 1945–1960.* Temple University Press, 1994.

Michel, Sonya. *Children's Interests/Mothers' Rights: The Shaping of America's Child Care Policy.* Yale University Press, 1999.

Michner, James A. *Kent State: What Happened and Why.* Random House, New York, 1971.

Milkman, Ruth. *Gender at Work: The Dynamics of Job Segregation by Sex during World War II.* University of Illinois Press, 1987.

Minkoff, Debra C. *Organizing for Equality: The Evolution of Women's and Racial-Ethnic Organizations in America, 1955–1985.* Rutgers University Press, New Jersey, 1995.

Moon, Danelle. "Educational Housekeepers: Female Reformers and the California Americanization Program, 1900–1927." In *California History: A Topical Approach,* ed. Gordon Morris Bakken, pp. 108–24. Harlan Davidson, 2003.

Moon, Danelle. "Female Politicians." In *Icons of the American West,* ed. Gordon M. Bakken. Vol. 2, pp. 399–420. Greenwood Press, 2008.

Moon, Danelle. "A Pocket of Quiet Persistence—In the Age of the Feminists Doldrums? Florence Kitchelt and the Connecticut Committee for the Equal Rights Amendment." *Connecticut History* 45 (Fall 2006): 201–28.

Moraga, Cherrie, and Gloria Anzaluda, eds. *This Bridge Called My Back: Writings by Radical Women of Color.* Kitchen Table: Women of Color Press, 1981, 1983.

Morrison, Joan, and Robert K. Morrison. *From Camelot to Kent State: The Sixties Experience in the Words of Those Who Live It.* Oxford University Press, 2001.

Muncy, Robyn. *Creating the Female Dominion in American Reform, 1890–1935.* Oxford University Press, 1991.

Nadasen, Premilla. "Welfare's a Green Problem: Cross-Race Coalitions in Welfare Rights Organizing." In *Feminist Coalitions: Historical Perspectives on Second-Wave Feminism in the United States,* ed. Stephanie Gilmore, pp. 178–224. University of Illinois Press, 2008.

Nadelson, Regina. *Who Is Angela Davis: The Biography of a Revolutionary.* Peter H. Wyden, New York, 1972.

Naples, Nancy A., ed. *Community Activism and Feminist Politics: Organizing Across Race, Class, and Gender.* Routledge, New York, 1998.

Odem, Mary. *Delinquent Daughters: Protecting and Policing Adolescent Female Sexuality in the United States, 1885–1920.* University of North Carolina Press, 1995.

Offen, Karen. *Globalizing Feminisms, 1789–1945.* Routledge, New York, 2010.

Payne, Charles. "Ella Baker and Models of Social Change." In *Women and Power in American History; A Reader, Vol. II from 1870,* ed. Kathryn Kish Sklar and Thomas Dublin, pp. 215–39. Prentice Hall, New Jersey, 1991.

Ramirez, Catherine E. *The Woman in the Zoot Suit; Gender, Nationalism, and the Cultural Politics of Memory.* Duke University Press, Durham, 2009.

Rivera-Guisti, Ivette. "How Did Women Needleworkers Influence New Deal Labor Policies in Puerto Rico?" In *Women and Social Movements in the U.S., 1600–2000,* eds. Kathryn Kish Sklar and Thomas Dublin. State University of New York, 2007.

Rhodri Jeffreys-Jones. *Changing Differences; Women and the Shaping of American Foreign Policy, 1917–1984.* Rutgers University Press, 1999.

Robnett, Belinda. *How Long? How Long? African American Women in the Struggle for Civil Rights.* Oxford University Press, New York, 1997.

Rose, Margaret. "Woman Power Will Stop Those Grapes: Chicana Organizers and Middle-Class Female Supporters in the Farm Workers' Grape Boycott in Philadelphia." In *Women and Power in American History; A Reader, Vol. II from 1870*, ed. Kathryn Kish Sklar and Thomas Dublin, pp. 240–53. Prentice Hall, New Jersey, 1991.

Rosen, Ruth. *The World Split Open: How the Modern Women's Movement Changed America.* Viking Press, 2000.

Rosenstone, Steven J., and John Mark Hansen. *Mobilization, Participation, and Democracy in America.* Macmillan Publishing Company, 1993.

Roth, Benita. *Separate Roads to Feminism; Black, Chicana, White Feminists Movements in America's Second Wave.* Cambridge University Press, 2004.

Royster Jacqueline Jones, ed. *Southern Horrors and Other Writings: The Anti-Lynching Campaign of Ida B. Wells, 1892–1900.* Bedford/St. Martin's, 1997.

Rupp, Leila J., and Verta Taylor. *Survival in the Doldrums: The American Women's Rights Movement 1945 to the 1960s.* Oxford University Press, 1987.

Schechter, Patricia Ann. *Ida B. Wells Barnett Against Racial Violence, 1886–1930 (Critical Documentary Essay).* Alexander Street Press, Alexandria, Virginia, 2009. http://www.aspresolver.com/aspresolver.asp?GILD;1001257422.

Scott, Anne Firor. *Natural Allies: Women's Associations in American History.* University of Illinois Press, Chicago, 1991.

Sicherman, Barbara. *Alice Hamilton: A Life in Letters.* Harvard University Press, Boston, 1984.

Sklar, Kathryn Kish. "How Have Recent Social Movements Shaped Civil Rights for Women? The 1994 Violence Against Women Act." In *Women and Social Movements in the U.S., 1600–2000*, eds. Kathryn Kish Sklar and Thomas Dublin. State University of New York, 2007.

Sklar, Kathryn Kish, and Thomas Dublin. *Women and Power in American History; A Reader, Vol. II from 1870.* Prentice Hall, New Jersey, 1991.

Sklar, Kathryn Kish and Beverly Wilson Palmer, eds. *The Selected Letters of Florence Kelly, 1869–1931.* University of Illinois Press, Chicago, 2009.

Sklar, Kathryn Kish and Thomas Dublin. "How Did the National Women's Conference in Houston in1977 Shape an Agenda for the Future?" In *Women and Social Movements in the U.S., 1600–2000*, eds. Kathryn Kish Sklar and Thomas Dublin. State University of New York, 2007.

Smith, Fran. *Breaking Ground: The Daring Women of the YWCA in the Santa Clara Valley, 1905–2005.* YWCA of Silicon Valley, 2005.

Solinger, Rickie. "Extreme Danger: Women Abortionists and Their Clients before *Roe v. Wade*." In *Not Just June Cleaver; Women and Gender in Postwar America, 1945–1960*, ed. Joanne Meyerowitz, pp. 335–57. Temple University Press, 1994.

Swerdlow, Amy. *Women Strike for Peace; Traditional Motherhood and Radical Politics.* University of Chicago Press, 1993.

Uniform Child Labor Laws, National Child Labor Committee, Proceedings of the Seventh Annual Conference, Birmingham, Alabama, March 9–12, 1911. (New York, 1912).

Valk, Anne. "Fighting for Abortion as a 'Health Right,' in Washington D.C." *Feminist Coalitions: Historical Perspectives on Second-Wave Feminism in the United States*, ed. Stephanie Gilmore, pp. 135–62. University of Illinois Press, 2008.

Verba, Sidney, Kay Lehman Scholzman, and Henry E. Brady. *Voice and Equality: Civic Voluntarism in American Politics*. Harvard University Press, 1995.

Ware, Susan. *Beyond Suffrage: Women in the New Deal*. Harvard University Press, 1981.

Weiss, Jessica. *To Have and To Hold: Marriage, the Baby Boom, and Social Change*. University of Chicago Press, 2000.

Wilson, William Julius. *The Bridge Over the Racial Divide; Rising Inequality and Coalition Politics*. University of California Press, Berkeley, 1999.

Younger, Louise. *In the Public Interest: The League of Women Voters, 1920–1970*. Greenwood Press, 1999.

DIGITAL RESOURCES

Kathryn Kish Sklar, and Thomas Dublin, eds. *Women and Social Movements in the U.S., 1600–2000*. State University of New York, 2007.

The National Park Service. "World War Two in the San Francisco Bay Area." Accessed through San Jose State University Library, August 27, 2010. http://www.nps.gov/history/nr/travel/wwiibayarea/index.htm.

FILM RESOURCES

Benshoff, Harry M. Malden. 2004. *America on Film: Representing Race, Class, Gender, and Sexuality at the Movies*. Film. Massachusetts, Blackwell Publications.

Creekmur, Corey K., and Alexander Doty, eds. 1995. *Lesbians and Film. In: Out in Culture: Gay, Lesbian, and Queer Essays on Popular Culture*. Film. Durham, North Carolina, Duke University Press.

The Fabulous Sixties, 1963. 1987. Videorecording. Document Associates Inc. Oak Forest, Illinois, MPI Home Video.

Fundi, the Story of Ella Baker. 1986. Videorecording. New York, First Run/Icarus Films.

Garnier, Katja von, Hilary Swank, Frances O'Connor, Julia Ormond, Anjelica Huston, Molly Parker, Patrick Dempsey, et al. 2004. *Iron Jawed Angels*. New York, HBO Video.

Johnson, Mary Ann, and Elisabeth P. Montgomery. 1992. *Women of Hull-House*. [Chicago, Ill.] Jane Addams' Hull-House Museum, University of Illinois at Chicago.

Joyce Melva Baker. 1980. *Images of Women in Film: The War Years, 1941–*
    1945. Film. Ann Arbor, Michigan, UMI Research Press.
McGrath, Alice Greenfield, and Bob Giges. 1996. *From Sleepy Lagoon to*
    Zoot Suit the Irreverent Path of Alice McGrath. Santa Cruz, California,
    Giges Productions.
Rothman, Ellen K. 1984. *Hands and Hearts: A History of Courtship in Ameri-*
    ca. New York, Basic Books.
Ruiz, Jose Luis, Hector Gala´n, Henry Cisneros, Mylene Moreno, Sabine R.
    Ulibarri, Toma´s Atencio, Moctesuma Esparza, et al. 1996. *Chicano!*
    The History of the Mexican American Civil Rights Movement. 1, Quest
    for a Homeland. Los Angeles, NLCC Educational Media [distributor].
Williams, Juan. 1987. *Eyes on the Prize: America's Civil Rights Years, 1954–*
    1965. New York, Viking.

WEBSITES ON WOMEN'S HISTORY—FILMS, RESOURCE GUIDES, AND MUSEUMS

Alice Paul Institute: http://www.alicepaul.org/researching_alice.htm.
American Women's History: A Research Guide, Middle Tennessee State Uni-
    versity http://frank.mtsu.edu/~kmiddlet/history/women.html.
Celebrating Women's History: 100 Amazing Libraries and Collections:
    http://www.elearningyellowpages.com/blog/2008/10/celebrating-
    womens-history-100-amazing-libraries-and-collections-on-the-web/.
International Museum of Women: http://www.imow.org/home/index.
National Women's Hall of Fame: http://www.greatwomen.org/.
National Women's History Museum: http://www.nwhm.org/.
The National Women's History Project: http://www.nwhp.org/.
Women History Month Films: http://blog.beliefnet.com/moviemom/
    2010/03/list-movies-for-womens-history.html.
Women's Rights Film and Tapes: http://www.winningthevote.org/res_
    films.html.

WOMEN'S HISTORY PRINT AND DIGITAL COLLECTIONS

Cornell University Library, Division of Rare Books and Manuscripts:
    http://rmc.library.cornell.edu/.
Iowa Women's Archives: http://www.lib.uiowa.edu/iwa/.
National Archives, American Women Gateway to Resources: http://
    memory.loc.gov/ammem/awhhtml/.
New York University, Tamiment Library and Robert F. Wagner Labor Ar-
    chives: http://www.nyu.edu/library/bobst/research/tam/index.
    html.
Rutgers University Libraries: http://www.libraries.rutgers.edu/rul/libs/
    scua/womens_fa/womenhomepage.shtml.

Sally Bingham Center for Women's History and Culture: http://library. duke.edu/specialcollections/bingham/.

San Jose State University Special Collections & Archives: http://library. sjsu.edu/sjsu-special-collections/sjsu-special-collections-and-archives.

Schlesinger Library, Radcliffe Institute for Advanced Study, Harvard University: http://www.radcliffe.edu/schlesinger_library.aspx.

Sophia Smith Collection: Women's History Archives at Smith College: http://www.smith.edu/libraries/libs/ssc/index.html.

Swarthmore College Peace Collection: http://www.swarthmore.edu/ library/peace/.

University of California, Berkeley, Bancroft Library: http://bancroft. berkeley.edu/.

University of Nevada Special Collections: http://knowledgecenter.unr. edu/materials/specoll/.

University of Texas, Harry Rasom Center: http://www.hrc.utexas.edu/.

University of Washington: http://www.lib.washington.edu/subject/ history/tm/women.html.

Yale University Library, Manuscripts and Archives: http://www.library. yale.edu/mssa/.

ORAL HISTORY COLLECTIONS

Columbia University, Oral History Research Office: http://www. columbia.edu/cu/lweb/indiv/oral/.

New York University, Tamiment Library, University of Nevada Special Collections & Archives, Oral History Program: http://www.nyu. edu/library/bobst/research/tam/.

Regional Oral History Office, Bancroft Library, UC Berkeley: http://bancroft. berkeley.edu/ROHO/index.html.

The T. Harry Williams Center for Oral History Department, A Division of the LSU Libraries' Special Collections: http://www.lib.lsu.edu/ special/williams/.

University of Connecticut, Oral History Office: http://www.oralhistory. uconn.edu/.

University of Nevada Oral History Program: http://oralhistory.unr.edu/.

INDEX

About the Author

DANELLE MOON is the Director of Special Collections & Archives, a Full Librarian, and Adjunct Professor of History at San Jose State University. She holds an MLIS from Southern Connecticut State University and an MA in history from California State University, Fullerton. Her areas of expertise include women and politics, social reform during the Progressive Era history, California and the West, and archival management. She has written several articles and book chapters on the women and social movements in the 20th century.